WOMEN AND DISCOURSE IN THE FICTION OF MARGUERITE DURAS

Women and Discourse in the Fiction of Marguerite Duras

Love, Legends, Language

Susan D. Cohen

University of Massachusetts Press
Amherst

Printed in Hong Kong

First published in the USA 1993 by
The University of Massachusetts Press
Box 429
Amherst, Mass. 01004

LC 92–13945
ISBN 0–87023–827–2 (cloth); 828–0 (pbk.)

Library of Congress Cataloging-in-Publication Data
Cohen, Susan D.
    Women and discourse in the fiction of Marguerite Duras: love,
legends, language / Susan D. Cohen.
        p.   cm.
    Includes bibliographical references and index.
    ISBN 0–87023–827–2 (cloth). — ISBN 0–87023–828–0 (pbk.)
    1. Duras, Marguerite—Characters—Women.   2. Women and
    literature—France—History—20th century.   3. Discourse analysis.
    Literary.   4. Women in literature.   I. Title.
PQ2607 . U8245Z63   1993
843 ' . 912—dc20   92–13945
                                                              CIP

In memory of my mother, Celia Cohen.
For Lynn Landman, who inspires.

Contents

vii

Contents

Acknowledgments

I would like to thank the following people and institutions for encouragement with this project: Sonia Assa, Tom Bishop, Anna Cancogni, Josephine Diamond, Claire Duchen, Jacques Garelli, Leah Hewitt, Adele King, and The National Endowment for the Humanities and Barnard College for research grants.

The publisher and myself are grateful to the following for permission to publish material that has appeared in altered form elsewhere: *L'Esprit Créateur*, *Les Cahiers Renaud-Barrault* (Editions Gallimard). The Analytic Press and Peter Lang Publishing.

Introduction

How to theorize the oppression of women has been a subject of contention among feminists for several decades. Questions germane to literary criticism such as women's relation to language, the mediations of race and class, concepts of identity, difference and gender inform debates among and between French and Anglo-American feminists and enrich feminist theory, as does the engagement with other major discourses such as Marxism and postmodernism. These issues are central to the work of Marguerite Duras. Contemporary thought provides conceptual tools with which to analyze Duras' oeuvre and situate it theoretically.

In his essay "Discourse in the Novel," for example, Mikhail Bakhtin emphasizes the frequency with which discourse takes itself as a topic: "that one of the main subjects of human speech is discourse itself has up to now been insufficiently taken into consideration."[1] Broadening the concept to include the unspoken as well as the spoken word, Marguerite Duras' work focuses on language taken in a wider sense. In accord with modern linguistic and critical theories, Duras' fiction shows language to be constitutive as well as reflective of our place in the political, socioeconomic, racial and sexual configurations of our existence. Bakhtin demonstrates the importance of class and ethnicity, noting that "the individual's speech is inexorably merged with the sociolinguistic element."[2] However, as Patricia Yaeger observes, he neglects to factor in gender. Along with the other pertinent categories and certainly as profoundly, gender has affected people's access to and use of discourse. Yaeger shows the productiveness of "extending Bakhtin's analysis into the realm of gender – a variety of otherness that is fundamental to the structures and preoccupations of the novel."[3]

For Bakhtin, novels give expression to the centrifugal forces in language, which constitute heteroglossia: the various "languages" spoken by diverse social groups within a single language, or different languages within one country, or from nation to nation. These groups compete for a power that entails discursive and political hegemony. The dominant linguistico-political group marshalls centripetal forces and seeks to impose a "unitary language" in order to effect "concrete verbal and ideological unification and

1

centralization, which develop in vital connection with the process of socio-political and cultural centralization."[4] Bakhtin's historical outlook fosters awareness of the fact that, although unitary language seems always already there, it is not immutable. It struggles constantly to maintain dominance in the face of "the realities of heteroglossia."[5] As in language generally, in the novel "speech types" (heteroglossia) function dialogically in their social diversity.[6] Bakhtin forged the term "dialogism" to signify the perpetual confrontation and interaction between meanings.[7] Unitary language is always threatened by the inherently stronger force of heteroglossia. Monologue can not prevail, for it is of necessity in dialogical relation with a plural language world. Through the use of heteroglossia and dialogism, the prose writer de-centers unitary language and opens words to different meanings and social intentions.[8]

Because Bakhtin sees the novel as a theater of dialogism and heterglossia, he attributes to it a revolutionary structure. Most contemporary thinkers acknowledge the phallocentric character of reigning unitary languages, something attendant not simply on capitalism, but on the male-dominated structures of society, present within each class and traversing class as well. Bakhtin's unitary language corresponds to what today is called "dominant," "masculinist" or "phallo(logo)centric" language, terms suggestive of the links between domination and gender bias in society. Anne-Marie Houdebine affirms the diachronic and contingent nature of dominant masculinist language in her discussion of sexism with regard to the Saussurian concepts of "langue" (Language) and "parole" (speech):

> In a living language one can succeed in saying everything, including what is still only scarcely being stammered. On condition that this language be treated like a living, not a frozen language, that one play with its potentialities, listen to the words that are said in it, – those that are heard in it and not those one thinks one hears. For sexism resides more in speech, the reflection of mind sets, than in Language, more in language practises, indeed in the projections of listeners, than in Language: the same utterance can convey meanings x or y, connotations pejorative or not, according to the subjects listening to or proposing it. For what makes meaning in language exceeds linguistic categorization (lexical or syntactical); there has to be message, situation, speaker [. . .][9]

In the West, dominant language reflects and perpetuates a rationalist culture structured on hierarchical binarisms which institute distinction and separation for purposes of exploitation. To name is to claim, classify, objectify, dominate. Presupposing the primacy and normative status of one term, binarism posits the "second," "opposing" term as inferior or dangerous, something to be mastered, exploited, and/or repressed. As Simone de Beauvoir showed in 1949,[10] it invents Otherness, and Woman as a culturally constructed Other, denied subjectivity, reified and subordinated. Radical feminists such as Hélène Cixous contend that whatever the binary opposition, and despite the contradictions involved, dominant discourse associates the subordinated term with negatively marked attributes ascribed to women or femininity: "The entirety of symbolic systems – that is, everything that is said, that is organized as a discourse, art, religion, the family, language, everything that grips us, everything that makes us – everything is organized on the basis of hierarchical oppositions that go back to the opposition man/woman."[11] As examples of these dichotomies, Cixous lists: active/passive, culture/nature, day/night, father/mother, head/heart, logos/pathos, master/slave, form/matter.[12]

Within this "dualistic objective posture of Western rationality," as Jessica Benjamin asserts: "to be a woman is to be excluded from this rational individualism, to be either an object or a threat to it."[13] It also entails being barred from what Foucault calls "the proprietorship of discourse" which, he notes, is "reserved in fact (sometimes even in a statutory mode) for a determined group of individuals."[14] Having applied Patricia Yaeger's above-mentioned "extension" to Foucault's analyses and understood the exclusion of women as a *group* from the "proprietorship of discourse," many women are refusing object status to embrace the "threatening" position, to challenge dominant culture. Women writers, and Marguerite Duras among them, are effecting changes in dominant language which may justifiably be called gender-specific given women's particular socio-linguistic circumstances. They are doing this in a diversity of ways, from a variety of positions relative to differing circumstances of thought, class, race, and nationality.

Although through different elaborations, Hélène Cixous and Luce Irigaray have been the most influential and most controversial proponents of "écriture féminine" ("feminine writing"[15]), a concept they elaborated in the 1970s. Most feminists today recognize the importance of their "critique of phallocentrism in all the material

and ideological forms it has taken and [their] call for new representations of women's consciousness,"[16] and value their demys-
tification of dominant symbolic structures and representations as
well as their denunciation of the repression of women's sexuality
in masculinist discourses from philosophy to psychoanalysis. But
they also criticize both Cixous and Irigaray for the essentializing,
reifying implications of their definitions of feminine sexuality. More
specifically, many feminists critique the way in which their analyses
of the connections between the social and the sexual tend to slip
from cultural critique to universalizing, biologizing, a-historical
axioms. This leads Cixous and Irigaray to found feminine sexuality
on concepts of a feminine unconscious and unmediated physical
morphology, and to advocate a feminine speech and writing which
would emanate directly from the body, or from a feminine libidinal
economy. Consequently, in their work the repression of women's
bodies becomes the repression of Woman's body and women's
speech becomes Woman's speech.

Toril Moi, for example, applauds Cixous for linking sexuality
and textuality and for examining the articulation of desire through
language in literature, because this proceeds from a deconstructive
view of textuality. But she deplores the absence in Cixous of
"any specific analysis of the material factors preventing women
from writing,"[17] and for treating them as mythological archetypes
rather than social beings.[18] As for Irigaray, Moi feels that in her
attempt "to *name* the feminine" and to treat patriarchal power
as a monolithic force while ignoring its historical and economic
developments and contradictions, she undercuts her own "superb
critique of patriarchal thought."[19] As early as 1977, the Editorial
Collective of the newly founded journal *Questions féministes* made
similar objections, warning against assumptions that one can "speak
the body" in an unmediated way, and reminding us that "even our
'feminine' qualities, like our 'defects' are the product of the political
relation between men and women"[20] as it has developed historically
in the theater of contradictions that is capitalist patriarchy. Any
definition of "féminité" perpetuates binary thinking because it
defines women in terms of men and colludes with the use of
biology to rationalize oppression.[21]

Julia Kristeva rejects the concept of "feminine writing" and any
attempts to define women.[22] However, though she contests the idea
that women as writers must take sexual experience and libidinal
specificity as their starting point, her concept of a pre-oedipal,

pre-phallic "semiotic discourse" which challenges the (phallic) symbolic order[23] originates in the "blissful infantile fusion" with the mother in the Imaginary.[24] (And the mother's own experience of her body in maternity differentiates her from the phallic order.) Still, Kristeva maintains that the semiotic is the locus of a femininity defined through its positionality alone, as negativity rather than as gender. She does not exclude men from the semiotic (nor does Cixous from her "bi-sexuality"); indeed, she usually cites male avant garde writers (Joyce, Artaud, Mallarmé, Lautréamont, etc.) as its most successful exponents. For Kristeva, women's very marginality constitutes their revolutionary potential, and women should, along with other revolutionary movements (the male avant garde?) assume their negative function of rejection or explosion of social codes, and avoid the elaboration of alternative discourses.[25]

While Kristeva resists, importantly, the reification implicit in fixed identity, her restriction of the activity of marginal groups to negativity reduces potential impact from revolution to sporadic rebellion to threats easily absorbed. The anarchist tendencies implicit in her work, the problematic aspects, with regard to political agency, of the semiotic *qua* an unconscious force, and her recent swing towards the right have all been critiqued.[26] Moreover, her conflation of all dissidence elides the specificity of women's oppression.[27]

To proclaim fixed identity is indeed regressive, but, as Teresa de Lauretis indicates, *an* identity, though not of the traditional kind, is strategically necessary in the identification of women as a group oppressed *qua* women:

> a new conception of the subject is, in fact, emerging from feminist analyses of women's heterogeneous subjectivity and multiple identity [. . .] For if it is the case that the female subject is engendered across multiple representations of class, race, language and social relations, it is also the case that gender is a common denominator.[28]

De Lauretis opposes the practise of feminism to those branches of post-structuralist anti-humanism that advocate a concept of play cut off from concrete conditions,[29] and invokes "the epistemological priority which feminism has located in the personal, the subjective, the body, the symptomatic, the quotidian, as the very site of material inscription of the ideological; that is to say the ground where socio-political determinations take hold and are real-ized."[30]

Taking into account both post-humanist critiques of the subject and material conditions produced by representations of gender, race and class, feminism has been elaborating the concept of a shifting, non-stable, cross-cultural identity in order to articulate the experience of those elided and muted in dominant discourses, and in order to "open other possibilities of existing."[31] As elaborated in the sixties and seventies in response to Western leftist movements and philosophies which reduced oppression to class conflict, and whose adherents continued to practice the exploitation, denigration, and exclusion of women, the concept of gender at first contained universalizing implications from the position of bourgeois, white women, which other women severely criticized. Internal femin-ist debate and the impact on feminism of postmodernism and philosophical anti-humanism have modified the concept into a more nuanced category intended to address the complexities of socio-cultural differences between women.

In the ongoing feminist engagement with postmodernism, various positions have been adumbrated with respect to questions of gender and subjectivity. The recent volume *Feminism/Postmodernism*, for example, attests to the liveliness of the debate. In it Nancy Fraser and Linda Nicholson take issue with Lyotard's contention that because philosophical metanarrative fails to form a base for social analysis, criticism must be local and nontheoretical.[32] Rather than debilitating dispersal, they propose beginning with "the nature of the social object one wished to criticize," such as the oppression of women, and then proceeding with multiple methods, "large narratives," "historically and culturally specific sociologies of gender"[33] etc. Essentialist tendencies would be critiqued while the irreducibility of diverse factors (gender, race, class, nationality, etc.) would be maintained.

Inspired by Wittig's analyses, Judith Butler cautions that the category of woman has meaning only within "the conditions of oppression against which it has been formulated,"[34] and that only by refraining from assigning any fixity to gender identification will we understand gender "coherence" as a "regulatory fiction [. . .] rather than the common point of our liberation," the "effect" of politics, rather than its ground.[35] Butler would replace what she considers reified conceptions of gender with "complex and generative subject-positions as well as coalitional strategies that neither presuppose nor fix their constitutive subjects in place."[36] But Andreas Huyssen remarks that advanced capitalism has already dis-integrated the bourgeois subject, and adds his voice to those of feminists politically leery of the espousal of fragmentation. For the post structuralist denial of the subject "jettison[s] the chance of challenging the *ideology of the subject* (as male, white, and middle class) by developing alternative and different notions of subjectivity."[37]

With parallel logic, Susan Bordo doubts the political efficacy of discarding the concept of gender. While recognizing it as a concept, she considers it as "enabling" a construct as race or class. She worries that "feminist gender-scepticism [. . .] [might] now be operating in the service of the reproduction of white, male knowledge/power" by jumping the gun, so to speak, by refusing legitimacy and transforming capacity to the idea of "our [historically developed] Otherness."[38] Granted, all binarisms (male/female, white/black, west/east, etc.) are social (as opposed to natural) discursive creations, but each of these dualities "has had profound consequences for the construction of experience of those who live them."[39] One mustn't abandon the discussion of what is for a utopian what should be. The idealism and biologism of "écriture féminine" ought not be replaced by another idealism: the total erasure of the body, for it is in and starting from our bodies – as "constructed" by dominant forces – that women are subordinated and exploited.

If the "nowhere" of the objective Cartesian glance inhibited agency, so does the implied "everywhere" of endless differences. In attending to the differences among women produced by race and class, one must not deny commonalities. The "everywhere" stance erases the situatedness that informs our lives.[40] Bordo reminds us that "the most powerful strategies against liberal humanism have been those that demystify the 'human' (and its claims to 'neutral' perspective) *through* general categories of social identity [gender, for example] which give content and force to the notions of social interest, historical location, and cultural perspective."[41] Bordo does not advocate fixed conceptions of social identity. Rather, she believes that the tension between general categories and local differences must be maintained.[42]

As these analyses imply, "situatedness" is what enables one to take inflections of difference into account while articulating a base for political and critical action. In the "local" field of literature, this historical "situatedness," which is a function of historical exclusion and discreditation of women *qua* women, validates the attention to gender specificity within texts and with respect to the question of textual production. Whether or not the concept of a purely female literary tradition has permanent legitimacy or ultimate political desirability (it raises fears of ghettoization, marginalization, cooptation into binary thinking), its historically "situated" political usefulness can hardly be contested. The retrieval from oblivion of countless books by women, the challenge to the masculinist literary canon (successful in the United States to the point that major political figures as well as universities and publishers have seen the necessity of addressing it), and the large body of work on the subject attest to its productivity. As Martha Evans phrases it: "To emphasize the gender-bound nature of self-expression is not to claim it as the sole determinant of subjectivity, but rather to insist that it be considered as an essential and legitimate object of study for anyone who interprets the production of human meaning. To reject the relevance of this consideration in the study of literature is to repeat the very process by which women were excluded from it in the first place."[43]

Marguerite Duras' pronouncements on the subject of a women's literary tradition, and on the (French) feminist movement as a tactical tool have vacillated. Nevertheless, she consistently denounces the oppression of women and invokes the specificity of her womanhood with respect to her aesthetic production, through statements such as "it is as a woman that I cause things to be seen in this way."[44] Duras' fiction demonstrates her awareness of historical, socio-economic, racial, national and other factors mediating the experience of women, and uncovers and undermines fixed gender roles and identities in non-essentializing ways. Therefore, it can not be taken for an example of "écriture féminine." Particularities in women's writing do not issue, for her, from immutable, natural differences. Rather, the specificities of women's insertions into history, sexuality, language and art create different positionings, which affect cultural production: "We [women] do not write in the same place as men at all. And when women do not write in the place of [their own] desire, they are plagiarizing [men's writing]."[45] The place from which women start is the historically produced place of our oppression. Connections between sexuality and textuality are grounded in experience ordered by symbolic, political and material structures. Duras' texts ceaselessly probe the dominant use of language, women's access to speech and discursive strategies, how the symbolic order perpetuates sexual subordination, silence imposed and espoused, and alternate discursive avenues. In addition to describing and disclosing the givens of gender and subject positions, her work proposes rearticulations of them. This book tries to delineate, through close textual analyses, how one French woman writer's inflection of language on the one hand exposes the exclusion and denigration of women in and by dominant discourse, and on the other, proposes a non-oppressive handling of language.

Part I explores the modalities of this double practise-praxis in Duras' narrative strategies. In an interview with me, Duras remarked: "from the beginning of my life the problem, for me, has been one of knowing who was speaking when I spoke in my books . . . and if there is invention in my work, it is there."[46] This statement indicates the degree to which Duras is conscious of one of the most fundamental questions in contemporary literature. With the collapse of the notion of a metaphysically guaranteed truth and the correlative demise of the concept of objectivity, the classical stance of the omniscient narrator becomes inoperative. Attendant on the decentering of that discourse, twentieth century thought rejects the positivism implicit in an omniscient speaking subject, mouthpiece of a unitary language which subsumes all other speech under its legitimizing authority.

The attitude of narrative omniscience so prevalent in the nineteenth century has been replaced by a more or less continuous movement towards what I call an attitude of "ignorance." In response to a question I put to Duras on the subject, she identified this approach as her own: "Ignorance is the starting point of my work. If I am omniscient I do not write. It is in ignorance, in the impossibility of grasping [dans l'incapacité de saisir] that I write. I think this is a basic given common to all my books."[47] This narrative position is directly productive of many kinds of textual plurality. In Part I, I analyze the ways in which Duras' texts focus on the acts of narrating and writing, and how they emphasize the essential non-innocence of discourse. Going beyond restrictive dichotomies, Duras inscribes plurivocity in nearly all her texts, replacing "objectivity" not with the closure of a solipsistic "subjectivity" but with multiple possibilities. Omniscience fades into creative "ignorance." Speakers never possess all the facts, and this very absence of a single, verifiable referential given is what opens textuality – and intertextuality – in Duras' oeuvre.

The reactions of Duras' narrators and speakers to the ways "igno-rance" affects discourse and textual production is thematized, as is language itself, on nearly every textual level. Many of her internal narrators are "writers." How they approach narrative and speech with respect to dominant rationalist discourse correlates to how they assume gender and subject positions in the power relations articulated by the symbolic order, and to their efforts to maintain or challenge that order. Although the central focus is on gender in the manipulation of language, Duras does not reduce socio-political relations to that one denominator. Her texts almost always specify the speaking protagonists' class, race and ethnicity, and show these conditions coordinating with gender in the relation to language.

In Chapter 1, I explicate how narrative configurations in several texts incorporate and thematize "ignorance" as the fundamental structuring device. I discuss its repercussions on both narrators and protagonists. Chapter 2 extends the description of its functioning to intertextuality. Duras devises intertextual practises as a function of "ignorance," with the result that the very concept of intertextuality gets reformulated. Chapter 3 incorporates "ignorance," gender and textuality into analyses of how Duras approaches the subject of erotic discourse and literature through her own erotic texts. Despite or perhaps because of certain ambiguities and contradictions, and through techniques of framing and irony, stereotypes become self-deconstructive, or at the least are exposed as (self)destructive. I study the specificity of these texts, especially with respect to the erotic genre, and also indicate some of their connections to the rest of Duras' oeuvre. The continuity of basic concerns is evident: the pointed emphasis on narrative structure, the centrality of discourse in relation to gender, sexuality and erotic politics in our society, historical and economic contextualization, etc.

Throughout Part I, I show that Duras' female signature, her frequently present speaking "I," and non-traditional narrative structuring foreground the process of narration itself. Narration acquires an importance equal to that of plot or theme; discursive structures themselves are thematized, and telling a story becomes a story of telling.

Part II examines Duras' key "stylistic" and syntactic strategies. In a remark about her prose, Duras associates women with all silenced people, all those constituted as Other, and "feminized" in that sense:[48] "It is a style [. . .] of finding childhood again, the speech of children, of women, and the speech of the people [le parler populaire], also the speech of the world's border regions."[49] If, as Bakhtin holds, "the primary stylistic project of the novel is to create images of languages,"[50] then the images Duras proposes – to both sexes – come primarily from women's cultural spaces. The conception of language she advocates revalorizes and rearticulates elements relegated to the "feminine" domain. She reclaims the vast silences of women as the terrain of her discursive work:

> Duras: 'The silence in women is such that anything that falls into it has an enormous reverberation. Whereas in men this silence no longer exists.'
> Husserl-Kapit: 'Why do women possess it?'
> Duras: 'Because they *exist* in silence. [. . .] Because men have established the principle of virile force. And everything that emerged from this virile force – including words, unilateral words – compounded the silence of women.[. . .]
> Husserl-Kapit: 'Then the silence of women is imposed by men.'
> Duras: 'Oh, of course'.[51]

Duras' focus on women and our oppression as such (Fraser and Nicholson's above-cited "particular object one wishes to criticize") does not obscure inequalities separating men. As Marini puts it:

> Without denying the reality of oppression among men (a privileged theme of our revolutionary or anti-establishment writers and thinkers), she [Duras] shows how any man, be he the most oppressed, receives almost from birth the right to speak alone, about and in the name of women, on condition that he respect the between-men rules [les règles de l'entre-hommes]. Duras' works ceaselessly interlace differences of race, culture, class, nationality, language, generation and sex. But, at the bottom of the ladder, it's always a woman one finds, cumulating all the rejections [. . .][52]

Duras resituates silence with respect to speech, decenters words and divests them of their "unilateral" character. No longer in binary opposition, silence and speech together constitute a discourse which fosters receptive communication and creativity rather than domination. "Silence" correlates to the fundamental, productive narrative "ignorance" presented in Part I. Just as that "ignorance" avoids the equation of speech with dominating knowledge, her richly communicative "silences" enable her to deconstruct and avoid logocentrism. The silence Duras celebrates serves, like "ignorance," as source and component in a rearticulation of language which constitutes both a theme and a product in her fiction.

Chapter 4 analyzes Duras' use of silence and her approach to discourse in areas ranging from the thematic to the syntactic, from the lexical to page layout. Because *Le Vice-consul*[53] contains in profusion most of the techniques I describe, I take it as a base. Examples selected from others of Duras' texts further illustrate my review of these procedures. In Chapter 5, I discuss those features which, from narrative to grammatical, from onomastic to syntactic to poetic strategies, create the famous, ritual-like atmosphere of Duras' prose. The ultimate purpose of this book is to contribute to the elaboration of a poetics of Duras' fiction.

Part I
Strategies of Narration

1
"Ignorance" and Textuality

"It is not enough that you understand in what ignorance men and beasts live – you must also have and acquire the *will* to ignorance."

Nietzsche

INTRODUCTION

"From the beginning of my life the problem, for me, has been one of knowing who was speaking when I spoke in my books . . . and if there is invention in my work, it is there. For example," continues Duras concerning *Le Vice-consul*, "for the beggar, it took me months to know who was speaking, to tell the story of the beggar, and how someone knew."[1] The "secret," so to speak, of Duras' narrative structuring consists precisely in this: the "someone" in question, interposed voice or glance, does not "know." From the outset, the author renders him, or her, incapable of knowing. The "someone" speaks from an original, permanent, and textually productive "ignorance." Displacing the question of knowledge, Duras throws into relief gaps inherent in all narratives, in all relations to the world and to oneself. In her texts, this produces plurivocity and/or heteroglossia regardless of the internal narrative stance.

Duras' genius consists partly in rigging things, as it were, to inscribe a twofold "ignorance": the frequent impossibility of knowing who pronounces certain utterances, and her internal narrators' "ignorance" of their textual referent. She takes the definitive impossibility of adequation, this "ignorance," as her point of departure. It leads away from closure and opens multiple textual, discursive, and social possibilities.

15

LE VICE-CONSUL

Narrative voices and points of view proliferate in *Le Vice-consul*. Nothing is presented through what Duras calls "the inevitable realism of the direct and the trickery that represents."[2] Vision rarely functions in the singular, and Duras avoids creating an omniscient narrator to whom everything might be attributed. There does exist an implicitly first person narrator-writer whose "I" is never pronounced but which we infer from various deictics. Perceivable directly or indirectly throughout the text, this voice acts not as the repository of omniscience, but as a subversion of the concept of authoritative, univocal language. Further, *Le Vice-consul* poses the question of writing itself, directing us to the ultimate source, the signer. The pertinence of gender in this regard will soon become apparent.

Weaving itself among the various points of view, the narrator-writer's presence ranges from relative reticence to straightforward intervention. For example, the novel is set in Calcutta, India, and for a time the proper name functions like any real place name in literature. However, on page thirty-five, the narrator announces the intention to distort Indian geography and make Calcutta the capital, thus calling attention to the partially fictive character of all real toponyms in literary texts: "Five weeks ago Jean-Marc de H. arrived in a city on the shores of the Ganges, which will be the capital of India here, named Calcutta."[3] Had it appeared at the text's beginning, this statement would probably have functioned like stage directions, establishing extra-textually the setting of the drama to follow. But Duras inserts it late, after mentioning the city several times, so that it constitutes a startling interruption. The future tense jars the reader into assigning the double status of real and fictive to Calcutta. The deictic "here" does not refer only to that city; it points to a space inclusive of it. Proferred by an implicit "I" who is a writing narrator addressing readers, "here" designates the space and time of the novel itself, a work of fiction in process.

Appropriating a toponym already heavy with connotations (the East, mass poverty, colonialism) that she wishes to keep since she retains the name, Duras fictionalizes it through these dislocations. Writers of traditional realist fiction contrive to do the opposite. Gérard Genette emphasizes the conventional nature of Balzac's objective stance, for example, noting that despite Balzac's claims to truth and reality, his Paris both points to the real place and signifies a made-up city: "for the narrator-author is someone who 'knows' the Vauquer pension [in] the 'Paris' of *Le Père Goriot* [. . .] whereas Balzac only imagines it [. . .]"[4] The same double status applies to Calcutta in *Le Vice-consul*, but the text evokes it explicitly. Calcutta's fictional specificity itself is mitigated through its analogical equivalency to Lahore, and implicitly to any other poverty stricken Indian city: "This, which is Calcutta or Lahore, palm trees, leprosy, crepuscular light . . . " (V-C p. 32). Yet the toponym maintains its referentiality, functioning simultaneously in the three registers of reality, fiction, and symbol. Duras uses similar disruptive tactics in many of her texts, creating her particular form of distancing.

Le Vice-consul contains at least three stories: an indigent, uneducated young Indochinese girl unwittingly becomes pregnant, and is consequently forced to leave family and home. After wandering for ten years, begging now and then for food, she arrives in Calcutta, where she remains. Having shot and killed a number of defenceless Indian lepers, the French Vice-Consul at Lahore is stripped of his diplomatic duties. In Calcutta, he awaits the authorities' decision concerning his next post. Anne-Marie Stretter, wife of the French Ambassador to India, gives a reception in Calcutta. During the party, to which she has invited the Vice-Consul, the Indochinese beggar can be heard singing outside. She reappears at other moments in the text. Developed in counterpoint, these initially unconnected stories intertwine, meeting and separating in Calcutta, city of horror. One can count a fourth tale, that of Charles Rossett's initiation into white diplomatic India, during the course of which he encounters the three other protagonists.

"She's walking, writes Peter Morgan." This first sentence of the novel establishes a complex network of relations. "Duras"[5] identifies Peter Morgan as the writer of the ensuing segment, which is instantly relativized. From the start, several pairs of eyes are engaged: those of the beggar, fictionally projected by Peter Morgan, those of Peter Morgan, the would-be writer, those of the narrator, who presents him in that act of writing, and who in turn is "seen" by the ultimate "observer," the reader. Yet the text is organized in such a way that a first reading tends to neutralize this layered distancing. For Duras suspends reiteration of unambiguous attribution to Peter Morgan of the beggar's story until page twenty-four, so that the reader's awareness of the material's manipulation by a fictive writer slips to a level of presupposition easily forgotten. The fact that the story is written in the present tense also helps endow it with an immediacy and an intensity so strong that the effect of the initial distancing diminishes temporarily. Forgetting what we "know" about the fictionality involved, we accompany the young Indochinese girl on her terrible journey, and project into the present of her suffering, her hunger, her pregnancy, her separation from her mother, her painful loss of selfhood and her subsequent madness.

However, upheavals are caused by the abrupt reminder of Peter Morgan's authorship on page twenty-four, where "writes Peter Morgan" reappears, and by the lengthy interruption of his narrative soon thereafter (V-C, pp. 29–51). What the reader tended to ascribe to the beggar alone now seems equally construable in another perspective, yet one reading does not negate the other. Duras achieves this largely through the near total absence of punctuation marks or lexical elements indicating whether or not anyone – and who – is speaking other than the "writing" Peter Morgan. The paragraph in which the pregnant beggar discovers that men will give her money for sexual intercourse illustrates this: "With the money from the fishermen she goes to Pursat several times, she buys rice, cooks it in a tin can, they give her matches, she eats hot rice. The child is almost finished. The hunger of the first days will never return" (V-C, p. 23). The last sentence might read either as free indirect discourse in the beggar's point of view, or as a narrative anticipation of a future guaranteed by Morgan the "writer."

A striking instance of plural hermeneutical possibilities occurs on the novel's first page, where an abundance of pronouns and a lack of attributive marks inhibit univocal interpretation:

> How not to come back? One has to become lost. I don't know how. You will learn. I would like directions for getting lost. One has to be without second thoughts [arrière pensée], [. . .] ready to direct one's steps to the most hostile point of the horizon [. . .] She does it. She walks for days. [. . .] One has to learn that the point of the horizon that would draw you to it is, doubtless, not the most hostile one [. . .]. (V-C, p. 9)

Within this limited space, the beggar is designated by "I," "you" (familiar form), "one" ("on"), "she" and "you" (formal form). One might assimilate the various pronouns to the beggar's perspective and read the passage as a combination of indirect discourse and direct transcription of speech or thought, with the beggar addressing herself in an interior monologue of sorts, relayed by traditional third person narration ("She does it," etc.). (The monologue could also be a review by the beggar of a dialogue held with her mother as she threw her out.) Or one might receive it as a kind of conversation between Morgan and his character, transcribable as follows:

The Beggar (to herself or to Morgan):   'How not to come back?'
Morgan: 'One has to become lost.'
The Beggar: 'I don't know how.'
Morgan: 'You will learn.'
The Beggar: 'I would like directions for getting lost.'
Morgan: 'One has to be without second thoughts, ready to direct one's steps to the most hostile point of the horizon.'
[. . .]
Morgan (as narrator):   She does it. She walks for days.
[. . .]
Morgan: 'One has to learn that the point of the horizon that would draw you to it is, doubtless, not the most hostile one.'
[. . .]

Additional interpretations are possible. Peter Morgan's declaration, much later in the novel, that he has been taking "imaginary notes" (V-C, p. 157) on the young Indochinese woman introduces another level of uncertainty: did the text we read consist merely of notes? Would that explain the proliferation of pronouns? Will Morgan rearticulate his text around a single voice at some future point? Is he writing as we look over his shoulder with Duras? Typical of Durassian ambiguity, which permeates every aspect of *Le Vice-consul*, this plurality of possibilities remains unresolved. And it is precisely this irreducible quality that makes Durassian uncertainty, or "ignorance" productive.

The interruption of Morgan's text on page twenty-four and the numerous subsequent references to his "authorship" ("he writes," or "he stops writing,": pp. 24, 29, 51, 58, 69, 72) have other consequences, among which the most important is to shift the focus from the content of his narrative to the act of writing itself. Each allusion to his writing disrupts the diegetic hierarchy: Peter Morgan sinks from the level of author to that of character and the beggar accedes, from the status of Morgan's imaginary creature, to the same degree of intratextual reality as he. The intradiegetic contextualization of Morgan's writing, which is always referred to in the present tense, brings the reader to perceive it as an event occurring in alternation with others in the text.

Yet Morgan's other possible activities elicit little interest in the reader. In contrast to the other protagonists, Peter Morgan remains a figure strikingly devoid of personality. His textual function remains restricted to the role of "writer," his *raison d'être* in the novel, and the sole aspect developed by Duras. Equally or more important than what he writes are his reasons for writing. The shifting narrative levels and multiple perspectives combine with metaliterary interpolations ("he writes") to raise the question of the ethics of writing, which the text thematizes. Concepts of innocence, neutrality, and objectivity are demystified. What, how, and why one writes communicate one's approach to the world, and in this context the creation of a male intermediary voice in the figure of Peter Morgan has significance.

With the first reflections on his motivations for writing, he is shown immersed in the dynamics of appropriative domination: "Peter Morgan is a young man who desires to *take* the pain of Calcutta, to throw himself into it, so that it be done, and *so that his ignorance cease* with the taken pain" (V-C, p. 29 – emphasis added). Far from acknowledging that he is implicated by the suffering around him, he wants to "take" it. The underlined segment indicates that the knowledge he desires is contingent on this taking, and signals a *weltanschauung* which equates knowing with objectification and possession. Morgan wishes to possess Calcutta's pain not in order to keep it, but for the express purpose of ridding himself of it. Art for him serves as an expectorant, a cathartic act of sublimation through which he separates himself from Calcutta's squalor, symbolized, significantly, by a woman. Kristeva discusses the use of "that catharsis par excellence which is art"[6] as a process of control and differentiation from what she calls the "abject": "In symptoms, the abject invades me, I become it. With sublimation, I have a hold on it."[7] For her, on the one hand we lose ourselves in the abject in order to exist: "the sublime, the dazzlement in which I lose myself in order to be;"[8] and on the other hand, we separate ourselves from it, again in order to exist: "the immemorial violence with which a body separates itself from another in order to be."[9] According to this subject-object (abject) dichotomy, the abject object whose rejection one's existence requires, is, of course, woman. For

Kristeva this also describes the double dynamic of art: temporary projective identification followed by radical distinction.

Morgan, the white, European male artist will not belong to the same world as the inarticulate, mad, animal-like Indochinese beggar woman, figure of the poverty of the East. Marcelle Marini writes: "If it is her, then it isn't me. 'She' is that body roaming around, chained to its elementary appetites; 'I' belong to the civilized world of embassies."[10] Morgan's denial of shared humanity brings him the "exaltation" of a sublimation that is a form of elimination. Discussing his book in progress, he declares: "I get exalted [je m'exalte] over the pain of India" (V-C, p. 157). He then posits equivalence between his writing and what those he is addressing, Anne-Marie Stretter's "lovers," do to disassociate themselves from Calcutta: "We all do it, more or less, no?" (V-C, p. 157). (I insert inverted commas around the word "lovers" because a close reading of the text discloses that what these men love in Anne-Marie Stretter is her "feminine" role as intermediary, filter and maternal screen, protecting them from, precisely, the abject. One of them makes the distinction: "Anne-Marie,' says George Crawn, 'also has her own India, but it isn't in our cocktail' . . . " V-C, p. 158). Morgan's "we all do it" links the "lovers" to the rest of privileged white colonial society, which consigns the people of Calcutta to a category of Otherness in a hierarchy in which difference entails inferiority. (Anne-Marie Stretter rejects this by connecting herself to Calcutta.[11])

Separation is achieved by asserting one's humanity over and against what is implicitly constituted as quasi-animality, be it through the fences surrounding the white enclaves in Calcutta, the use to which Anne-Marie Stretter is put, or through cathartic art. This relieves the "lovers" of the responsibility of questioning colonialism. Repression and sublimation collude with oppression. The text's other male figures perpetuate these structures in the exercise of their official duties and/or by withdrawing into hobbies (the Ambassador's hunting) or alcohol (The Director of the European Circle), for, as the Ambassador affirms, "one can not look things in the face" (V-C, p. 119). Although the Vice-Consul behaves with greater complexity, rejecting diplomatic codes, he reacts to India in the mode of murderous violence. Unable to make even the initial contact necessary for sublimation, he attempts to destroy the abject. Shooting lepers, those living symbols of India's massive suffering, he seeks his catharsis in the firing of a gun. The phallic imagery is especially pertinent with respect to this character, whose other, connected salient trait is his virginity. Impotent in the sense that he is unable to love, his sole sorties from this state are this symbolic rape-murder of a feminized "India" and a coercive advance towards Anne-Marie Stretter.[12]

Peter Morgan's motivations for writing reveal a questionable attitude towards the beggar and towards women in general. After each pause in his "writing," he leaves his lodgings in order to observe the beggar, the real thing (sic), and one is struck by the reification this involves. She provides the raw material for his work-in-progress. That from among the masses he singles out a woman is not incidental, for his own Western ideology associates inarticulate, powerless, chaotic suffering with the feminine, as it does the unclean. Triply reified by her gender, her foreignness, and her madness, the beggar constitutes the perfect object of research for the male writing subject. In the rationalistic-scientific spirit, he studies the silenced and therefore unresisting abject object he has appropriated discursively: "She is dirty like nature itself [. . .] I would like not to leave that level, of her filth [. . .] I would like to analyze that filth, to tell what it is made of [. . .]" (V-C, p. 182). In response to the question "Why her?" Morgan carries the objectification one step further. Explaining that he has chosen the beggar because "nothing more can happen to her" (V-C, p. 157), he denies her the essential component of life: change. He adopts the Pygmalion course, which deprives her of any existence other than that which he chooses to confer on her, as one of his interlocutors remarks: "'I think that what he means,' says Michael Richard, 'is even more; he would like to give her existence only in he [sic] who would watch her live. *She* would feel nothing'" (V-C, p. 182).

Thus the male writer will speak in place of the conveniently mute female. Morgan will further palliate ignorance of his "referent" by occupying even her internal discursive space: "Peter Morgan would like now to substitute the bric-à-brac of his memory for the abolished memory of the beggar. Without that, Peter Morgan would find himself at a loss for words to account for the beggar of Calcutta" (V-C, p. 73). An "ignorance" which would acknowledge the Other as subject is rejected. Conceptualized as a silenced object, the Other perforce becomes a mysterious referent, which incites the dominant desire for knowledge of it – as an object. The narrating subject's "ignorance" can now "cease" because he "takes" not "the pain of Calcutta" (V-C, p. 29), but the symbol he makes of it (the beggar), and incorporates that into his symbolic universe. In this way, Morgan will "account for the beggar of Calcutta" and avoid what he fears most: a loss of words.[13]

In the scene of the "lovers'" discussion of Morgan's writing (V-C, pp. 179–183), we learn that Anne-Marie Stretter's person is to furnish the material for the only other female character in his book. Therefore, she too must undergo the reifying transformation. She too must be reduced to silence, so that a man can represent her, founding his existence on her non-existence, his discourse on her silence. The very textual organization of the lengthy passage exposes the workings of this mechanism. For Anne-Marie Stretter's silence is self imposed. It takes the guise of an implausible, probably simulated sleeping, and lasts the entire duration of the men's conversation. Moreover, "Duras'" insistent references to her silence (nine in four pages) suggest another function. More than a support for male discourse, Anne-Marie Stretter's silence is a refusal of the reifying discussion of the beggar. Duras uses it as an example of passive resistance. Miming with her own person the mute corporeal entity representing the beggar, object and source of the men's speech, Anne-Marie Stretter exposes what dominant discourse does to women. At the same time, her silence constitutes a rejection of that discourse, and expresses solidarity with the other woman, across boundaries of race and class.

Literary objectification relays social objectification. Ultimately, in the men's speech Anne-Marie Stretter and the beggar meet in the uniform designated area of non-subjectivity. The symbolic mechanisms which deny women discourse deny them difference. Not only do they refuse women positively marked difference from men, they assimilate women into the object Woman, reinforcing the contrast between that object and (male) subjects. In the "lovers'" literary discussion, the men effect a gradual conflation of the beggar with Anne-Marie Stretter, until the two seem to merge into one. "The violence goes very far," notes Marini, "[Anne-Marie Stretter is] progressively assimilated to the beggar."[14]

Metonymic and onomastic devices as well as thematic ones expose this homogenization into "the feminine." Anne-Marie Stretter's name disappears for most of the conversation. Divested of the only individualizing marker possible in the third person, she joins the beggar on the physical level by dozing, figuring an inert, inarticulate female body (the beggar is usually asleep when Morgan observes her), and merges with her on the discursive level in the third person pronoun "she." Emile Benveniste shows linguistically as Martin

Buber does philosophically, that intersubjectivity exists solely
between "I" and "you." The third person, linguistic category of
interchangeability, non-personhood, absence of personhood, implicitly reifies.[15] At times the second person appears, but without its
function of direct address, for the men neither expect nor await a
response. The "you" slips back each time into the third person "she"
or "her," which begins to apply indifferently to Anne-Marie Stretter
and the beggar. Progressively "she" loses referential specificity, as
in the following remark by one of the "lovers": "'[. . .] no more
boredom for her.' – George Crawn laughs – 'that's why we're here,
in principle. Never, never the slightest suspicion of boredom . . . '
She sleeps" (V-C, pp. 181).

Whereas the "lovers" are deaf to the message of Anne-Marie
Stretter's silence, "Duras'" interventions in the scene ensure that
the reader hears it. Because these intercalations usually contain
Anne-Marie Stretter's name, they simultaneously throw into relief
her deindividuation by the "lovers" and counterbalance it. This
other, female voice dialogizes the univocity of the men's discourse.
One of the most forceful examples occurs in a typically Durassian
manipulation of repetition. George Crawn speculates about the
beggar in Morgan's projected novel: "she makes useless speeches
in the profound silence" (V-C, p. 181). A few paragraphs later,
Michael Richard repeats the last part of the sentence. Having different speakers utter nearly identical words has many consequences
in Duras' texts. Here it produces a boomerang effect. The shift
works metonymically. Immediately after Morgan's speech about
analyzing the beggar's filth, pronounced while he looks at the
sleeping Anne-Marie Stretter (an indication of his conflation of
the two women), "Duras" inserts the remark: "Why speak to that
sleeping woman?" (V-C, p. 182). Referring to Anne-Marie Stretter's
silence, this prepares a new contextual referent for the repeated
phrase. As if in answer to the query, Michael Richard repeats
Crawn's words, but in the singular: "Useless speech and profound
silence . . . " (V-C, p. 182). The minute alteration is crucial, for the
words now allude not to the beggar's speeches but to the speech just
made by Morgan, "futile" in its bad faith. And "profound silence"
now refers to the sleeping Anne-Marie Stretter. But as always when
the silence is hers, it sheds the connotation of emptiness.[16] In the first
instance "profound" emphasizes the vacuum of muteness within
and surrounding the beggar; in the second, it acquires meanings of
fullness and depth – and resistance.

Other passages thematizing writing in *Le Vice-consul* pose the question of the ethics of aesthetics. The drunken director of Calcutta's European Circle exclaims that what he has seen in India would "make a wonderful book" if he "knew how to write." " . . . 'These countries [. . .] have such charm . . . " (V-C, p. 74). Immediately contiguous to an episode in which the starving beggar gives away the child she can not feed, the director's cliché seems grotesque. Juxtaposing the two scenes implicitly condemns the reduction of massive poverty to the picturesque through "art."

Plurality of perspectives persists throughout *Le Vice-consul*. Characters are rarely present without some form of secondary voice or vision interposed between them and the reader. We observe these intermediaries themselves as they talk, write, or see. At those infrequent points when characters appear alone, dislocations in third person narration and the play of pronouns, the present tense, deictics and diegetic elements decenter the single perspective. At one point the solitary Vice-Consul's glance sweeps over the city: "The Vice-Consul of Lahore looks at Calcutta, the smoke, the Ganges, the sprinklers, she who sleeps [the beggar] [. . .] again he looks at the stone and the palm trees, the sprinklers, the woman who sleeps, the agglomerations of lepers on the river bank, the pilgrims, this which is Calcutta [. . .]" (V-C, p. 32). Although the text states that the Vice-Consul sees the beggar, nothing indicates that he distinguishes her from the innumerable lepers and beggars. He has not yet met Peter Morgan and will not be privy to the conversations concerning his book. At this juncture, then, the beggar has no significance for him. Moreover, he later affirms that he has never noticed her: " [. . .] 'that madwoman who swims in the Ganges, she is intriguing, has he seen her?' asks Charles Rossett. 'No.'" (V-C, p. 174).

Because deictics presuppose an "I", "you," and "now" contemporary with the act and setting of discourse, they belong to the intersubjective order.[17] The word "this" introduces the reader along with the implied narrating "I." As with the beggar section, this produces contrasting effects of distancing, which usually inhibits verisimilitude, and intensification, for the intersubjectivity is situated in the here and now of the novel's action. The poignancy of the beggar's story actually increases. Only the double perspective can reactivate it here, since the Vice-Consul, not having noticed the beggar, could not mention her were the segment set solely in his point of view. The anaphorical referential power of "she who sleeps," then, works not for him but for the reader. Through individuation of the beggar on a different narrative level, the double perspective implicitly denounces the Vice-Consul's reification of the poor of India into a mass associated with other objects in the scenery. The contrast has repercussions extending to issues of colonialism, race and gender, which are further discussed later in this study.

A scene in which Charles Rossett is alone makes the point through manipulation of the pronouns "on" and "nous" (we), of whose malleability Duras makes rich use. An Indian servant rouses Rossett from an afternoon nap. Referring to the dream he has just had, Duras employs "we" instead of the anticipated third person "he", the proper name, or the first person singular: "We dreamed of a rosy woman, a rosy reader, rosy [rose liseuse rose] who would read Proust in the acid wind of a far away English Channel" (V-C, p. 47). The ambiguity of the speaking source produces several hermeneutical possibilities, which, in typically Durassian fashion, circulate together. Who utters the sentence? It might be a projection into Rossett's thoughts, in which case "we" would designate an aggrandized but undemarcated subjectivity, a function described by Benveniste.[18] This would accord with the sketchily delimited personhood of someone first emerging from sleep and with Rossett's uneasy sense of selfhood caused by his inability to "get used" to Calcutta. The context of impoverished India, with a member of the white ambassadorial society surrounded by obsequious native servants also brings to mind the royal we of privilege, albeit ironically given Rossett's malaise. If spoken only by "Duras", "we" conveys contempt for the character either being addressed or spoken for, and whose nostalgic dream of France it implicitly mocks. Finally, an equally tenable reading could assign the "we" to the Indian servant, who would utter it or think it with deference or disdain. Purposeful imprecision, then, compounded by lack of quotation marks, makes it difficult to identify the speaker of the sentence.

The exaggerated repetition of the word "rosy" within the syntagma "rosy woman, rosy reader, rosy," and of the entire phrase in the same paragraph heightens the sarcasm of the latter two perspectives. The insistence on skin color underscores the racist structures of colonialism and the sexism accompanying them. Inferentially contrasted to the dark skinned Indians, the white woman is the symbol of refinement, protected, privileged – and desexualized. In his dream, Rossett finds her boring compared to the image not, to be sure, of Indian women, but of the sun-tanned Anne-Marie Stretter.

"We dreamed that at the side of that rosy woman rosy reader we felt a certain boredom/longing [ennui] for something else that is found around here, in the somber light, a woman's form in white shorts [Stretter]" (V-C, p. 47). At the novel's end, Duras again switches a locution from one narrative source to another. The rosy female reader reappears in the Vice-Consul's voice: "She [his aunt] is looking for a wife for me [. . .] She would read, rosy reader with rosy cheeks, Proust. [. . .] the little goose from Neuilly, she is white" (V-C, p. 211). This shifts derision from the aunt and the imagined fiancée to the Vice-Consul, again connecting his disparagement of women, his murders of Indian lepers and his impotence. Retrospectively the "we" in the Rossett dream scene can read as inclusive of the Vice-Consul and the white diplomats, designating the collective white male colonial imagination. Like Rossett, the diplomats as well as the Vice-Consul fantasize about Anne-Marie Stretter.[19]

Duras makes great use of the highly mobile third person French pronoun "on," which usually designates a collectivity: "one," "they," or, more informally, "we," but which can address a diminished "you" or even substitute for "I".[20] When it replaces "you", "on" carries with it the attenuation of personhood inherent in the third person. If "on" is used instead of "tu" in questions directed to children (Has "on" been good?) it connotes the child's inferior status. Duras' manipulation of "on" in the scene with Rossett also produces a plurality contingent on narrative ambiguity: "An Indian servant wakes Charles Rossett. Through the half-open door, the head appears, with cunning and prudence. Monsieur must wake up. 'On' opens 'on's' eyes, 'on' has forgotten, like every afternoon, 'on' has forgotten Calcutta" (V-C, p. 47). The discursive source remains unspecified, which permits additional permutations. Whether read as "you" or "he," in the narrator's voice or the Indian servant's thought or speech, "on" conveys disdain for the representative of white colonialist power. Additionally, it is impossible to decide who, Rossett or "Duras," speaks or thinks the words "cunning" and "prudence."

When, on the same page, "on" designates Rossett and his servant in rapid succession and a hackneyed colonialist comment on native inefficiency follows, there occurs a further ricochetting of disparagment: "'On' [Rossett] wants some tea. And [Rossett wants] 'on' [the servant] to open the shutters. [On veut du thé. Et que l'on ouvre les volets.] There, the shutters squeak, for they will never know how to manipulate them." Like the beggar, the lepers, and all Indians, the servant remains nameless and unindividuated, depersonalized through use of the third person, collectivized in the plural "they." Exposed by Duras, denigration shifts from the Indians to the white man. The discursive move that denies personhood to "natives" in order to justify exploitation is deconstructed. The play on narrative ambiguity shatters the single viewpoint, and the situation is presented from several simultaneous perspectives: that of white society, that of the Indian(s), that of Duras. As though to drive home the point, Duras thematizes the question of vision in the startling sentence immediately contiguous to the derogatory remark: " . . . for they will never know how to manipulate them. Where is the gaze?"

The lengthy reception scene at the French embassy (V-C, pp. 92–164) offers the greatest plurality of voice and perspective. One might liken it to Greek tragedy, in which focus and point of view shift from one protagonist to another, relayed by a chorus. But it would be in a form inclusive of stage directions by an "author" who does not vanish during performances. It is the writer-narrator who sets the scene, informing us of the number of guests and describing the ballroom: "[. . .] those fine grates on the windows through which one would see the gardens as though through a mist, no one is looking" [V-C, p. 93]. (An intertextual reference to the ball scene of *Le Ravissement de Lol V. Stein* points to the signer: "The rooms are vast. They are those of a summer casino at a sea resort [. . .]" [V-C, p. 93]).

After these preliminaries, the writer-narrator continues to orchestrate what follows. She alternately speaks as "author" and goes from one character's point of view to another's, communicating directly or indirectly what various people do and say, what they remember, what they think, and even what they will say or remember. Yet it must be reiterated that "Duras" does not assume the stance of traditional omniscient narration. She varies point of view in the interests of deconstructing omniscience, univocity, and objectivity. In the reception scene this functions mostly dialogically, to unseat white colonial society from its throne of symbolic-discursive universality. Duras localizes that society within the novel through a personification which casts its perspective as but one among many. It is revealed to be ideological and eminently fallible. Unlike the Greek chorus, an informed and objective judge, it is both a biased intratextual commentator and an actor in the diegesis. The reader watches as it misjudges, misunderstands, and misinterprets.

Although the white community is represented by a great diversity of grammatical forms covering the gamut of unidentified voices,[21] the pronoun designating it most often is "on." Rather than personifying, actually, this pronoun collectivizes impersonality. In contrast to the personal form "we," which emphasizes the subjective "I" contained in it, "on," an impersonal, third person form, de-emphasizes subjectivity in favor of a generality linguistically projected as unanimous. (As in "En France on parle français": in France one speaks French.) Through a process of condensation which causes "on" to precipitate out as but one voice among others, Duras relativizes the impersonal and demystifies its assumed universality. The reader observes an "on" which no longer stands for everyone. The reception scene abounds in presentations in the form of "on" says, "on" remarks, etc., which renders its bad faith particularly visible. The decentering of white colonial discourse through all these techniques constitutes one of the novel's most stunning achievements.

One more "voice," the beggar's silent one, increases the heteroglossia dialogizing the voice of white society. I amplify Bakhtin's term to include a certain silence as a category of non verbal yet "vocal" social contestation. Duras makes great use of women's silence in her texts.[22] Intradiegetically the beggar's has become empty muteness, but extradiegetically Duras' rendition of it gives it voice for the reader. The beggar is reintroduced periodically, in counterpoint to the ambassadorial party. Incarnating Otherness in her poverty, race, gender, foreignness, and madness, she represents disruption itself. Therefore, "on" excludes her, fencing her out and not listening to her or thinking about her. Outside the embassy gates, as she waits for the distribution of leftovers, "She is talking, saying something no one would understand" (V-C, p. 149). Implied by the conditional "would understand," the absent subordinate clause (presumably "if anyone were to listen") suggests in turn an equally absent yet obvious "but no one does" (except Anne-Marie Stretter[23]). These interruptions of the reception scene counterpose the beggar's hunger to the embassy's luxury. Unlike "on," the reader cannot avoid her or the questions raised by her reduction to muteness.

The contrast is made possible by Duras' use of intermediary voices, through which she can avoid direct representation, denounce the ideology subtending it and yet at the same time convey a story's intensity. Peter Morgan's unfinished notes about the beggar, for example, are Marguerite Duras' finished product – but only part of it. The narrative structure enables her to distance herself from Morgan's attitude. The thematization of writing introduces "Duras" and directs us to the signer. We see the problems raised by the "trickery" of direct representation – Morgan's stance – and Duras' solution of it: indirect representation with as its source an "ignorance" one does not seek to overcome.

MODERATO CANTABILE, DIX HEURES ET DEMIE DU SOIR EN ÉTÉ

How do narrative "ignorance" and plurality of voice, its Durassian corollary, manifest themselves in the author's other texts? What strikes the reader is the diversity of Duras' technical invention. It is as if the very premise of non-adequate narrative discourse generated multiple approaches. Sometimes an incident, witnessed neither by the text's protagonists nor by the narrator, but which fascinates them, shapes the text's matrix. Confronted after the "fact" with an inherently unknowable event, they speculate about it, and their wondering engenders new relationships and the text itself.

In *Moderato Cantabile*, a crime of passion has been committed in a café. It remains doubly unknowable, because the novel's main characters did not witness it, and the murderer, who appears but briefly, refuses to explain his act. Soon we learn that he has gone mad, which further inhibits learning "the truth." Yet the impossibility of elucidation is precisely what attracts Anne Desbaresdes and Chauvin to the café, induces their initial meeting and subsequent encounters, and produces the multi-tiered textuality which constitutes the novel. Although Anne and Chauvin return daily to discuss the crime, they do not attempt to ascertain facts. To the contrary, they begin each meeting with reiterations of their ignorance. Their first conversation opens with statements confirming the inaccessibility of "the truth": "[Anne] 'And evidently one can not know why?' [. . .] [Chauvin] 'I would like to be able to tell you, but I know nothing certain.' [Anne] 'Perhaps no one knows?' [Chauvin] 'He knew. Now he has gone mad, [and has been] locked up since last night. As for her, she is dead.'"[24] This is followed on the one hand by successive declarations of ignorance, such as "I do not know" (M-C p. 27) and "I know nothing" (M-C, pp. 41, 54, 84, 85, 111, etc.), and on the other hand, by insistent mutual requests to talk about the crime.

Whenever the two meet at the café, they discuss the murder they know nothing about. They fabricate versions only to negate any truth value of their suppositions, declaring, for example, that they have been lying (M-C, pp. 59, 87) or making things up (M-C, p. 43). In a cooperative effort *not* to know, then, Anne continually begs Chauvin to speak about the murder, while he orders her to say anything at all about it: "Hurry up and speak. Invent" (M-C, p. 59).

"Ignorance" repeatedly invoked forms the foundation of their relationship. Only once the field has been ritually cleared at the beginning of each rendezvous, disencumbering the terrain, so to speak, of fact, do Anne and Chauvin proceed to what really matters: their excursion into imagination. They continue to return to the blank scene of the crime in order to construct their own scene. "Ignorance" enables them to invent a story with which, moreover, they identify so strongly that they "act it out" verbally. Akin to the crucial moment in psychoanalysis, they imitate what they recount, except that here they are creating fictions instead of remembering "fact." They project into an imaginary past, the absent source of the fictions they create and of their new relationship. The occurrence obsessing them – passionate love culminating in the murder of a woman at her request – veers out of the visual and the concrete into the verbal. Gradually, discourse displaces "reality" in the realm of experience itself. Although Anne and Chauvin have no sexual contact, their verbal intercourse carries enough performative power to make of Anne "that adulterous woman," a title conferred on her by the narrator (M-C, p. 114). The novel culminates with a fusion of imagination and experience – again in the performative – in which the two protagonists substitute themselves discursively for the original couple. Through speech acts, they "enact" the passionate crime. After transforming the deeds of the original couple into words, they treat their own words as deeds, living, loving, dying in the performative: "'I wish you were dead,' says Chauvin. 'Done,' [c'est fait] says Anne Desbaresdes" (M-C, p. 114). A speech act itself, the text ends with the end of the verbal performance, as Anne Desbaresdes disappears in the "sunset", the "red light" (M-C, p. 115) of which bathes both her and the café in the symbolic color of blood.

Dix heures et demie du soir en été, Duras' other novel revolving around a crime of passion, centers on two elusive acts which captivate the heroine, Maria: a man's murder of his young wife and her lover in Spain, and the imminent lovemaking between

Maria's husband, Pierre, and their friend Claire. Maria witnesses neither one; the former took place before her arrival in the small Spanish town, and the latter is structurally exclusive of her. The two stories of betrayal parallel each other and intersect in Maria's fascinated "ignorance."

Despite its outwardly classical form, the novel is not traditional. Duras appears to have chosen a seemingly omniscient attitude for the express purpose of undermining it. She achieves this in part by rendering the point of view ambiguous in key passages. One can not determine, for example, whether an omniscient narrator describes the love scene between Maria's husband and Claire,[25] or if it is the indirect transcription of something Maria imagines (or dreams). Several factors contribute to the reader's "ignorance." Maria has announced that she is going to sleep on a bench in the dining room of the hotel where the three French tourists have stopped for lunch. But numerous contradictory allusions make it impossible to ascertain whether or not she sleeps. Claire remarks: "She's sleeping" (D-H, p. 168). On the next page a question, the discursive source of which might be any of the protagonists or the narrator alone, throws the assertion into doubt: "Is Maria sleeping?" (D-H, p. 169). Pierre declares: "She is not sleeping" (D-H, p. 170). Maria herself seems not to know: "She thinks that she is sleeping" (D-H, p. 172) and "Maria is sleeping. She [Maria] is certain of it. If she pushed it, she would dream. But she doesn't push it. She doesn't dream. It's admirable, this sudden calm following the discovery of her awakening. She wasn't sleeping, then" (D-H, p. 173).[26] The narrative source of this last sentence also remains unclear. Consequently, the reader does not know in whose perspective to cast the images of Pierre's and Claire's lovemaking (D-H, pp. 170–175), or whether or not Maria is lying when she subsequently claims to have slept so well during the couple's absence (D-H, p. 175).

The present tense heightens the ambiguity. Interspersed with it, there occur declarative sentences in the future, a form of literary anticipation usually indicative of an omniscient narrator. Yet Duras deconstructs that stance through the use of questions and expressions of uncertainty. For example, concerning Pierre in the hotel room with Claire, seen by the narrator or imagined by Maria: "He will know later that he saw her in the frame of the open window, between the olive trees. Will he know it later?" (D-H, p. 172). Pierre then tells Claire that she is beautiful, but again doubt is interjected: "You are beautiful. God, but you are. Or perhaps no word will be pronounced" (D-H, p. 172). These devices shatter the omniscient stance, pluralizing narrative possibilities.

Pierre's compliment to Claire compounds the confusion of levels anaphorically, because it echoes words appearing much earlier in the novel, in a passage equally difficult to assign with certainty to Maria or the narrator (we have seen how this manipulation of repetition functions in *Le Vice-consul*): "Where can they have found a place to meet this evening, in this hotel? Where will he take off that light skirt, this very night? How beautiful she is. How beautiful you are, God but you are. Their forms have disappeared completely from that balcony with the rain" (D-H, p. 51). The interrogative form, the absence of any punctuation indicating a speaker and the switch from the third person to the second add to the "ignorance" concerning the narrative source. When the phrases recur, they do not clarify. Maria might be imagining the words; she might be overhearing them; the narrator might be speaking them. Contextually, what "counts" is their possibility. Whether or not they were "really uttered," their existence on the page activates signification.

In several of Duras' texts an absent character forms the focal point of an entire narrative. In *L'Après-midi de Monsieur Andesmas*, an elderly man awaiting his daughter, and a woman whose husband is perhaps beginning an affair with her, indulge in anguished mutual questioning about her. The novel consists of the man's solitary waiting, then of their conversation, waiting together, and their interaction. The young girl never appears. In *Le Marin de Gibraltar*, *Hiroshima mon amour* and *Savannah Bay*, textuality is also generated by a central character's absence. The refusal to "represent directly," a constant in Duras' oeuvre, frees imagination and textuality from the confines of adequation.

PHANTASM AND NARRATION IN *LE RAVISSEMENT DE LOL V. STEIN*

"Comme tout récit à la première personne, *Alexis* est le portrait d'une voix."

Marguerite Yourcenar

Whenever the intermediary narrating voice is a male "writer," a woman's madness ensures her silence, the narrator's "ignorance," and his textual productivity. Partial in *Le Vice-consul* (Peter Morgan's writing and speaking in place of the psychotic beggar), this format contains all of *Le Ravissement de Lol V. Stein*, which has a rare narrative structure: a female author, a male narrating "writer," and a female protagonist upon whom he claims to be focusing. This text undermines the unity of the single internal narrator, dramatizes the destructiveness of the drive to unitary language and depicts its essential failure.

On the night of a summer ball at the T. Beach casino, nineteen-year-old Lola Valérie Stein is abandoned by her fiancé, Michael Richardson, who goes off with another woman. Lol plunges into a profound crisis that will culminate in insanity. Fixated on the impossible vision of her own absence, she tries obsessively but unsuccessfully to imagine the lovemaking of the newly formed couple that excludes her. Her madness takes the form of a blank phantasmal scene for which, after failing to compose it through imagination alone, she seeks more concrete support. By way of another couple, Jacques Hold and Tatiana Karl (her childhood friend who had attended the ball with her), Lol reconstructs the scene. Although she will never witness it, the knowledge of its enactment places her phantasm on firmer ground. But not just any couple making love can serve this purpose. Because Lol's phantasm requires that she be replaced and forgotten again and again, because she lives for this incessant annihilation, the man involved must love her and abandon her repeatedly. Such a role implies conscious cooperation on his part.[27] In order to obtain it, Lol selects her man, seduces him, and makes him her accomplice. For "love" of Lol (we shall see some of the questionable aspects of this "love") Jacques Hold consents to continue to see Tatiana[28] and thus to "abandon" Lol each time he has sex with Tatiana in the Hôtel des Bois.

Hold's eagerness to play his designated part becomes problematical, given the novel's structure. Since his is the narrating voice, this willingness elicits questions of "who": who is living the phantasm; who is speaking; who is seeing; whose story is being told? The answer is at once double, for Hold becomes part of Lol's phantasmal world, and single, for Lol is neither the one who sees nor the one who speaks. Indeed, the "story" the narrator recounts is not simply Lol's. It is primarily his, that is, the story of his own entry into phantasm. And the novel itself tells yet another tale: the story of his narration.

Hold cooperates so readily because he has become fascinated by an unlived moment in someone else's past. What he desires is to penetrate that past: "She is the night of T. Beach. Soon, when I kiss her, the door will open, I will enter" (Rav, p. 121). Not content to duplicate Michael Richardson's conduct, he wants to blend with him, to experience directly those past events. He means to accompany Lol figuratively and literally on her voyage back to T. Beach, to follow her into her imagined memory: "Here is the moment of my access into Lol V. Stein's memory" (Rav, p. 202). However, in his haste to invade her phantasm, he does violence both to himself and to her. Love and fascination cross the boundary into obsession and disregard. Hold overlooks the fact that one does not come and go at will in the world of insanity; at risk is the coherence of the self. Mesmerized by *his* desires, he embraces and even longs for this disintegration: "I desire [. . .] to be part of the thing Lol lies about. Let her carry me off [. . .] let her pulverize me with the rest [. . .]" (Rav, p. 124). In a sort of ritual de-naming ceremony with Lol, he enacts his depersonalization onomastically. The moment she utters his name, he experiences an internal fissure. His own name names him no longer: "Who had noticed the inconsistency of the belief in that person so named if not she [. . .] For the first time my name pronounced does not name" (Rav, p. 131).

While this extraordinary scene marks Hold's passage into phantasm, it does not herald participation in a world shared with Lol. By its very nature, phantasm severs one from the world of others and from time. (Lol lives locked in an imaginary past.) Phantasm isolates, shuts one into a state akin to dreaming as Ludwig Binswanger notes: "The individual's images, his feelings [. . .] belong to him alone, he lives completely in his own world, and being alone means, psychologically, dreaming – whether or not there is at this time a physiological state of sleep."[29] Lol's world remains perforce sealed to Hold. Therefore, his claims of penetrating what he himself refers to as her dream ("Lol dreams [. . .] That dream contaminates me" – Rav, p. 217) are indicative of his, not her illusions. All the more so given that Lol lives attuned to the eminently private moment of her own extinction. The role assigned to Hold reinforces her exclusion – and his. Thus in its very configuration, Lol's phantasm precludes togetherness. One may conclude that Lol and Hold do not share the same phantasm.

The dynamics of Hold's phantasm involve a complex nexus of cruelty, (self) destruction and perversion, articulated around a desire for knowledge defined as possession. Lol represents a mystery

("What was this tranquil ghost hiding [. . .]?" – Rav, p. 92) he would like to elucidate for the knowledge it will bring him about *himself*: "But what is it about myself that I am ignorant of to such a degree and that she summons me to know?" (Rav, p. 123). Uninterested in an "ignorance" which acknowledges otherness without trying to absorb it, Hold embarks on an essentially epistemological undertaking, as Michèle Montrelay observes: "Jacques Hold [. . .] he who knows that a woman's 'madness' attracts him most vitally [le sollicite au plus vif] because it turns his anxiety into that burning curiosity which is the epistemological drive."[30] The text is punctuated with his exclamations of frustration at the impossibility of knowing Lol, but also with statements expressing the excitement afforded him by a woman who eludes full "possession."

Lol retains his interest precisely because she has "a secret [. . .] that she will never disclose to him, he *knows* it" (Rav, p. 150 – emphasis added). She "has gone off towards something else, vaguer, endless, she will go off towards something else that I will never *know*, endless" (Rav, p. 179 – emphasis added). The narrator transforms into antithetical declarations of knowledge the very "ignorance" which ensures the continuation of his quest: "What I know for certain are the stakes of this victory: the retreat of clarity" (Rav, p. 127). Not knowing Lol becomes knowing her: "Now, alone among all these falsifiers, I know: I know nothing. That was my first discovery about her: to know nothing about Lol was already to know her. One could, it seemed to me, know still less, less and less about Lol" (Rav, p. 94). Thus Lol's impenetrability guarantees at once knowledge and mystery, possession and the chase: "Since I know – have I ever known anything to such a degree? – that she is unknowable to me, one can not be closer to a human being than I am to her, closer than she is to herself [. . .]" (Rav, p. 192). Despair on the one hand, delight on the other, for the dynamics of traditional masculine "possession" turn women into objects of knowledge to be had, and, once had, discarded with ennui. In order to avoid boredom, the narrator maintains the dialectic knowledge – ignorance, counterbalancing efforts to know and epistemological frustration ("[. . .] she is hiding something" – Rav, p. 197) with efforts not to know ("You mustn't tell me everything" – Rav, p. 196).

Hold tires of Tatiana and despises her because he thinks he knows her, and her body, "better than Tatiana herself" (Rav, p. 155). The discovery that he will never succeed in knowing Lol secures his interest, which lies in the perpetual repetition of his

own phantasmal quest for knowledge, renewable precisely because
it goes unsatisfied. Cruelty and perversion come into play. Moved
by a desire for endless knowledge-possession rather than by love,
Hold has no thought of helping Lol out of neurosis. Her madness
must be perpetuated, for it causes her to escape his "trap," ("My
hands become the trap in which to immobilize her" – Rav, p. 125)
and continue to attract him. When Lol voices her fear of incumbent
insanity, and, in an indirect appeal, expresses her loss of identity, he
exhorts her not to change: "[Lol:] 'I don't understand who is in my
place.' [. . . Hold:] Don't change'" (Rav, p. 160). When she suffers:
"I say nothing, do not come to her aid" (Rav, p. 153).

In addition to encouraging Lol to remain neurotic, Hold induces
the crisis which propels her into psychosis. She commits the existentially fatal error of deciding to spend a night alone with him. This
alters her phantasmal structure, reducing the necessary trio into a
duo, in which she has the wrong role, something Hold understands
perfectly: "The crisis is here. Our situation, at this moment, in this
room where she and I are alone, has set it off" (Rav, p. 217). Although
he perceives that Lol's fragile equilibrium is breaking, he aggravates
matters, undressing her when she won't do it herself, lying in order
to keep her in the room ("Let's go,' says Lol. 'I say the police would
arrest us" – Rav, p. 218) and touching her despite her protestations
of pain ("Oh, how you're hurting me.' – I continue" – Rav, p. 218).
The shaky identity Lol had constructed depended on her phantasm's
triangular structure. When she is alone with Hold in the hotel room
that identity can not sustain itself. She asks frantically who she is. It
is then that Hold provokes her descent into madness, by calling her
Tatiana: "She asks, 'who is it ?' She groans, asks me to tell her. I say,
'Tatiana Karl, for example'" (Rav, p. 218). In order to reconstruct the
triadic structure of her phantasm, Lol seizes on Hold's suggestion
that she be Tatiana. Her personality splits, and she refers to herself
alternately as Tatiana and as Lol (Rav, p. 219). This rectifies things
onomastically, but at the price of Lol's psychic ruin.

Hold's disregard for Lol is matched by his perverse cruelty to
Tatiana. Aware that she realizes he does not love her and that
she wishes he did (Rav, p. 175), he takes pleasure in a grotesque
parody of love. He speaks lovingly to her, enjoying the certainty
that she does not believe him: "Doubtless she did not believe that
they [his words] were addressed to her" (Rav, p. 142). He persists far
beyond the exigencies of Lol's phantasm, relishing the insult in his
false declarations, phantasizing more and more violent effects. He

considers his lying protestations now an annihilating punishment
that will cover Tatiana's "shame" (Rav, p. 183); now a cup of poison
he administers slowly, the better to savor her suffering ("I say, 'I love
you.' Once the words are pronounced, my mouth remained open so
that they would pour out to the last drop" – Rav, pp. 184–185); now
a physical attack ([. . .] but the blow is dealt, and Tatiana felled"
– Rav, p. 185). His erotic phantasies involving her couple sex with
death (of the woman), exposing an association basic to the dominant
symbolic order: "Soon, soon, in less than two days, I will possess all
of Tatiana Karl, completely, until her end" (Rav, p. 107). He reaches
a paroxysm of imagined violence when during sex he simulates her
murder. Covering her head with the bed sheet, he "possesses" her
"decapitated body," symbol of severed selfhood, of the reduction of
women to silent flesh: "He hides Tatiana's face under the sheets and
thus has her decapitated body in his hands, entirely at his disposal.
He turns it, raises it, disposes of it as he wishes [. . .]" (Rav, p. 156).
He phantasizes further brutality: "Her hot, gagged body, I plunge
into it [. . .] I graft myself onto it, I pump Tatiana's blood [. . .]
Beneath me she slowly becomes bloodless" (Rav, p. 194).

Consistent with dominant binarism, Hold consigns Lol and
Tatiana to opposite poles of the virgin/whore dichotomy. To
Tatiana, the illicit, ever available lover, devolves the latter role.
Along with boredom, (carnal) knowledge breeds contempt. Hold
mocks Tatiana's "air [. . .] of false shame," (Rav, p. 155). If submission to sex devalues women, female desire removes all worth
entirely. Black haired, sensual Tatiana has an "insatiable body whose
existence is indifferent to him" (Rav, p. 155). The adulterous woman
is scorned like the (as a) prostitute. Metaphors merge the two;
Tatiana's "body of an adulteress" (Rav, p. 67) becomes a "body
of a whore," (Rav, p. 91) whose "wound [. . .] calls out ceaselessly
[for the phallus and] [. . .] it is whole only in a hotel bed" (Rav,
p. 91). Tatiana is an "admirable whore" (Rav, p. 136). In contrast to
the dark woman-whore, blond modest Lol (Rav, p. 193) is a virginal
girl: "Virginity of Lol pronouncing that [his] name!" (Rav, p. 131).
Innocent like a child, "She has a childlike odor, like talcum powder"
(Rav, p. 157). With "that well-behaved stiffness of a grown boarding
school girl," (Rav, p. 170), she moves like a child (Rav, p. 172) and her
"sweet" face and body are "drowned in the sweetness [douceur] of
an interminable childhood [. . .]" (Rav, p. 205).

With her "air of remorse," (Rav, p. 155) eyes "of a gravity ravaged
by ineffable remorse," (Rav, p. 67) and body showing signs of wear

(her breasts are "already rather spoiled" – Rav, p. 75), Tatiana pays the wages of sin. The ultimate punishment for her free love will be death, meted out symbolically in bed by Jacques Hold. Then, after "killing" the "whore," Hold will deflower the ever youthful "virgin": "I lie down next to her [Lol's] closed body" (Rav, p. 218) – in the very same hotel room. (The flower metaphor had appeared earlier. Lol's fingers "[. . .] have, for me, the newness of a flower [. . .] Lol's hair has the floral texture of her hands" – Rav, p. 132). But, after intercourse, virgins resemble other women. They incur the same symbolic debasement and elicit the boredom and violence attendant on "possession." Although catastrophic for Lol, her personality split provides a perfect solution for Hold. It resolves the contradiction between her "virginity" and her obvious knowledge of sex. As Tatiana, she "begs to be taken again," and is so "knowing" that "there was no longer any difference between her and Tatiana Karl [. . .]" (Rav, p. 219). As Lol, she "begs [. . .] to be left alone, [feels] hunted, tries to flee from the room, from the bed [. . .]" – Rav, p. 219). The man can enjoy the lust of the whore and the frightened timidity of the violated virgin all in one woman. Thus Hold's phantasm moves along perverse, sadistic lines, and occupies a space quite different from Lol's.

The text, then, recounts two phantasms, but has only one narrator. The narrating voice belongs to Jacques Hold. Yet, if the narrator and the male protagonist are the same "human being," they do not coincide. Analysis of the text's narrative structure reveals the importance of this factor in the other "story," that of narrative voice.

Although the book is written in the first person,"I"'s identity remains concealed for more than one third of the text. Only on page eighty-five does the narrator disclose his name, and only on page eighty-seven does he explicitly define his relationship to Tatiana Karl. One might suppose that, concerned with creating suspense and respecting the chronology of a story he relates through the eyes of the heroine, the narrator reserves the introduction of his name for the moment when Lol actually learns it. But this hypothesis collapses because the text contains two protagonists, Hold and Lol, because the former has more weight by virtue of his narrative stance, because the narrator maintains no distance from his text, which is actually non-linear, and because the eyes through which everything is seen and the voice expressing that vision, are always only his.

On the one hand, the name "Jacques Hold" solves several

mysteries. Pronouns converge: the speaking "I," "me," but also "he," and "the man" – Tatiana's lover, whom Lol had followed through the streets of S. Tahla. On the other hand, despite the cessation of narrative deceit, no linguistic unity of person ensues. Even after naming himself, the narrator does not merge "I" with "he."

Before page eighty-five, the narrator does state that he enjoys an intense personal relationship with Lol. Still, enough ambiguity persists (due, in part, to his use of the third person to designate himself in that section) so that the moment of onomastic identification comes as a surprise. The pause created by the blank space on page eighty-five, followed by the entirely blank page eighty-six, breaks the textual flow, drawing the reader backwards rather than forwards. One must reread the text up to that point in order to grasp the extent of the narrative deception and to begin to appreciate the complexity of the narrator's relationship to his text. We discover that "Jacques Hold," "he," is also the "I" who is "writing," who, *qua* author (he refers to "the reader" on page thirteen) has been manipulating information he already possessed. Further, instead of presenting his text as objective, the writing narrator repeatedly proclaims the opposite. If at first he often documents his information ("Tatiana says," "they say," etc.), quite soon he repudiates the principal source, informing the reader that he no longer believes Tatiana (Rav, p. 12). (It is not coincidental that the source Hold negates is a woman. In *his* text, he deprives women of discourse either by discrediting what they say – Tatiana, Lol's mother – or by speaking in their place – Lol.) Having dissipated the factual stance, he announces that the story of the ball will be a mixture of Tatiana's report and his own invention. Thereafter, he furnishes a sort of anti-documentation, punctuating the narrative with a mélange of "outside" sources and personal statements such as "I think," I'm making this up," so that fact and imagination merge. What emerges is a single vision and existential "truth," reality, in other words, as projected by the narrator, who states as early as page twelve: "I am going to tell *my* story of Lol V. Stein" (emphasis added).

In an early declaration of intent, he informs us that he has filtered what he has learned about Lol's past, choosing to relate only a minimum. Lol's life as such does not interest this "writer." Only that part of her existence which relates to him contains significance. He devotes so much space to the ball because of its central role in *his* entry into Lol's life, that is, into (his) phantasm: "I don't want to

know the nineteen years preceding that night any more than I say
[. . .] because the presence of her adolescence in this story might
attenuate in the reader's eyes this woman's crushing presence in
my life" (Rav, pp. 12–13). With the same vocabulary of possession,
he explains how he will manipulate Lol textually: he will "take
her," "at the moment she seems to *me* to begin moving towards
meeting *me*" (Rav, p. 13 – emphasis added). This correlates to the
rebirth imagery and to Lol's "virginity." She gets reborn when *he* –
a demonic "saviour" – enters the picture, and the mother of three
becomes a virgin (mother) when she pronounces *his* name: "The
virginity of Lol pronouncing that [his] name!" (Rav, p. 131).

Lol's "crushing presence" in Jacques Hold's diegetic life as
character and in his narration is phantasmically projected. The
word "presence" provides a key to the novel. From the very
first sentences, the textual discourse is situated in the here and
now: "Lol V. Stein was born [est née] here, in S. Tahla" (Rav,
p. 9). With certain exceptions I analyze shortly, the verbal tense
predominating is the present. It includes the passé composé which,
as Benveniste shows, establishes a "living link" to the act of speech
in the process of being made (in the present) and, therefore, to the
speaker. This makes the passé composé an "autobiographical form
par excellence."[31] As Erwin Straus writes, the passé composé is
"meant as present," and "cannot be detached from myself as the
one who is narrating, experiencing, thinking."[32] Many passages
beginning in that form slip into the present. They usually contain
deictics, another sign of the narrator's present/presence. The text
is narrated in the present, not by someone simply reporting past
events in his life, or experiencing them for the first time as he writes,
but by someone living them in a perpetual and perpetually repeated
present. It is an iterative present, not unlike that of stage directions
in scripts, for a drama designed to be perpetually reenacted.

Reiteration characterizes the narrative from content to syntagmatic configuration. Repetitions of whole scenes, paragraphs,
sentences and words must be situated not on the diegetic but
on the narrative level. Pontalis and Laplanche define phantasm
as an "imaginary scenario in which the subject is present,
and which figures, in a fashion more or less distorted by
defensive processes, the satisfaction of a desire [. . .] [it is]
repetitive behavior."[33] The subject of the narratively enacted
and re-enacted phantasm is none other than the "I" announced
in the first paragraph of the text, and who speaks in the perpetually

repeating present of the recurrent waking dream that constitutes the novel.

The continual textual repetitions issue not from Lol but from the narrator, who, as speaker, is already caught in the phantasmal world he constructed as a character. For example, on page ninety-three, the narrator repeats data concerning Lol's adolescence which were already provided in the text's opening pages. Much the same information reappears yet again on page one hundred nineteen. This can not be explained as a desire to inform the reader. Given the narrator's stated intention to speak very little of Lol's past, the triple reiteration becomes additionally symptomatic, especially when one observes that each time he repeats something, he does so practically verbatim. The narrator is far too obsessively involved to be able to monitor his narrative. Far from being the simple narration of a phantasm, *Le Ravissement de Lol V. Stein* is a phantasmal narrative in which the narrator himself is caught.

Several "slips" indicate his loss of control. He cites one of Lol's mother's remarks in the present tense, leading one to conclude that he consults her as he consults Tatiana: "Lol, says Mme Stein, was taken back to S. Tahla, and she stayed in her room for a few weeks without going out at all" (Rav, p. 23). Yet we subsequently learn that Lol's mother died years ago, before he met Lol, so that he could not have spoken with her. In the passage describing Tatiana's introduction of him to Lol, the narrator "writes": "Tatiana, now, the one who at any second is going to scream my name" (Rav, p. 83). For the narrator already obsessed with Lol at the time of the "writing," the impact of his name about to be mentioned (by *him* as writer) for the first time in the text, may resound to his own ears as a scream. But if anyone screams here, it is the narrator, not Tatiana, whom he portrays in the act of calmly making the introduction: "Tatiana introduces Pierre Beugner, her husband, and Jacques Hold, one of their friends, to Lol [. . .]" (Rav, p. 85).

The phantasmal character of the narrator's discourse manifests itself markedly in repetitions of the ball scene, which he continually redescribes and re-evokes, in addition to simulating its sequel over and over at the hotel. Initially, he relates it in the passé simple (Rav, pp. 13–21), the French verbal form of the historical, "objective" past. This sets the ball at a temporal zero, the point from which the narrator's "chronicle time" would be measured. Benveniste explains that "chronicle time" founds communal life, by fixing an axis which must remain stationary. Time is then counted in regular intervals before and after it.[34] Yet even as he first recounts the ball, the narrator has ceased to project it as past. It is already "this famous ball," (Rav, p. 10) present, as the deictic implies. The subsequent recapitulations of the scene in the present tense show that it has already changed from a historical event to a phantasmically repeated present that obsesses both narrator and narrative from the outset. The ordered discourse of chronicle time gives way to the temporality of phantasmal discourse, as Benveniste explains it must when the axis of temporal reference is displaced by an individual.[35] This occurs throughout the book in slips from the passé simple to the present, interjections in the latter such as "I see," and alternation of the two forms, so that the passé simple gets absorbed into "now, the present, the present alone, which turns, turns in the dust" not only when Hold meets Lol on page eight-five, but from the text's very beginning.

Almost nothing in the text happens just once. Episodes of pursuit and of "voyeurism" recur frequently, often in inverted form: Lol follows Jacques Hold who in turn follows her, only to be followed again by her, etc. Lol takes up a position of false voyeur outside the hotel[36] and Hold actually spies twice on her and Tatiana (Rav, pp. 105 and 171). The last event of the text, when Lol again lies outside the hotel window where Hold awaits Tatiana, constitutes less a final episode than another instance of the same scene ceaselessly repeated, opening on yet another immobile series enclosed within the walls of the phantasmal ballroom where time does not advance.

On the syntagmatic level, repetition occurs extraordinarily frequently. To cite but a few random examples: "ceaselessly, she will go towards something else that I will never know, ceaselessly" (Rav, p. 179); "the sea subsides, subsides" (Rav, p. 211); "he walked, walked" (Rav, p. 63); "I begin again, perhaps, perhaps" (Rav, p. 195). The phrase about Tatiana "naked under her black hair naked, naked, black hair" (Rav, p. 134) is repeated so often that meaning collapses: "the sentence explodes, it shatters meaning [. . .] I don't understand it, I don't even understand any longer that it doesn't mean anything" (Rav, p. 135).

I can now propose an elucidation of the phenomenon of non-coincidence between the narrating "I" and Jacques Hold. In famous linguistic analyses Benveniste demonstrates that first person narratives contain a double "I": the speaking "I" and the "I" to which the utterance refers, the character in the diegesis. While this distinction does apply here, temporality is not limited to the relatively simple contrast between the present of narration and the past of plot. A multiplicity of pronominal references must be reconciled within this text's complex structure. Before the name Jacques Hold appears, the speaking "I" does contrast to an unidentified character, "I", but also to "he" and "the man." Instead of simplifying matters, the naming of Jacques Hold complicates them further. Moreover, other allusive pronouns such as "we" and "one" [on] must be accounted for as well.

The observation that discursive disarray usually reflects existential, psychological malaise can afford some clarification. The splintering of narrational self-reference corresponds to fissures in the narrator's identity. The various "persons" can not merge because the pronouns do not refer to the same self. Existentially, psychologically, linguistically, Jacques Hold is not the same person as the narrator; unlike the former, the latter has "survived"[37] the scattering of his personality ritually enacted in the above mentioned "de-naming" scene. The very un-French patronymic "Hold" is motivated. Jacques Hold attempts to get a hold on Lol, Tatiana and his text, but loses his grip, especially on himself. The onomastic signifier no longer names (Rav, p. 131) because the self it signified has disappeared. Once he divests himself of his name, there remains no appellation for him beside "I". This shifter has a role to play in "I"'s phantasmal hopes of blending with Michael Richardson. The narrator confirms "I"'s anonymity when he "renames" himself, less misleadingly than on the first occasion: "For the first time my name pronounced does not name. [. . .] *I* am the man in S. Tahla she [Lol] has decided to follow" (Rav, p. 131 – emphasis added). This onomastic depersonalization empties the first person pronoun and prepares the phantasized fusion of identity effected through the use of "on" at the end of the scene: "The eternal Richardson, the man of T. Beach, is going to be useful. 'On' will mix with him pell-mell, all that will merge into one, 'on' will no longer recognize who is who, before or after, 'on' will lose sight of 'on's' self, of 'on's' name [. . .] [on va se perdre de vue, de nom]" (Rav, pp. 131–132). Thus, after initially designating a first person singular ("on" will mix with "him"), "on substitutes for the first person plural "we." The narrower "I" widens into a blurred phantasmal "I – we."

Precisely because "I" is no longer Jacques Hold, the two can not coincide on the narrative level. In its very structure, the sentence in which the name Jacques Hold first appears both evokes a unity which no longer obtains, and expresses the present disunity. It lists a series of elements, but leaves "I" unmentioned and implicitly separate: "Tatiana introduces her husband, Pierre Beugner, to Lol, and Jacques Hold, one of their friends – the distance is covered – me [moi]" (Rav, p. 85). "The value of emphasis or contrast peculiar to 'moi' with respect to 'I' (je)"[38] distinguishes it from "I." Benveniste notes the onomastic role of the autonomous pronoun: "The pronoun 'moi' acts as a proper name."[39] In the above sequence it functions appositively, its antecedent being not "I" but Jacques Hold and/or "one of their friends." This has great significance. On the "I" side of the "I"/Jacques Hold dichotomy, a certain anonymity has developed. On the other side, a more radical depersonalization has taken place. No longer naming "I", Jacques Hold names no one.

The name Jacques Hold, which continues to appear regularly, is reserved almost exclusively for the man who sleeps with Tatiana, and is consistently accompanied by third person forms. For example, at the end of the first scene in Lol's home, which focuses mostly on Lol and is written in the first person, when the narrator speaks once again as Tatiana's lover he switches to the third person and "me" reappears: "Lol gets up too. Opposite her, behind Tatiana, me. He has made a mistake, he thinks. It is not him Lol V. Stein is seeking. It's a question of someone else. [. . .] Tatiana turns towards Jacques Hold: 'Are you coming?' Jacques Hold says 'no'" (Rav, p. 128). (Just after the narrator reveals his name, he writes: "I am Tatiana Karl's lover" – Rav, p. 87. This single instance unambiguously linking the first person to Tatiana occurs just before the subjective coherence it suggests dissolves in the diegesis. It has, of course, already done so on the narrative level. Later, when "I" tells Tatiana he loves her, the reader and "I" know "I" is lying, that "I" neither means he loves Tatiana nor refers to Jacques Hold.)

This division and the gradual emptying of the referential content of the name Jacques Hold are clearest in the hotel scenes. The first takes place before the narrator divulges his name (Rav, pp. 71–76). Therefore, the use of the anonymous third person ("the man," "he," "him") for the as yet unidentified man with Tatiana seems logical if one reads the episode as an indirect presentation from Lol's point of view. However, narrational interjections in the first person and in the present tense mar the unity of that perspective. At this point in the text, the reader can not situate the "I" who says, for example, that he sees how Lol reaches the rye field ("I see how she gets there" – Rav, p. 72), that he remembers ("I remember: the man comes over" – Rav, p. 75), and that he sees Lol ("Lol, I see her, she doesn't move" –Rav,

p. 75). Retrospectively, the reader can interpret the distribution of the referential elements. Here, like in several earlier sections, as well as in the rest of the text, "I" occurs when the narrator thinks directly of Lol, and the third person designates Tatiana's lover.

In the second hotel scene (Rav, pp. 139–146), a dichotomy in verbal forms parallels the pronominal and onomastic split. Whenever the narrator projects towards Lol, he "writes" in the first person and the passé composé, the form linked to the speaker. For example, "I" takes Tatiana to the window to show Lol they are there: "I asked her [je lui ai demandé] to come with me to the window [. . .] I was standing behind her. Thus, I showed [J'ai montré] Tatiana to her" (Rav, p. 141). But "I" vanishes when he turns his attention from Lol and "possesses" Tatiana. In "I"'s place, there appears Jacques Hold, in the third person, which constitutes him as distinct from the narrator. The use of the passé simple, the form of purported absence of relation between speaker and content, further emphasizes this detachment: "Jacques Hold possessed [posséda] Tatiana Karl mercilessly" (Rav, p. 142). As the pace of alternation quickens, the contrast sharpens: "I" went back [je suis allé] to the window [to look at Lol]. [. . .] He went back [il regagna] to the bed, lay down [s'allongea] next to Tatiana Karl" (Rav, p. 145). And "She [Tatiana] made a date with him [lui donna rendez-vous] for three days later, fearing he wouldn't accept. He accepted [il accepta]" (Rav, p. 145), as opposed to "I" when Tatiana has left the room and "I" concentrates on Lol: "When she was gone [a été partie] I turned out the lights [j'ai éteint] so that Lol could go [. . .]" (Rav, p. 146).

But the distinct personae prove difficult to maintain. By the third hotel scene (Rav, pp. 187–190), the narrating "I" has separated himself so thoroughly from Jacques Hold, whom he no longer wants to be, that he can no longer be him. Jacques Hold has become nobody: "She [Lol] loves, loves the one who must love Tatiana. No one. No one in me loves Tatiana" (Rav, p. 154). The narrator's awareness catches up with the linguistic manifestation of the "nobody", the absence of personhood inherent in the third person form. In the third scene, the name Jacques Hold has disappeared, and with it the person who sleeps with Tatiana. Therefore, "I" finds himself impotent. Only Jacques Hold can "take" Tatiana; "I" can not even try: "*I* don't even try to take her, *I* know *I* would be incapable [impuissant] of doing so" (Rav, p. 188 – emphasis added). Jacques Hold remains absent from the episode, told in the first person and in the present tense, for the man with Tatiana thinks only of Lol.[40]

Were the narrator able to adhere to his original literary plan to tell a story in which events unfold chronologically, the fourth hotel scene would be the last. Jacques Hold having disappeared, "I" would remain impotent; Tatiana would know why; they would separate and the phantasm would come apart. But in the conflict between "rational" and phantasmal discourse, the phantasmal need for repetition prevails. The brevity with which the narrator evokes the scene allows him to avoid articulating the structural alteration a definitive break with Tatiana would entail. Instead of depicting the rendezvous, he merely alludes to it: "Night was falling when I arrived at the Hôtel des Bois. Lol had preceded us. She was sleeping in the rye field, tired, tired from our trip" (Rav, p. 221). Sketching only the outlines of the scene, the narrator suggests that it will be enacted as usual, another in a continuing series. The participants reassemble, and we are to suppose they will behave in the prescribed manner, regardless of what has happened in "external" "chronicle" time. Consistent with this phantasmal temporality, the narrator explicitly rejected the concept of an end a bit earlier: "I deny the end that will probably come to separate us, its disheartening simplicity, for from the moment I deny that one I accept the other one, the one which has to be invented, which I don't know, which no one has invented yet: the endless end, the endless beginning of Lol V. Stein" (Rav, p. 214). If the novel finishes with the fourth hotel episode, it serves, then, less to conclude than to refuel the perpetual repetition intrinsic to the narrator's phantasm.

On both the diegetic and the narrative levels, the subject of *Le Ravissement de Lol V. Stein* is thus the tale of the narrator's continuing phantasm, to which priority Lol's story is subordinated. But the narrator is subject in a more crucial sense. He, and only he says "I", in contrast to Lol's inability to express herself. When Lol fell down in a "dead" faint at the end of the ball, she fell silent as well, not uttering a word for several days. Later, she speaks first a prefabricated discourse, composed solely of responses programmed by societal prescriptions of how a bourgeois housewife should speak, then in a more personal yet phantasmal discourse which cuts her off from the world rather than connecting her to it, and reflects her basic alienation from language.[41] Mostly, she does not speak at all: "Lol is silent in life" (Rav, p. 54). Lol's silence conveys the demise of her subjectivity. Devoid of self, she remains voiceless: "[. . .] Lol stands there [Lol se tient], torn, with no voice to call for help [. . .], she is no one" (Rav, p. 53) and "What had she done during those hours of

the day for ten years [. . .] [the years of her marriage to Bedford] She
wasn't able to say [. . .] She was unable to say how [she had spent
her time], nothing" (Rav, p. 50).

It is the narrating "I" who notes Lol's silence, and who asserts his
self contrastively to it. Benveniste demonstrates the link between
subjectivity and the ability (one might add, opportunity) to assert
it by saying "I".[42] As sole possessor of discourse, the narrator
alone constitutes subjectivity, however phantasmally, whereas Lol
remains the voiceless object of his text. Moreover, the narrating "I"
connects his "love" for Lol to her muteness: "I returned to the
window; she was still there, [. . .] alone in that field in a way that
she could communicate to no one. I discovered that about her at the
same time I discovered my love[. . .]" (Rav, p. 145). "I" delights in
Lol's silence because it enhances her mysteriousness, but especially
because it enables him to articulate everything as a function of his
subjectivity, to which he sacrifices both Lol and Tatiana. If Lol does
speak, he will take her words: "I desire like someone overwhelmed
with thirst to drink the foggy and insipid milk of the speech that
comes out of Lol V. Stein [. . .]" (Rav, p. 124).

Lol must remain silent/silenced so that the narrator/writer can
appropriate her phantasm, her person, her story. Remembering
Freud's contention that muteness in dreams is a common representation of death, and that this novel is a sort of phantasmal dream,
one may conclude that Lol's silence, upon which "I"'s cannibalistic
voice is predicated, correlates to her "death," desired, encouraged,
ensured by him. In the narrator's phantasmal murdering of Tatiana,
to "kill" her means above all to silence her, pouring the poison of
his words down her throat, "decapitating" and gagging her in bed.
The putting to death that is sexual intercourse for him is repeatedly
represented as a silencing : "Again I have to shut Tatiana up [through
sex] under the sheet" (Rav, p. 157). Projected by the narrator, Lol's
repeated "velvet annihilation" in the rye field outside the hotel room
(Rav, p. 56) and her psychic death caused by his onomastic and
physical violence when he is alone with her[43] accomplish the same
purpose. The narrator's text, then, exists at the price of the "murder"
of two women.

Beyond the fissure in the narrator's voice, which subverts the
unity and closure of the single narrator within the text, his gender
refers the reader to the female signer. External yet highly pertinent,
her presence enables us to perceive a triple narrative function. The
narrator's "writing" acts simultaneously as a screen (he closes out

or invalidates other discourses), a mirror (the speaker of a text is also spoken by it, especially in first person narratives, as Benveniste notes: "Saying I, I can not not speak about myself"[44]), and a window (Duras' structural presence renders his speech transparent, objectifying it in Bakhtin's sense of presenting it as something to be analyzed and through which we "read" other, silenced discourses).

Martha Evans makes the important point that "while Duras' repetition of male narrative strategies permits her to deconstruct those strategies from within, it also allows her to dramatize the relationship between male tradition and the writing she produces as a woman."[45] However, she concludes from Lol's inability to articulate her desire, that Duras defines the "asymmetry of male and female desire in terms of oblivion and indifference" and that consequently "the shift from male to female narrative" and desire "is a voyage into madness."[46] This affects the author: "the transgression of writing drives both Duras and her character to the edge of madness."[47] I would argue that this applies in Duras only to those female characters already silenced and isolated. As my foregoing study and subsequent analyses show, it is not the shift to narrative but its deprivation that drives Duras' women mad. It will be seen that, if anything, access to discourse preserves Duras' heroines – and Duras – from insanity.

L'AMANTE ANGLAISE, LE MARIN DE GIBRALTAR, LE CAMION

In L'Amante anglaise plurality of voice revolves around a woman's madness and a male "writer"'s planned expropriation of her discourse and her story. Situated on the same diegetic level as the others, the unnamed "writer" interrogates three people about a murder committed by the woman, Claire Lannes. Neither the café owner nor Claire's husband knows the "truth" of what happened, not having witnessed the crime, and the murderess, questioned last, is considered insane. The text's narrative structure calls to mind the film "Rashomon," in which opposing accounts of a rape and murder are recounted successively by several people, with the difference that all of them had been present during the events.

In "Rashomon" the equivalence of each version's claim to truth, based on assertions of empirical knowledge, results in a relativistic impasse. In L'Amante anglaise, the plurality issues from "ignorance," avowed in the case of the first two speakers, and double for Claire

Lannes. Externally, on the one hand: this "crazy" woman's discourse is discredited as irrational ravings, dismissed as a form of
invalid "ignorance." Internally on the other hand: perfectly conscious of this mechanism, Claire reverses the situation, propelling
the investigators (the police inspectors and the "writer") into a
different "ignorance" by declining to disclose where she has hidden
the head of her victim. She subverts the "writer's" quest for truth
through ironic manipulation of her supposed madness: Claire: "So
I'm crazy? What is your answer if I ask you if I'm crazy?" The
"writer": "I also answer yes." Claire: "So you are talking to a
madwoman." "Writer": "Yes." Claire: What a madwoman says
doesn't count. So why ask me where the head is, since what I
say doesn't count."[48] This constitutes the most productive level of
all. For Claire's refusal to dispel official ignorance enables her (and
Duras) to textualize. Her silence on that one point forms the condition of her discourse, because, were she to provide the requested
information and satisfy the ambient desire for rational clarity and
totality, the missing piece in the puzzle would fit, the mystery of
the crime would be solved, and no one would talk or listen to her
any longer. The world would resume its repression of her.[49] Worse,
if she succumbed to the demand for order and clarity, she would be
eliminated, as she herself remarks: "I know that the more criminals
speak clearly, the more they are killed" (A-A, p. 142). (One might
read a pun in Claire's first name, which in French means "clear.").

L'Amante anglaise introduces another facet of plurivocity through
the interrogating "writer"'s initial statement that he is taping
everything that is being said. Like Peter Morgan's "notes," and
similar to the structure of many of Duras' texts, the ambiguous
status of what we read elicits a number of questions, which remain
open: Are we to project as present with the taping? Are we reading
Duras' or the "writer"'s transcription of the taped sessions? The
first sentence of the text informs the reader, along with the other
characters, not only of the taping in progress, but that a book is
beginning to be written: "Everything said here is being taped. A
book on the Viorme crime is beginning to be made" (A-A, p. 9).
Because the novel consists entirely of direct questions and answers
in the first and second persons, one remains unsure whether the
"book" has reached completion or not, and, finally, of just what it
is we are reading.

Several of the thematized structural components discussed so
far figure in Duras' earlier *Le Marin de Gibraltar*, (1952) generally

considered a rather traditional novel. Possible feminine madness inspiring a male narrator also a "writer," circularity and uncertainty produced by the inscription of that "writer"'s activity (is the book being written, about to be written, already written, whose book are we reading), the central gap of an absent story or character founding narrative "ignorance" and therefore textually productive; all these are present to some degree. The female protagonist's "irrational" worldwide search for a former lover prompts her present lover, narrator and prospective writer, to comment: "Perhaps you are a bit insane, after all."[50] Although he seems to love Anna, his announced intention to transmute her story and their love affair into a novel (Mar, p. 204) perforce distances him, rendering his motivations slightly suspect. Like Jacques Hold, he prefers the titillation of being with a beautiful, perhaps mad, and here very wealthy woman to the more ordinary pleasures of his previous lover's company. Once again a potential male writer will take possession of a woman's story – and of the woman. Desire to accumulate material for his future book as well as (more than?) his interest in the woman impel the hero-narrator's persistent demands that she recount her adventures with the missing man. When she proves reluctant ("I don't feel like talking,' she said, a little pleadingly," objecting that "It is not something that can be told") he orders her to continue: "Well then,' I said, 'invent what you want, but you have to talk to me" (Mar, p. 217). Her life seems to count mostly for the material it will provide him for his book.

Aware, probably, that she attracts him to the extent that she corresponds to certain fictions about rich, mad, exciting women attainable yet unattainable (she still loves and seeks someone else while loving the narrator), and that her life feeds the fiction he plans to write, Anna often responds with "a soft irony," as the narrator himself remarks (Mar, p. 217). After failing to find her ex-lover in Africa, for example, despite her profound disappointment, she reminds the narrator to include the episode in his book (Mar, p. 428). Upon learning that her yacht has been destroyed in a fire, she comments: "There's something that will lighten up your novel" (Mar, p. 429). Ultimately, the fact that the novel actually written is written by a woman, Duras, injects even further irony.

When the author appears named *qua* author in her texts, this adds other narrative dimensions which subvert textual closure and authoritative narration, through additional forms of "ignorance," circularity, and plurality. In the text/film *Le Camion*, "Duras" herself and a famous male actor read from a manuscript written by Duras. The published text names them, thus recreating onomastically the recognition achieved visually on screen in the film: "Two people are there, seated at the table: Gérard Depardieu and Marguerite Duras. On the table, manuscripts. The story of the film is, then, read. They will read this story."[51] But the reading is not equally apportioned. Depardieu asks questions and now and then proposes possible lines for the "characters". Mostly, however, "Duras"/Duras[52] reads all the roles, simultaneously to Depardieu and to the public. She speaks in the hypothetical past-conditional mode or in the future anterior, telling the plot of what "would have been a film" (Cam, p. 11), in which a middle-aged woman hitch-hiker "would have been picked up" by a truck driver.

"Duras"/Duras explicitly sets the story in the mode of the potential and the variable. From time to time she indicates alternative fictional developments, introducing them with some form of "or else":

> M.D.: 'Outdoors, still, the sublime nudity of the Beauce hills. Or else: Sublime desert of an immigrant land [d'une terre immigrée]'.
>
> (Cam, p. 19)

> G.D.: 'What is she doing waiting on that road?'
> M.D.: 'There would have been several explanations. She could have gone from one place to another for personal reasons, for example, her car breaks down and she has to go to her family, the place is deserted, she stops the first vehicle that passes by [. . .] (pause)'.
> G.D.: 'Or else?'
> M.D.: 'Nothing. [She would do it out of] idleness.'
>
> (Cam, pp. 38–39)

> [. . .]
> M.D.: 'She could also be going to the home of her daughter, who just had a baby.'
>
> (Cam, p. 50)

To the last example "Duras" adds in a footnote that were the story to proceed from the idea that the lady is going to visit her daughter, it would constitute but one possible textual direction: "N.B. The narrative that follows is, of course, indefinitely interchangeable"

(Cam, p. 50). Thus the "author" inscribed in *Le Camion* furnishes not *the* answers but answers, creating an "ignorance" which fosters multiple textual possibilities.

Positively marked "ignorance," the Durassian opposite of closure, operates visually as well. In the film, viewers see Marguerite Duras and Gérard Depardieu talking and reading, relayed by travelling sequences of a truck in an industrial region outside Paris. The lady and the truck driver, projected in an unfilmed future anterior, do not appear. Nevertheless, Duras repeatedly asks Depardieu, "You see?" to which he usually replies in the affirmative. This device transposes seeing out of the visual into an imaginary free of imposed images.[53] What Duras "shows" is mainly a text, written and read by her, heard and read by Depardieu. He also figures "the reader" in general. Since most of the story is read to him, he is "the listener" as well – an internal narratee. Like most listeners in collocutive circumstances, he participates, voicing reactions and interpretations. Duras' inscription of the writer, the reader, and the listener creates a *mise en abyme* which admits the real receivers of the text/film as yet more pluralizing "voices."

Finally, *Le Camion* dislodges the role of the actor from its customary locus. In an interview appended to the published text, the author states that Depardieu had not seen his lines previous to the filming: "The film is read pages in hand, and, for Depardieu, it is read for the first time, and the attention he pays to reading it is seen in the film. I say elsewhere in the film at a certain point: 'No rehearsal of the text would have been envisaged.' Now I think that that was in order to avoid acting. If we had read the text beforehand, if we had rehearsed it, even just to read it afterwards, we would have acted" (Cam, pp. 86–87).

One effect of this subversion of the actor's activity (it prevents the actor from acting) is to focus on that very process. The shift from acting to reading displaces not reality but convention. Traditionally, actors do "read" their roles, but from memory. Realism requires the pretence that they are neither reading nor acting, that they *are* the characters. In *Le Camion*, acting consists of enacting reading. This disjunction of the actor from the character is found in the majority of Duras' recent cinematic and theatrical texts. In an afterword pertaining to a possible staging of *La Maladie de la mort*, for example, Duras stipulates procedures similar to those used in *Le Camion*. (It will be noted that Duras never repeats exactly the same structure.):

Only the young woman would say her role from memory. Never the man. The man would read the text, either standing still or walking around the young woman. The man in the story [celui dont il est question dans l'histoire] would never be represented. Even when he would address the young woman, it would be through the intercession of the man reading his story. Here, acting would be replaced by reading. I always believe that nothing replaces the reading of a text, that nothing replaces the lack of memory of the text, nothing, no acting.[54]

Actors, then, no longer act in the traditional sense. Instead of incarnating characters, their bodies refer to them visually, as Duras explains concerning *Vera Baxter*: "And what the actors are going to do is bring this abyss [abîme], Vera Baxter, to us to see."[55] In *India Song*, the actors' bodies function as vehicles to evoke, not represent, characters long dead. Duras states: " [. . .] I think that the actor is there [on screen] in order to be in the image, to people [peupler] the image. What is talked about is not the actor but the story. [. . .] The actor peoples the image while a narration takes place which he/she does not master, does not act. There is no acting."[56]

Duras calls actors "speakers" [diseurs] in her preface to *Le Navire Night*, and notes that in that instance as well, they had no access to the scenario prior to the filming: "I did not distribute the text of *Le Navire Night* to the people who spoke it in the film. There are only dashes in front of the sentences, in order to indicate that the speaker should probably change at such and such a point in the narrative."[57] Like the actor's physical presence with respect to the character, the actor's speech points towards or "indicates,"[58] a story rather than representing it. Duras' actors lend their voices (and bodies) to texts like the audience and the reader lend an ear and/or an eye. Further, the various listening, speaking and seeing activities are rarely directed at the same thing at the same time. For not only does Duras subvert coincidence between the actors and the characters, she also often separates the actors' voices from their physical presence.[59]

As a result of these disruptions of traditional mimetic conventions, acting begins to resemble narration: "Because in [the staged] *Savannah Bay* there are no characters. It is an attempt to make theater out of a text. The text is carried by two people who could blend with the characters but who are not the characters. They are Madeleine Renaud and Bulle Ogier."[60] Duras does not deny the hermeneutic nature of this "carrying." Like all "speakers": narrators, authors, readers, listeners, Duras' actors constitute a set of "interpreters," as performers are so aptly called in French (interprètes). Their interpretations add another dimension to the sharing of a text with the public. A further, diachronic variation comes into play in the theater "There new voices will take charge of it [the text], the voices of the actors. These voices get renewed in the course of years and centuries."[61] Each performance can create an additional version, not necessarily corresponding to the author's particular vision: "I know that when my role is finished, they [the actresses] will do what they want. And even if it turns out to be another Savannah Bay, it will nevertheless still be a *Savannah Bay*. But I think that on certain evenings, who knows why, it will come close to the one I saw when I was writing the book and when I was listening to it."[62] Because they are structurally inscribed in the published texts, the voices of these public readers that Duras' actors are, speak, as it were, in the reader's imagination. The written text indicates their pluralizing narrative function, to which the reader adds yet another interpretive level.

2

Intertextualities

"Un coup de dès jamais n'abolira . . . "

Mallarmé

INTRODUCTION

The author's transpositions from novel to novel, and from novel to play to film, raise questions of intertextuality and inter-genres. Duras' practice is not based on the principles of simultaneity, continuity and non-contradiction so fruitfully developed by Balzac in another period. Avoiding the construction of a (chrono) logical edifice rooted in an outdated conception of verisimilitude, when this writer reintroduces elements from one text to another, she alters them. Contradiction functions both as a deconsructive strategy and as one productive of a more contemporary truth. Otherwise stated, Duras reaffirms on the intertextual level what she expresses within each distinct text: that, rather than attempting mimesis of an (inaccessible) objective reality, her writing is concerned with fictions, with non-objective reality, with social conventions communicated and changeable through those fictions. Her texts do not claim to report occurrences fixed in some immutable, experiential past. They advance possible narratives of possible stories, and one must keep both variables in mind. Intertextually speaking, each work functions like a variant of a missing original. That the definitive version remains always already lacking constitutes the *a priori* of her textual productivity. Thus the mutability which founds narrational "ignorance" operates on this plane of Duras' literary production as well.

It, too, takes many forms. The author often returns to earlier stories in later narratives, sometimes allusively, sometimes constituting series, but to which she denies conventional continuity. Certain events will be re-enacted or recalled in new contexts and time sequences which rarely correspond exactly to what preceded. Characters reappear in "disorderly" fashion, and may undergo significant alteration. Anne-Marie Stretter, for example, has the same physical characteristics in *Le Ravissement de Lol V. Stein, Le Vice-consul* and *India Song*, yet numerous details prevent one text from functioning tidily as sequel to the other. Dates do not coincide. Stretter seems the same age in the first two novels whereas Michael Richardson, twenty-five when he meets her in *Le Ravissement de Lol V. Stein*, is thirty-five in *Le Vice-consul*. Moreover, his name changes from Richardson to Richard in the later text, and back to Richardson in *India Song*. The accounts of the couple's meeting and of the length of their affair conflict. The ball at T. Beach, site of their encounter in the first novel, disappears from the second, in which Michael Richard informs a companion that he met Anne-Marie Stretter in Calcutta. Their love affair, which in the first novel reportedly ended after a few months (Rav, p. 120), has lasted for two years in the second and is continuing. *India Song* reintroduces Lol and the ball.

Duras explores many other modalities of passage from one text to another. The story of a murder and dismemberment inspired the quite different *Les Viaducs de la Seine et Oise* and *L'Amante anglaise*. Nearly identical plots inform the plays *Suzanna Andler* and *Vera Baxter*. The female protagonist's lover in each text is named Michel Cayre, but his structural position changes due to the addition of another character in the second book. Frequently one title refers to works in different genres. *Le Square, L'Amante anglaise* and *Des Journées entières dans les arbres* name novels and plays. Different stories can have the same title, as with the *Aurélia Steiners*. Finally, Duras' films or plays produced from her written texts almost always vary the content.

I do not conclude, with certain critics, that each of Duras' texts "annuls," "cannibalizes," or "erases" its predecessor,[1] for such readings imply a linearity foreign to her artistic undertaking. Duras' "rewriting" neither corrects nor destroys. It opens and pluralizes. Far from nullifying previous texts, later ones recall them in order to interact with them, naming them, referring to scenes from them, repeating speeches, or presenting different renditions, usually through insertion into new narrative configurations. Otherwise stated, Marguerite Duras transfers to the activity of writing something commonly accepted as an aspect of reading: if books do not remain hermeneutically stationary, if rereading never discloses the same text, if the work is mobile for the reader, it is for the writer as well. And the author may "rewrite" it, developing other fictional avenues. (The "or else" on the scale of the whole story.) The new work does not invalidate earlier ones, it "repeats" them, differently, maintaining the anaphorical charge of whichever elements recur, in an open play that has nothing nihilistic abut it.

Duras' work discloses the "ignorance," the essential absence on which textuality depends. Because no reporting can completely cover an event, additional narratives are always possible, as she explains regarding *L'Amant*: "Tomorrow I can begin another book starting with this same link which is missing in the telling of my life. And, maybe that book will be as full as the other, as this one, and as a hundred others could be in the same way."[2] The recent *L'Amant de la Chine du Nord* fulfills this prophecy, taking up that "missing link" and joining it to other thematic and structural permutations.

Noting what changes and what does not from one text to an other, the reader realizes that each one constitutes a single, never definite "proposition" (a word much used by the author with reference to her texts), new each time, indefinitely valid along with the others. Linearity fades before an open-ended, *a posteriori* simultaneity, which places the reader before irreducible multiplicity.

INTRATEXTUAL INTERTEXTUALITY

"External Voices"

India Song

Among these "propositions," *India Song* contains an intertextuality so full of innovations that it expands the very meaning of the term. Taking up parts of *Le Vice-consul* as well as harking back to the story of Lol V. Stein, *India Song* revolves around and issues from a narrative ignorance due initially to death: the intra-diegetic protagonists have been dead for many years when the narrative begins. Anonymous, invisible but gendered voices "tell" the tale. Perhaps because "the voices did know it [the story], or read it, a *long time ago*" (emphasis added). "[. . .] none remembers it completely [. . .]"[3] The speakers have been transferred from another text, parts of which they duplicate: "Certain voices from *La Femme du Gange* have been displaced here. And, in the same way, certain of their speeches" (Ind, p. 10 – "general remarks"). The voices construct a narrative "made of debris of memory, in the course of which a sentence will emerge, intact, from the forgotten [l'oubli]" (Ind, p. 40). Projecting towards something they barely remember, they (re)create a past not their own. Its equivocal "truth" status results from the impossibility of verification, from faulty memory, from the implied interchangeability in memory of knowing and reading. Did the speakers "know" the events as witnesses? Were they told the story? If they read it, what did they read, Duras' novels or something else? In contrast to classical techniques, Duras' manipulation of narration undermines her speakers' authority. Filtered through the disembodied voices, these ambiguities open the play of intertextual reference to the earlier works.

"Duras'" presence in the text complicates the structure. It is she who, *qua* author, first qualifies the story as mostly forgotten and presents the intermediary voices relating to it, and relating it. Then the speakers themselves constantly reiterate their ignorance. *India Song*'s "narrators" function primarily as questioners, both of the tale and of the telling. Indeed, they speak mostly in the interrogative mood. .

"Duras" states that the narrating voices speak as though they were reading, but does not specify what. Often parts of their speeches are placed within quotation marks, playfully compounding the ambiguity. For example: "Voice 1 (*as if it were being read*): 'Michael Richardson was engaged to a young girl from S. Thala. Lola Valérie Stein. The marriage was to take place in the autumn. Then there was that ball. The S. Thala ball [. . .]'" (Ind, p. 15). In part II, guests at the reception discuss Anne-Marie Stretter's past in similar fashion: "*Some women are speaking:* 'The ambassador.' – 'You knew that he had taken her away from a general administrator in a remote outpost in French Indochina?' [. . .] – 'You don't remember?: " . . . slow sloop with blinds, slow upriver trip on the Mekong towards Savannakhet . . . wide flowing [river] in the middle of the virgin forest'" [. . .]" (Ind, pp. 67–68). Punctuation marks the second half as textual citations. Nevertheless, both halves of the passage are near verbatim quotes from *Le Vice-consul* (pp. 98 and 165), as is the first passage from *Le Ravissement de Lol V. Stein*. Thus a plethora of intertextual references, including exact reproductions, improvisations and contradictions, "conjugates" with new elements to create another narrative permutation. (I borrow the word from *La Femme du Gange*, which intertwines (the) stories of Lol V. Stein and

Anne-Marie Stretter with that of *L'Amour*: "The conjugated nights of the Ganges and S. Tahla."[4])

A series of "general remarks" at the beginning of *India Song* explicitly posits intertextual "ignorance" as the pre-condition of textuality and intertextuality:

> The characters evoked in this story have been dislodged from the book entitled *Le Vice-consul*, and projected into new narrative regions. It is therefore no longer possible to bring them back to the book and to read in *India Song* a cinematographic or theatrical adaptation of *Le Vice-consul*. Even if an episode from that book has been taken up here almost in its entirety, its link to the new narrative changes the reading of it, its vision. [. . .] The fact that India Song penetrates and discloses a region not explored in *Le Vice-consul* would not have been sufficient reason to write it. What was, was the discovery, made in *La Femme du Gange*, of the means of disclosure [dévoilement], of exploration: the voices external to the narrative.[5] This discovery permitted [me] to shift the narrative into forgetfulness in order to leave it at the disposal of memories other than that of the author [. . .] Deforming, creative memories (Ind, pp. 9–10).

Forgetting and distortion are positively connoted as a (perhaps the) creative principle of (inter)textuality. The apposition at the end of the passage implies synonymy between "deforming" and "creating," which together define memory and its narratives. This creative movement is purposely illogical rather than logical, passionate rather than dispassionate, calculated for open (in)coherence rather than for closed coherence. The "remarks on Voices one and two" connect this to gender. Female, these voices are in love with each other and mad: "Voices one and two are *women's* voices. [. . .] They are tied to each other by a love affair. [. . .] The voices of these women are stricken with madness [. . .] The memory they have of the story is illogical, anarchic. They rave most of the time. Their delirium is at once calm and burning" (Ind, p. 11). Extraordinarily overdetermined, the "external voices'" "ignorance" is the "deforming" source, embraced as (re)creation. Connecting women's discourse to creativity dialogizes dominant society's tendency to dismiss it as mere raving.

If the principle of Duras' intertextuality is "the means of disclosure," the insertion of a story into "new narrative regions," into "other memories," one might speak of an intratextual intertextuality within individual texts. In so much of Duras' work, the narrating voices are "external" – they relate something in which they did not directly participate. But one must contextualize this exteriority. External to the past event, the speakers are not external to the present narrative, much of which issues from them. Instead of rigid separation there is a doubly imbricated relation: the voices color the story and the story affects the voices. Continuing her presentation of the female speakers, Duras writes: "Sometimes they talk about this love, theirs. Most of the time, they talk about the other love, the other story. But this other story brings us back to theirs. Just as theirs does to the story of *India Song* [. . .] It is when they slide towards their own story that they will be the most present. Which means that they will be that way almost always, since the love story of *India Song*, in a constant slippage, juxtaposes itself to theirs" (Ind, pp. 11–12).

Thus, from two "texts": the absent referent/text, and the discourses referring to/narrating/creating it, a single yet plural text emerges, new and more numerous with each "repetition," never definitive. Duras' co-operative plurivocity contrasts to Bakhtin's essentially conflictual conception of heteroglossia. For Bakhtin, the word encounters "in its path toward the object the fundamental and richly varied *opposition* of another's word."[6] When unitary truth and discursive control are not the goals, variation need not entail dispute. Dialogue need not imply struggle for domination. While it does for certain of Duras' narrators, in those texts which are plurally narrated, such conflict does not obtain. The speakers accept "ignorance" as the productive foundation of their discourses, and engage in collaborative efforts. (This occurs in *India Song, La Femme du Gange, Savannah Bay, Le Camion*, and, on different narrative levels, in *Moderato Cantabile, Hiroshima mon amour, Le Navire Night, Vera Baxter ou les plages de l'Atlantique*, and *Agatha*.)

India Song is divided into five sections. The female voices (one and two) "narrate" part one. Part two consists of the embassy reception, in which the external voices are replaced by those of various anonymous guests commenting on the actions of the named "protagonists," who also speak from time to time. Male voices (three and four) "narrate" part three, most of part four, in which one also hears a few of the protagonists, and part five. The female voices return briefly in part three, "mixing" (Ind, p. 113) with the male voices, but the two sets of speakers never address each other. When

Voice three becomes aware of the female voices, it frightens him to learn that the men were not alone in relating (to) the tale at hand. His partner remains deaf to female discourse: "Voice three (*fright*): 'Voices, suddenly, near us . . . ? Do you hear?' Voice four (*pause*). 'No.' Voice three: 'Very young . . . women?' Voice four (*pause*) "I hear nothing" (Ind, pp. 114–115). It is noteworthy that among the speakers, male Voice four, "the one that has forgotten the story the least, [that] knows it almost in its entirety" (Ind, p. 105), is the one to reject the possibility of other speakers.

Thus the text exposes the men's fear and reluctance to recognize other discourses, yet at the same time inscribes plurivocity. The message is that there are always other voices, other visions. This is emphasized from the beginning, when "Duras" introduces the female voices into the opening description, assumed until then by her: "While, very slowly, the darkness dissipates, there are, suddenly, voices. Others besides us were looking at, hearing what we thought we were alone in looking at, in hearing. They are women" (Ind, p. 13). That those for whose voices room must be made are female constitutes another indication of Duras' awareness of the social silencing of women and another of her corrective strategies.

Verbally registered in the written text, the much remarked separation of voice from image in the film version further corrodes concepts of univocity and adequation. The four speakers remain disembodied. Unlike traditional off-screen narrators, they entertain no inherent connections to what they "narrate" other than narration itself. (The narrators discussed in chapter 1 have some connection with what they tell, albeit after what interests them has taken place. Morgan sees the beggar, Hold meets Lol, the narrator in *Le Marin de Gibraltar* meets Anna, who had known the sailor, the woman had known the German soldier in *Hiroshima mon amour*, the interrogator meets Claire in *L'Amante anglaise* and in *Moderato Cantabile*, Anne and Chauvin tryst in the café where the "story" took place, etc.). Moreover, in *India Song*, the speakers address each other, not the reading or viewing public. This sets the voices apart, making characters of these "narrators" on another fictive level.

The foreword to *La Femme du Gange* explains how this type of external voices functions: "*They speak to each other. They are ignorant of the presence of the spectator.* It is not, then, a commentary. If the Voices are in S. Tahla like the other voices in the film, they are not linked to them in any way. Nor are they off-screen Voices in the usual acceptation of the word: they do not facilitate the unfolding [déroulement] of the film; to the contrary, they hamper it, trouble it" (Fem, p. 103).

In *India Song* the guests at the reception also remain invisible. In a production in which "[. . .] on stage [or screen], rigorously, no word will be pronounced" (Ind, p. 58), the disjunction affects those we do see as well, because Duras also disconnects the "protagonists'" bodies from their voices. When before us they do not speak. When they do, they remain hidden. In addition to dismantling literary, theatrical, and cinematic realism, these techniques deconstruct the idea of a self-present subject. Because the actors never are where their voices are, one is led to reconsider the simultaneity of seeing and hearing, and the unity of presence and speech. The actors in the film *India Song* underwent the disorienting process of sundering their physical from their verbal "acting."[7] After they recorded the sound track, they were filmed as they heard their own and other voices played back. For the most part other people's voices are heard while they move, and what is said rarely corresponds to what is seen. For example, when the unseen "speakers" describe Anne-Marie Stretter's white dress, on screen she is wearing black. For the "actors," their own pre-recorded words become part of yet another text, with which they inter-act. All this fragmentation aims, as always in Duras, at constructive destructuration. Far from reducing meaning, it expands it: "So you see," remarks Duras in an interview about *India Song*, "when they [the actors] speak and hear their own words, speech resonates infinitely more. [. . .] The field opens, the field of speech opens infinitely more. I think that's it, and everything takes on double meanings because of that."[8]

Like *Le Camion*, *India Song* proposes textual alternatives intratextually in the mode of "or else." The text occasionally actualizes them, incorporating them in fleshed-out scenes replete with characters and their lines. Pages one hundred thirty-four to one hundred thirty-seven present two renditions of a conversation about the beggar: "First version: We hear, from fairly far away, the conversation between Georges Crawn and the Stretters' guest" (Ind, p. 134). The conversation follows. "Second version: Voices three and four relate the conversation which took place between Georges Crawn and the Stretters' guest [. . .]" (Ind, p. 136),[9] and a different discussion is then presented. As always when Marguerite Duras varies narrative structures, she alters content. One is reminded of Paul Valéry's call for inclusive plurality:

Perhaps it would be interesting *one* time to make a work which would show, at each one of its knots [noeuds], the diversity that can present itself to the mind at those points [. . .] the illusion of a *possible at each moment*, which seems to me more truthful.[10]

What affords the structural capacity for inscribing the "either/or" is Marguerite Duras' highly original manipulation of "stage directions." I place the expression within quotation marks because their function far exceeds customary usage. Intended for potential directors and actors, traditional didascalia constitute succinct production hints and little more. Performance eliminates them, retaining only the dialogues – the faithfully reproduced "story." In *India Song*, they occupy an enormous amount of textual space, ranging from a single line to several pages. Moreover, they are directed to the reader. These two factors undermine the homology suggested, rather disingenuously, in the subtitle "text, theater, film." Despite a layout similar to the format of theater or film scenarios, the multi-genre character of this text functions mostly conceptually. In the "stage directions" the author refers simultaneously to her readers and her spectators,[11] but they occupy different positions. This being a written text, all the allusions are received by a real reader, who imagines the inscribed viewers (and readers) along with everything the book evokes. The written and the reader encompass the viewer and visual elements, which, with the "stage directions," constitute intratextual components of the book *qua* book. The published text stands independently as a literary work. Not only does the film *India Song* not adhere to the published text, Duras published a transcription of the film itself, which differs substantially from the first text.

Parallel techniques are used with other texts that formally resemble scripts. (*Agatha*, the *Aurélia Steiners*, *Savannah Bay*, *Vera Baxter*, etc.). In the theater, the changes and/or additions made during rehearsals introduce another diachronic variable. Duras distinguishes this purposeful instability from the concept of correction: "Question: 'It appears that you work a lot on your dialogues during rehearsals of your plays?' Duras: 'Yes, that is to say, I write new ones every day, which is different. [. . .] I can not stop a text."[12]

The literary, diegetic nature of Duras' "stage directions" is confirmed in those texts which refer internally to another medium. The book *Nathalie Granger* contains a scene absent from the film.

"Duras" discusses it in a "stage direction," entitles it "unfilmed sequence," and presents it in a type face different from the rest.[13] Its inclusion in the book signals it as an integral textual element, like the "didascalia" and authorial notes placed at the bottom of the page. Certain of the latter add "either/or" interpretational hints. For example, "Duras" comments on a dialogue in a "note": "The thing can be understood in two ways" (Nat, p. 54), and furnishes both readings. A "stage direction" in *Agatha* provides information (and a specifically literary experience) to the reader which it expressly qualifies as unavailable to any spectator, since it lies beyond the purview of visible mimesis: "They remain there with their eyes closed. Still the softness, the cracked voice, broken by an unbearable emotion, not actable [non jouable], not representable."[14]

Published with the subtitle "scenario and dialogues," *Hiroshima mon amour* incorporates a great deal of material absent from the movie but integral to the text *qua* text. This includes dialogues specifically designated as eliminated from the film, a "synopsis," a "foreword," footnotes which mention ways in which the film differs from the text, lengthy "didascalia," and "appendices." "Duras" stresses that the latter are "work separate from the script."[15] They consist of thirty-three pages of fictional passages with titles. Some refer to scenes in the film. More than simply describing the shots; they expand the fiction, adding descriptions, perspectives, and episodes. Certain of them are written in the first person voice of the female protagonist. Here too, notes are interjected in the either/or mode, such as " [the woman's] mother was either Jewish or separated from her husband" (Hir, p. 127).

Lastly, the disappearance of the "stage directions" from a performed or filmed text constitutes another major difference between it and the written work. Structural erasure of "didascalia" removes the inscribed reader and the very important, very present "author." In *India Song* it also entails deletion of the character of the beggar, present in the text (in the "didascalia"), absent in the film. Thus, although the first *India Song*, "text, theater, film" does suggest three genres, they remain potential. What is actual is the text figuring all three simultaneously. Neither a novel, nor a theater scenario, nor a film script, this text blurs the lines between genres.

India Song's greatly expanded "stage directions" are, then, part of the story. The reader imagines people interacting with each other in a film or play, "spoken" in part by the voices and "narrated" in part by the "author" in the "stage directions." These "directions" afford a forum for the "author's" voice. Descriptions go beyond the simply informative and attain a poetic quality, another factor distinguishing them from traditional didascalia. Duras generally writes her "stage directions" in the same poetic prose characteristic of all her texts. For example: "The beggar sticks out her bald head and looks – night bird" (Ind, p. 88), and "A ceiling fan revolves, but with nightmarish slowness" (Ind, p. 15). The same long "stage direction" contains a playful allusion to the fiction under construction: "Nothing moves, nothing, except that ventilator of nightmarish 'fictiveness'" (p. 15).

One also finds overt intertextual references in *India Song*'s "stage directions": "Anne-Marie Stretter will wear a black dress – the one she wore at the ball at S. Tahla – the one described in *Le Ravissement de Lol V. Stein*" (Ind, p. 57). With regard to the speakers, the voice of the "stage directions" oscillates between a stance of having more knowledge than they and one of having less. When it sees more than they do, it conveys that supplemental information. It also comments on the speakers, apprising us of their emotions, both prescriptively: "Voice two: *moan* [. . .] Voice three: *fright*" (Ind, p. 114), and retrospectively: after Voice two states that Michael Richardson left India after Anne-Marie Stretter's death: "The sentence was said with one breath, as though slowly recited" (Ind, p. 17). The latter, reactive stance implies an "authorial" "ignorance" of what the voices were going to say and how. In the same "stage direction" the "ignorant" "author" deduces "new" knowledge from their speeches: "Voice two: 'After her death, he left India.' *Silence.* [. . .] The woman dressed in black, who is before us, is, therefore, dead."

The "author" frequently situates herself in the same space as the reader-narratee, naming this community "we:" "We are in the same place in the embassy as before" (Ind, p. 107). This "we" does not always "see" the same thing at the same time as the speakers. When the text opens, the reading "we" perceives (imagines) Anne-Marie Stretter before Voice one does (Ind, p. 16). Later, "we" see the Vice-Consul in the park two pages before the voices do: "The tall skinny man dressed in white enters the park. The voices haven't seen him" (Ind, p. 44). The voices also miss some of what he does during those two pages. At other times, author, speakers and reader-narratee "look" together at the "screen" or "stage" imagined in the text. Yet the real reader is, of course, external to all of this. The inscribed reader is a fictive co-presence who has read and been moved by Duras' earlier books, as the following "stage direction" implies: "When they [the voices] speak about the story we see unfolding before us, they will rediscover it at the same time we do, therefore with the same fear and, who knows, perhaps with the same emotion" (Ind, p. 12).

Thus Duras' "stage directions" introduce an additional narrative dimension, a voice functioning as an agent both of intratextual and intertextual intertextuality.[16] The constant shifting of narrative position plays on "ignorance" at every level. Multiple narrative splitting conveys the partial, relative nature of narration and the potential, variable nature of narrative. Consistent with her approach in nearly all her work, "Duras'" voice represents neither omniscience nor a closed subjective view. "Stage directions" retain part of the purpose the term implies, but shift function and locus. From imperatives to be obeyed on screen or stage and absorbed in the acting, they become suggestions for possible performances on the stage/screen that is the reader's imagination, "stagings" in which they remain present.

Le Navire Night

"Intratextual intertextuality" informs *Le Navire Night,* which deserves mention for its interesting articulation of "ignorance." Preceding the title page, several pages written in the first person discuss the genesis of the text and subsequent film, and include indications one can consider "stage directions". After that, we find no "didascalia" other than a few notes at the bottom of the page, one of which informs us that a passage we have just read does not figure in the film (Nav, p. 62).

"Duras" opens with the assertion that an acquaintance of hers told her the story, in which he had been a protagonist. Having thus affirmed the tale's veracity, she proceeds to subvert this very traditional subterfuge by consigning the telling to other, intermediary voices. Like in *India Song,* anonymous and invisible "external" speakers "narrate." In this text their number and gender are not specified. Duras simply calls them "sayers" [diseurs]. Their "ignorance" is assured, since "only about ten people knew of [the story's] existence" (Nav, p. 7). Several factors prevent them from functioning as actors. They remain uncharacterized, make no reference to themselves, and simply read a text in the third person. No roles are assigned. "Duras" states in the text: "I did not distribute the text of *Le Navire Night* to those who said it in the film. There were only dashes in front of the sentences, to indicate that the sayer [diseur] should probably change at such and such a point in the narrative" (Nav, p. 10).

Another narrative dislocation introduces the "author" in several first person descriptions of a trip she made to Athens – something unrelated to the central story. A distinct type face separates these sections from the text they interrupt. Yet the Athens segments contain enough metonymical possibilities for the reader to connect them with the other story. One technique is antithesis. With its overwhelming, repeatedly evoked absence of love ("this lack of loving" – Nav, pp. 22, 62, 74) in the terrible mid-day heat, Athens figures the opposite of the love-filled city of Paris, where the other story takes place. Both are passionately told, and a contrastive link is established. Relation is fostered further through the anaphorical and oxymoronic use of the word night, from the title and the main story, to describe mid-day Athens: " [. . .] night in the brightness. The silence of the night in full sunlight, The sun at its zenith and the silence of the night. The silence at the center of the sky and the silence of the night" (Nav, p. 22).

Within the central story, "ignorance" affects the "source": the male protagonist never sees his female partner, learns almost nothing about her, and knows only her voice. Their intense love affair takes place over the telephone. Significantly, it is the woman who sets these terms, who slowly initiates the man into an 'ignorance" receptive to love. "It is she, F, who directs things. [qui mène l'histoire] [. . .] who, little by little, makes them both get accustomed to things. *She* knows nothing, invents" (Nav, p. 33).[17]

The man compounds the internal "ignorance" of the story when he gives it to another ear/voice, to Duras. This mirrors what Duras does when she projects speakers other than herself, who "say" a text. Her comments concerning the man's reaction to her "version" express her fundamental approach to narration: "I gave the text in its first form to J.M. He read it. He said that 'everything was true but that he recognized nothing.' [. . .] We no longer spoke about the story. [. . .] After having read this becoming [ce devenir] – written by someone else – of his own adventure, J.M. remained silent, but as though he were constantly on the verge of speaking. I think he must have discovered that other narratives of his story would have been possible [. . .] that they were possible like they were possible for any story" (Nav, pp. 8–9).

"Internal External Voices"

Savannah Bay

"Identity destroys creation"

Gertrude Stein

Several of Duras' texts feature female narrators involved in the stories they recount. They were witnesses (*Savannah Bay*) or figured directly as protagonists, "imaginary" (the *Aurélia Steiners*) or "real" (*L'Amant*). These narrating women adopt an external approach to events to which they were internal. Through connected strategies of forgetting and fabrication, they create an "ignorance" which becomes the source of open textual production. Memory, always in-adequate, non-objective, correlates to imagination. *Savannah Bay* thematizes this process, and Madeleine, an intradiegetic "narrator" demonstrates it. *Savannah Bay* is plural within itself due to Madeleine's willful forgetfulness on the one hand, and her innumerable variations of the story sought after by the Young Woman on the other. In contrast to the interposed male narrators in Duras' texts, Madeleine incarnates what Duras considers a feminine awareness of the properties of an "ignorance" resulting from a certain absence and exclusion.

"There is nothing true in reality, nothing." This declaration by Duras[18] is not meant to incite one to seek truth or reject reality, but to direct one towards what shapes her literary project. Paul de Man called literary consciousness "the persistent and renewed naming of this void."[19] Duras' work is concerned not with emptiness but with the generative capacity of "ignorance." *Savannah Bay* presents the workings of an "ignorance" which informs all narrative.

A young girl who had just given birth committed suicide twenty-five or thirty years ago. Madeleine, her now elderly mother, is apparently losing her memory. The Young Girl's child, now the Young Woman, knows little of the event, and, of course, does not remember it. Thus structurally inscribed "ignorance" – a dead girl, an elderly woman subject to forgetfulness, and a young woman who can not have known – sets in motion a text which, once again, begins after events rendered unverifiable. The already tenuous data dissipate further, to the point of dissolving completely. On this and on every textual level, as the "stage directions" inform us, "nothing is sure."[20] Since the Young Girl's body was never found, she "probably" died. By refraining from assigning proper names to the Young Girl and the Young Woman, Duras inhibits classificatory social identification, which she rejects in general, and particularly for women. Madeleine, the only named character, lacks the patronymic which would have anchored her in dominant society. Consequently, an often playful doubt permeates the relationship between the three women: "Madeleine: 'Are you my grand-daughter?' Young Woman: 'Perhaps.' Madeleine: 'My grand-daughter? My daughter?' Young Woman: 'Yes, perhaps'" (Sav, p. 13).

On another level, authorial interventions perpetuate uncertainty at the very moment they purport to resolve it. "Duras" writes in a "stage direction": "[. . .] the third one, absent, dead, no doubt, no doubt the girl of the White Rock – one of Madeleine's children, the one who is the Young Woman's mother" (Sav, p. 39). Instead of eliminating ambiguity, the words "no doubt" augment it. A note at the bottom of the page further sabotages the very information it seems to confirm, for it states the "author's" viewpoint in the guise of a subjective option: "I adhere personally to that proposition." This type of intervention presented in the mode of opinion is one more strategy Duras deploys to distinguish her stance from that of omniscience. She uses it in several texts when speaking as "author." For example, in Le Camion: "Gérard Depardieu: 'Will that relationship happen?' Marguerite Duras: 'Perhaps never.' G.D.: 'What do you think?' M.D.: 'Never'" (Cam, p. 17), and in La Maladie de la mort: "I ["Duras"] don't know if you [the male protagonist] perceive the muted and far away rumble of her pleasure [. . .] I don't believe so" (Mal, p. 15).

Vanished events, vacillating memory, uncertain identity convey neither existentialist anxiety, nor a post structuralist draining of meaning. Duras' "ignorance" founds a world view (and textual practice) which embraces and produces multiplicity in difference: different voices, different perspectives, different texts. The bad faith of positivistic rationalism is always already discredited. What all of Duras' work undermines is less an already devalorized rationalism than the need, desire, or nostalgia for it. Far from leading to an anxious or empty impasse, this attitude leads to the unlimited creativity of play. In French the word "jeu" has a rich diversity of meanings, including play, acting, game, gambling, action, all of which the author mobilizes in Savannah Bay. The reader is cautioned in a "stage direction": "Here it should no longer be clear what is make believe [comédie]. [It is] as though it is simply entirely in the 'jeu' of the two women" (Sav, p. 39). Together the two women act/play (with) the story of the Young Girl, which is non-present, like all stories, all histories. Its absence founds both their play (jeu) and their mutual love, "the very strong love that ties them to each other through the third, absent one, dead, no doubt" (Sav, p. 39). The two women adopt shifting roles much like in children's games. Now one or the other speaks as narrator; now they "act" the roles of the Young Girl and her lover, sharing the imagined lines of both. Or they play mother and daughter to each other, switching parts back and forth. Sometimes they project the story out of the "family romance," for example onto a stranger encountered (perhaps) by Madeleine in a café; at others they situate it in various cities where "the story could have taken place" (Sav, p. 73). Or they locate it in that ultimate site of "play" – a theater – where Madeleine would have or might have acted a part in the story adapted for the stage – and we recognize a now familiar Durassian *mise en abyme*. But play (le jeu) pervades an even more internal level: if Madeleine, who forgets everything, enters so easily into this playing that she directs it most of the time, it is because she has not forgotten how to do the one thing she has spent her life doing: play acting (jouer): "Madeleine; (*as though just discovering it*) 'Well . . . I was . . . I was an actress. That's what I did. An actress.' Jeune Femme: 'An actress in the theater.' Madeleine: 'Yes.' Jeune Femme: 'Nothing else.' Madeleine: 'Nothing.'" (Sav, p. 29). She knows the triple relationship between (textual) play and death and life. First, each time one "plays" (jouer) on stage one is divested of oneself, and theater depends on this forgetting, this "death": "For months on end I had the experience of dying each evening in the theater" (Sav, p. 69). (One can draw the analogy with writing. Marguerite Duras declares both "When I write I am separated from myself,"[21] and "When I write, I do not die."[22] The death of the positivistic subject caused by writing opens another, less circumscribed self to life and to love.)

Second, Madeleine knows that everything is play (jeu): "Whatever part I acted during that whole period, that pain found its way into the role; it acted (jouait) too, it showed me one could act anything" (Sav, p. 69). Last, she knows that theater, like writing, like life, revolves around the play of "ignorance": "But [. . .] almost nothing is ever played [joué] in the theater . . . everything is always as if . . . as if it were possible . . . " (Sav, p. 64).

In *Savannah Bay* the *en abyme* structure opens out in every direction at once. Not only is Madeleine a former actress aware that her profession defines her, *en abyme*, but Duras wrote the part for a real actress named Madeleine Renaud, who will coincide with the character she plays and breach the fictive framework when, in response to the Young Woman's question about whether she met the man from the café in "a place like this," she exclaims, "But this is a theater!" (Sav, p. 65). It would be futile to seek to determine whether the "real" or the fictive actress utters these words. Both elude us in the play of "theater," which encompasses everything, and which "begins" (Sav, p. 31) only after Madeleine puts on a costume, which, because she dons it on stage, simultaneously reveals and conceals the ungraspable absence – "ignorance" from which all play (jeu) emanates.

If "nothing is ever played in the theater," nevertheless something is at stake (en jeu) in this gambling play of possibilities, and that is the Young Woman's very capacity for play. We witness her vacillation between whole-hearted participation in play / a play predicated on the impossibility of possessing her own past on the one hand, and, on the other, her anguished, sporadically recurring need to know what her story, her history "really was." To be sure, the Young Woman cheerfully acknowledges the uncertainty which Madeleine can not or will not dispel:

> Young Woman: 'Tell me the story again.' [. . .]
> Madeleine: 'Every day you want that story.'
> Young Woman: 'Yes."
> Madeleine: '[Repeating it] every day makes me mix up the dates, the people, the places . . . ' *Laughs of the two women.*
> Young Woman: 'You make more and more mistakes.'
> Madeleine: 'Is that also what you want?'
> Young Woman: (*laughing*)   'Yes.'

(Sav, pp. 29–30)

Yet, at first, she accepts this "theater" in the hopes of working through Madeleine's numerous narrative distortions in order to satisfy her "passion for knowledge" (Sav, p. 19) by somehow managing to situate herself with regard to the past: "It is on Madeleine's failing memory that she [the Young Woman] builds the memory of her childhood, of her birth. Theater begins [le théâtre commence], far off, painful" (Sav, p. 31). When play goes too far, that is, when Madeleine's sabotage threatens to fragment her story beyond recognition, the Young Woman panics: "Madeleine: 'On that point, at least I believe so, my memory is clear. But who knows? Unless I got it from that book I gave you [. . .]' Young Woman: 'No, stop, I beg you. *(Pause)*. Let's begin again' [. . .]" (Sav, p. 59). Such attempts to grasp the past fitfully reassert themselves. The Young Woman struggles with a "violent desire to apprehend the unknowable of the past through Madeleine's life, through consecrated texts. Failure" (Sav, p. 55).

Nevertheless, the Young Woman's visits to Madeleine gradually lead her to accept and even desire this "failure." Their "play" effects a Butorian "modification" of the Young Woman, whom Madeleine teaches not only how to play, but how to play to lose. The goal is not to recover a past which by virtue of its nature as past remains unattainable, but to accede to the "splendor" of Madeleine's self-dispossession, "her child-like lostness, the accomplishment of her majesty" (Sav, p. 10). That despite her initial resistance, the Young Woman understands the stakes in her bouts with Madeleine becomes evident early on, when she alludes to the day she will cease her visits, and with them her efforts to wrench her history, and Madeleine, out of the realm of the forgotten: "One day, one evening, I'll leave you for good. I'll close the door, there, and it will be over" (Sav, p. 23). *Savannah Bay* itself, which constitutes the final session of this apprenticeship of "ignorance," ends with just such a gesture of departure. The Young Woman has accepted the dispossession of her unknowable past, and it, along with Madeleine and the text itself, fades into darkness as the curtain, real or textual, falls.

The Young Woman succeeds in "failure" by ridding herself of a certain thirst for origins, for identity. Not just any "I" is at stake (en jeu), however, in this game. What is played out is the "I" constructed by dominant society and continually challenged in Duras' work. Delimited by the patronymic, which classifies and eliminates (women), it is the patriarchal "I" that dis-integrates. *Savannah Bay* deconstructs the classical "quest for origins," which, like "the Oedipus complex," names a principally masculinist desire to construct identity through and against the father, while the objectified mother, background or prize, is excluded from the male play of subjectivity. Identity thus conceived implies self-presence, which governs dominant desires for autogenesis, as described for example by such critics as Harold Bloom and Michel Beaujour, though in different contexts. Beaujour expounds the theme of modern *man's* nostalgia and misfortune, for which he implicitly blames the (silent) mother: "But his [sic] curse is simply a function of his *birth*: expelled from the maternal bosom, marked by the sign of the ego, condemned to wandering and conquest (to the transformation of the world) or to the reverse: interminable writing."[23] This definition of endless writing as the other side of conquest, and of conquest as the telos of wandering, accords with Lacan's theory that the mother's body is the original lost object (sic), which drives forward narrative in ceaseless attempts to recover the lost "thing."[24] Bloom's writing *conquistadores* set out to re-enact Freud's murder of the father. Ridding themselves of all "influence," creating themselves through the negation of others, they will possess literature (another displaced female object?).[25]

Feminist psychoanalysts and theorists critique this exclusionary focus on the male child and the male subject and address the question of female subjectivity. Through different theoretical elaborations, both French and Anglo-American thinkers concentrate on the pre-oedipal mother-child (especially mother-daughter) bond as their point of departure. Shirley Garner, Claire Kahane and Maedelon Sprengnether note: "while Anglo-American theories and their feminist revisions proceed from an assumption of unmediated presence embodied in the mother, French psychoanalysis constitutes its myth of origin from absence. [. . .] Lacanians insist on her loss."[26] Feminist Lacanians[27] accept Lacan's generalization of this loss as an originary "lack in the subject, displaced and veiled by language but persisting as unconscious desire," and appreciate the liberating potential in his postulate that sexual identity is a fiction. Other feminists reject his "totalizing equation of the symbolic with the law of the Father and his privileging of the phallus."[28] They refuse exclusion from the symbolic, and seek the construction of women's subjectivity in and through language.[29]

Connecting subjectivity, language and writing, feminist literary critics are theorizing the relational quality inherent in the construction of feminine identity within patriarchal societies, and the centrality of the mother-daughter relation in that ongoing process, as found in women's autobiographical texts.[30] They formulate a non self-present, non reified subject mediated through psychoanalytic factors and through socio-historical factors of race, ethnicity, and class.[31] This subject has agency through language, functioning as a force of constitutive, non-adequate co-presence, rather than only under the sign of phallic absence.[32] Duras' three texts "spoken" (*Savannah Bay*), "written" (the *Aurélia Steiners*), or narrated (*L'Amant*) by women thematize questions of identity and autobiography and replace traditional concepts with one articulated through a language informed by "ignorance."

In *Savannah Bay* two female subjects speaking (narrating, creating) in collaboration develop an other "family romance." The open, unlimited quality of Madeleine's narratives issues from the recognition of the plurality of origins and relational possibilities. Cixous writes of "the beginning, or rather the beginnings, the manner of beginning, not at a single point by the phallus, but of beginning on all sides at once, that is feminine inscription."[33] Duras' multiple textual "beginnings," intra- and intertextual "writings" and "rewritings" emanating from various textual "points" show women inscribing themselves in different parameters of discursive-familial configurations. *Savannah Bay*'s "stage directions" explicitly portray parental origins embraced in "ignorance" as a source of *love* and a function of shared discourse: "She [Madeleine] talks, relayed by the Young Woman, retells this narrative which is about the uncontrollable and mysterious parental origins of their love" (Sav, p. 50).

Readers encounter numerous mother-child relationships of intense love and mutual comprehension in Duras' work (in *Un Barrage contre le Pacifique, Des Journées entières dans les arbres, Moderato Cantabile, Le Vice-consul, Nathalie Granger, Dix Heures et demie du soir en été, Agatha, Aurélia Steiner, L'Amant, La Pluie d'été* and *L'Amant de la Chine du Nord*.) In *L'Amant* Duras also alludes to the "hatred" felt by the children towards their desperate, mad mother. But she portrays that resentment as a function of the widow's dire economic straits and consequent semi-insanity.[34] In *Le Vice-consul*, poverty and alienation motivate the beggar's mother to expel her, as starvation motivates the beggar's "hatred" of the child she is carrying. Yet mother-daughter relations in both directions furnish the only communication the beggar experiences, and their rupture, as Mieke Bal points out, is what causes her madness.[35] In *La Pluie d'été* the mother's occasional "hatred" of her children, with whom she otherwise enjoys a relation of great reciprocal love and understanding, is clearly linked to the large family's economic difficulties and the restrictions on her this produces. In Duras, maternal resentment stems from material circumstances and/or the frustrations attendant on the social assignment of mothering to women and, in the bourgeoisie, of the frequent confinement of women to that role.[36]

In *Savannah Bay*, the Young Woman's quest ends not with the knowledge-possession of patriarchal identity, but with her liberation from it. Duras has often stressed the gender specificity of what the Young Woman learns: that "one is never anyone in a society, and women are the ones who know it [. . .] Women are the ones who destroy the social image. Women know that they do not know who they are and that one can not know, and they know that it is a trap to think one knows."[37] Nearly all of Duras' female characters know that "they are no one." The expression of this knowledge often elicits repressive sanctions from a dominant society mistrustful of its subversive potential. When women "tell," they risk the "banishment" (into madness and/or marginality) evoked in Emily Dickinson's famous poem: "I'm nobody! Who are you?/ Are you nobody, too?/ Then there's a pair of us – don't tell!/ They'd banish us, you know [. . .]" One can cite all the women pronounced insane: Claire Lannes, Anna, Lol, the woman in *Le Navire Night*, Alissa in *Détruire, dit-elle*, etc. The driver's reaction in *Le Camion* is representative. He asks the lady, "Who are you?' [. . .] [She answers] 'I don't know how to answer you. Your logic escapes me. If someone asks me who I am I get confused.' He says: 'I knew there was something wrong with you'" (Cam, p. 62). Duras' oeuvre exposes this victimization and proposes models of women who escape it, for example in *Savanah Bay*, the *Aurélia Steiners*, and *L'Amant*.

As the Young Woman in *Savannah Bay* completes her apprenticeship of "ignorance," she achieves an open identity that can be shared with Madeleine. Near the text's end, the two women speak interchangeably, donning the same first person "I" for the roles in the story, which they "narrate" and "perform" in yet another version (Sav, pp. 75–90). Freed from proper names (most importantly from the socially delimiting one, the patronymic) and from concomitant concerns for property or propriety, the two women project towards the same absence, the same "ignorance." In this way, they release a playful "I" which floats between them. This un(de)limited, shared and plural "I" makes everything possible: textuality, contextuality, love. It should be stressed that Duras is not calling for disintegration into "the oceanic passivity of indifferentiation," to use Jane Gallop's phrase. One must distinguish between subjectivity and reified identity. Duras' subjects know with feminists like Gallop that "identity must be continually assumed and immediately called into question."[38] Set loose from dominant categories, the Durassian "I" catalyzes narrative, enabling the speakers to relate (to) memory in other ways.

In *Savannah Bay*, Duras chooses a character "too old to distinguish between this past and its representation" (Sav, p. 31). Madeleine will not and/or can not produce definitive memories ("Madeleine [*lying*]: "I don't know any more" – Sav, p. 55), because she knows that attempts to recapture things past inevitably fail. The past can not be im-mediately or accurately present. Embracing memory's intrinsic instability, Marguerite Duras abolishes the binary opposition between it and forgetting. From the opening dedication to the protagonist on, *Savannah Bay* is a text about memory founded on forgetting and structured by play (jeu): "You don't know who you are any longer, who you have been you know you've acted [jouer], you no longer know what roles you played, what roles you play, you act/play [tu joues], you know you must act/play, you no longer know what, you act [you know] neither what your roles are, nor who your children are, alive or dead" (Sav, p. 7). This play is, of course, textual play. The search for things past, which is memory, always culminates in fiction, for to remember is to choose a text. One remembers one's past like one recalls a text, as Madeleine implies: "Yes, one begins to doubt what happened, who died, who remained alive, which book it was, which city, who, who suffers, who knows the story, who made it" (Sav, p. 70). The past is re-presentation, texts (re)produced by creative-deforming memories. Madeleine (and soon the Young Woman) welcomes the "ignorance" mediating her "I" and its texts.

Ridding oneself of the will to possess the past, freeing one's "I," "losing" one's memory this way, opens it to others, and one of Marguerite Duras' innovations is to focus on this process. In *Savannah Bay* and in so many other texts where the story has receded in time, someone's "past" can be experienced, that is *told* by/with others. Memory, the epitome of private property, becomes public.[39] Like the song with which *Savannah Bay* opens, it "concerns all memories equally" (Sav, p. 10). So that, for example, the twin voices of the very young girls "narrating" *La Femme du Gange* can "remember" things they never experienced: "Voice 1: 'Sometimes, also, I remember things I did not know.' [. . .] Voice 2: '[. . .] sometimes another memory comes to me' . . . " (Fem, pp. 128–129). Correlatively, this "memory" founded on absence

and forgetting becomes plural, the source of unlimited narrative
possibilities.

The Young Woman questions Madeleine less, finally, about what
happened than about what Madeleine *says*: "Madeleine: 'He had
light eyes?' Young Woman: 'I think so. You said blue.' Madeleine:
'No, I said light. (*pause*). I also said: eyes . . . I don't know any
more.' (*pause*). Today I say light eyes'" (Sav, p. 80). At first the Young
Woman does have a "violent desire to apprehend the unknowable of
the past," *but* "through consecrated texts," (Sav, p. 55) and the plural
is noteworthy. The event's textual nature is constantly emphasized
lexically as well as narratively and thematically. It is " theater" (Sav,
p. 31) "legend" (Sav, p. 32) "story" (Sav, pp. 29, 39) "narratives,"
(Sav, pp. 32, 30) "book," (Sav, p. 59) and "texts" (Sav, pp. 35, 55).
Madeleine evokes the multiplicity engendered by the "unknowable
of the past" in response to a "correction" made by the Young
Woman: "Oh, it's possible, you know, with all these texts . . . "
(Sav, p. 35).

"Ignorance," source and matter of this textual play, leads one
to reconsider the word "text" in connection with weaving. The
French "texte" and "tisser" (to weave) are derived from the Latin
"texere." Far from weaving texts in order to cover (repress) what
the dominant symbolic order construes as empty and/or obscene,
as a negatively marked feminine absence, Duras devotes her fiction
to uncovering and revalorizing it. This deconstructs the pejorative,
phallogocentral metaphors relating to a posited "lack" in the female
sexual apparatus (and implicitly in the "feminine" discursive apparatus), seen as something to hide and reduce – to nothing.[40] Duras'
gaps are the fecund principle of textuality, which open the text to
voice and variation, as intimated in *La Femme du Gange*: "And, too,
they [the narrating female voices] could doubtless have arrived at
a film completely different from this one. On condition that it be
vacant, [. . .] made of holes" (Fem, p. 104).

Durassian textual play is at once joyfull and serious, for what is
at play, at stake (en jeu) is life. (Remember that Madeleine "died"
each time she "played" on stage). If, as de Man notes, "the aesthetic
entity belongs to the same class as the toy,"[41] then so does life.
Duras resituates play, with all its polysemy, at life's core, where it
is associated with a positively marked loss (of the objective attitude
towards identity and truth), childhood, and women. "Someone who
is not all lost, who has an answer for everything, that is appalling.
Yes, woman has the incomparable grace of being constantly lost.

Being lost is superb. It relates to childhood. [ça relève de l'enfance] All children are lost. I love that quality in women."[42]

Duras wrote *Savannah Bay* in the conditional, the French verbal form of make-believe. An "unreal" tense,[43] it escapes linear temporality. Because it heralds fiction, the conditional releases children (here Madeleine and the Young Woman) from social identity, freeing them to play many parts. Most often, the two women set the imaginary stage through use of the conditional before proceeding to the present of their characters.[44] For example: "Young Woman: 'He would have returned by way of the river road. [. . .]' Madeleine: 'He would have come close to her [. . .]' Young Woman: 'He would have said certain words [. . .]' Madeleine: 'They would have left the white rock.' [A "stage direction":] *They speak like other people, like the lovers would have spoken.* Madeleine: 'You are not too tired?' Young Woman: 'You swim so far out'" (Sav, pp. 43–44).[45] (The French conditional also has the function of the English "alleged," indicating the unproven nature of an ensuing narrative.)

That in *Savannah Bay* the "action" consists of an actress and a woman who visits her so that she will act/play with her throws into relief the connections between women, fiction and children, the first actresses and actors. This entails another key element in Duras: "répétition" which in French signifies both rehearsal and repetition. In one sense, everything is repetition-rehearsal; in another, repetition does not exist. Children at play act as though they were rehearsing an unwritten text which changes with each "performance" or in the course of a single one. In Madeleine's and the Young Woman's "theater," each repetition/rehearsal composes a different variation of an always already missing original script.[46]

If in *Savannah Bay* everything revolves around forgetfulness and uncertainty, Madeleine is nevertheless sure of one thing, which symbolizes Duras' thought. It is the white rock, site of the Young Girl's encounter with the Young Man: "I am sure of almost nothing. The white rock – of that I am sure" (Sav, p. 32). She is certain because the white rock is both a metaphor and a metonymy for "ignorance." Jutting out from "the middle of the sea" (Sav, p. 32), that "fullness-emptiness" so central to Duras' oeuvre, it figures the text. Like the rock, the story (all textuality) juts out of the fecund "emptiness that surrounds everything, bottomless, endless, it is sonorous: the sea" (Ind, p. 139), just as the Young Girl is brought forth from the water by the Young Man, just as the Young Woman brings Madeleine out of silence by means of the song. The white rock breaches the sea like the written page breaches the void of the unwritten, and both disclose the presence of the "absence" that is there. The key to the symbol lies in its whiteness, or blankness, (the French "blanc" means both). Continually washed over by waves, the white rock figures the page, always imminently blank, ready for writing to begin anew.[47] The stone is "burning, white/blank like the name" (Sav, p. 51) – and names do not appear in this text, having been bleached, whited out – in French "blanchi." Except for the name Madeleine, the very singleness of which calls attention to the surrounding onomastic absence like the white rock calls attention to the sea around it. Always available, then, the white rock figures multiple textual possibilities, plurality as a function of the "ignorance" surrounding and washing over everything, making everything possible: life, love, texts.

Aurélia Steiner

> "On écrit toujours pour la première fois."
>
> Marguerite Duras

A number of Marguerite Duras' heroines lead bourgeois lives, locked in silent idleness as someone's wife, lives which frequently culminate in madness, sometimes in suicide or murder. In contrast with these women smothering essentially for want of discursive options, Aurélia Steiner "saves" herself through artistic work, like Madeleine in *Savannah Bay*. Both have the crucial and, for women, rare opportunity of articulating their own stories. Aurélia Steiner is the only woman writer in Duras' literary production besides "Duras" herself. "Written" and narrated by a young woman with the same name as the title and the female protagonist, the three *Aurélia Steiner* texts take the form of anonymous letters in reverse. Anonymity is displaced from the writer, who identifies herself, to the person(s) to whom she writes. At each text's end, she asserts her "authorship" with the same name, age, and occupation, but varies geographical location:

> My name is Aurélia Steiner.
> I live in Melbourne, where my parents are professors.
> I am eighteen years old.

I write."[48]

"My name is Aurélia Steiner.
I live in Vancouver, where my parents are professors.
I am eighteen years old.
I write.

(Aur, p. 166)

My name is Aurélia Steiner.
I live in Paris, where my parents are professors.
I am eighteen years old.
I write.

(Aur, p. 200)

Signed and "sent," that is, "published",[49] these open letters address a non-specific, un-named "you" sometimes singular, sometimes plural. Although not amorphous ("you" shapes the lovers and the protagonist's parents), its referents remain obscure. The narrating writer has never met these absent "you"s, who are dead or imaginary. Discrepancies between the three *Aurélia Steiner*s and, within the individual texts, between the diegesis and the "facts" noted in each signing compound uncertainty. For example, the parents of Aurélia the writing narrator/protagonist are dead in each story, but those of Aurélia the signer are alive.

This writing woman creates axiomatic "ignorance" to open textual options. Aurélia declares on the first page of *Aurélia*-Melbourne:[50] "I write [to] you all the time [. . .] I am going to write you perhaps a thousand letters." On the first page of *Aurélia*-Vancouver: "I am in this room where I write [to] you every day" (Aur, p. 139). At the end of *Aurélia*-Paris: "Still [toujours] this room where I write [to] you" (Aur, p. 199). I place "to" in parentheses because the "you" in "I write you" can read as an indirect or direct object. Aurélia's writing creates both the "you" to whom she writes and her "I."

"Ignorance" opens space for difference: different texts, sexual difference, different relationships – and the three texts correlate difference to love. The *Aurélia Steiner*s are love letters which write relationships without the subject-object structure. In other words, in a woman's words, Aurélia creates identities and sexual and family romances predicating love between subjects. These love letters are literary appeals which create models of what they call for. Duras remarks: "The sentence Aurélia Steiner says at the end: 'I write.' Her call [appel] is not 'I am calling' but 'I am writing.'"[51]

Aurélia-Melbourne addresses an imaginary, anonymous, absent male lover. Writing negates the man's death, perennially decreed by society: "They [on] say that you are in an equatorial land where you supposedly died long ago, in the heat, buried in charnel houses of plague, of war also, and also in a German death camp in Poland. [. . .] I see that it isn't true. That when I write [to] you no one is dead" (Aur, pp. 119–120). Implicitly affirmative beckoning questions of "where" and "who" replace society's repressive "nowhere": "Where are you? How to reach you?" (Aur, p. 118). "What are you doing?" (Aur, p. 119). "But who are you?" (Aur, p. 126).

Aurélia posits love as contextualized in history: "Never, never do I separate you from our love. From your history" (Aur, p. 128), and avoids mind/body dichotomies: "I do not separate you from your body" (Aur, p. 134). "I do not separate you from me" (Aur, p. 134). A non-objectifying gaze joins without abolishing difference. Aurélia's text realizes the desire to be seen in one's sexual difference and loved as different, and articulates that at/as the end of the millenial violence done to Otherness: "There was killing here. Did you know it? [. . .] Thousands and thousands of years. The bloodied river. [. . .] For a very, very long time, nothing. And then, once, your eyes. Your eyes on me. First the liquid empty blue of your eyes. And then you saw me" (Aur, pp. 128–129).[52]

The first person narrator "writing" the text, inscribes her lover as an interlocutor, someone heard and quoted: "You used to say, '[. . . .]'" (Aur, p. 132). Reciprocal love between adult speaking subjects counters the dominant scenario, symbolized by the dying, leprous, white cat. Prowling outside Aurélia's room the cat cries out a desire for possession "masquerading as the wish to belong."[53] "There is that cat, skinny, white [. . .] he frightens me, he is screaming, he is lost, he wants to belong, and I don't want [that] any more [moi, je ne veux plus]" (Aur, pp. 118–119). Aurélia rejects a dependence which perpetuates relations of possession. The last part of the sentence reads either "I no longer want the cat to belong," or "I no longer want to belong," an ambiguity inclusive of both sides of the coin of possession. Resisting such catcalls, Aurélia escapes reification.

Once dead, the white cat becomes one of several figures of blank/white (blanc) space, tabulae rasae akin to Madeleine's white rock. They clear the way for Aurélia's repeatedly formulated question: How can we live our love? The cat has disappeared as has the city evoked by the imagined lover: "You had said to me: that submerged city is our obscure land" (Aur, p. 132). Both absences free a "blank" space in which the lovers might invent their love. The "blank" left by the dead cat provides her with the means of reaching him: "Fog rises in the garden. [. . .] I see it. It spreads over you. Over me. [. . .] It is through that mad, skinny cat, now dead, through this garden immobile around it, that I reach you. Through this white whiteness [or blank blankness], this infinite fog, that I reach your body" (Aur, pp. 133–134). The blank space elicits writing. Immediately after these lines come the statements of Aurélia's name and identity as a woman writer, which end the text and provide an answer to her initial questions. Through the blank of "ignorance," she can "give you letters of my life now" (Aur, p. 117). She can articulate and fictively grant her wish for reciprocal love, while simultaneously inflecting language with its expression, "sending" it to the public as an other possible model.

In *Aurélia*-Vancouver, a daughter spins a decentered family romance in which love circulates in all possible permutations between child, father, and mother. A "white rectangle" (Aur, pp. 149, 151, 156, 158), the assembly yard in a Nazi concentration camp where her parents die at the moment of her birth, figures another blank space from which narrative will issue.

Identity, relations and the text emerge from initial figures of immobility and radical separation. Aurélia's text tells these beginnings at its own inception, through the image of a seascape of suspended life: "The sky is dark. Before me there is the sea. Today it is flat, heavy, as though of a density of iron, with no more strength to move" (Aur, p. 139, the text's first page). A black line symbolizing blocked communication closes the horizon: "Between the sky and the water there is a wide, thick, sooty black line. It covers the whole horizon; its regularity is that of a giant, sure crossing-out [rature], of the importance of unsurmountable difference. It could cause fear" (Aur, p. 139).

With the very description of the dividing line, Aurélia crosses it, defusing the principle of binarism. Contact is not barred. Difference is not feared. As she "writes" the moribund scene, the flow of her ink begins to resuscitate life. Once again the impetus comes from a love call. In the somber atmosphere preventing Aurélia from seeing her image in the "dead glass" (Aur, p. 141), the mirror reflecting the deadened sea,[54] she declares love for the unknown father she is about to write: "I love you with all my strength. I do not know you" (Aur, p. 140). This catalyzes the creative motion, producing a sea change in "the depths" between the horizon and the beach (Aur, p. 140) and Aurélia "begins to see again" (Aur, p. 141). Life begins to flow, as suggested by the profusion of birth images associated with the resuscitated sea: "Before me a color is born," and "the sea becomes transparent, shiny with the brilliance of nocturnal organs, [. . .] of flesh" (Aur, p. 141). This sets in motion the homonymic play between "la mer" and "la mère" (the sea and the mother). Re-writing the static and the lifeless engenders life and text. The looking glass opens and Aurélia begins to see what she is imagining: an identity always already in relation. Her looking is a showing, a conversation constitutive of both "I" and "you": "I look at myself. [. . .] Do you see? Blue the eyes, beneath black hair. How I love you, seeing myself. [. . .] I smile at you and tell you my name. I call myself Aurélia Steiner. I am your child. You are not informed of my existence. [. . .] I am informed about/by you through me. [informée de vous à travers moi]" (Aur, pp. 142–143).

Because "de" is ambiguous here, "informée" can read "informed about," or "given form by." This imagined mutual generation *with* others works in both directions. Aurélia's blue eyes and dark hair come from her "father's" part in her creation (Aur, p. 145). Crossing the "line," Aurélia in turn "creates" him, and stresses the textual nature of this endeavor: "I construct your voice [. . .] The voice of the millenial sleeper, your voice written as of now" (Aur, p. 146). Although she "would have heard" him call our her name (Aur, p. 146), he remains markedly nameless: "I do not know his name" (Aur, p. 160). Purposeful onomastic "ignorance" thwarts the classifying and proprietary tendencies of patriarchy. Neither needy nor desirous of a name-of-the-father, Aurélia writes a father who gives love rather than law.

Aurélia-Vancouver's central scene of loving family origins is set in opposition to an emblem of hyper-rationalized, dominating law at its most murderous: a Nazi camp. Interned because of the decreed intolerable otherness of being Jewish, Aurélia's invented father dies for love of another Other: he is hanged in the camp for stealing soup to feed his newborn female child (Aur, p. 158).

Nearby, watching him die while she herself dies in childbirth, lies the mother, also Jewish. With her last gesture she protectively hides her infant (Aur, p. 160). "You" now becomes the mother, to whom the "writer" Aurélia Steiner gives the same name as to herself *qua* writer and infant. This effects continuity and solidarity, not dissolution in fusion or Oedipal replacement. It figures (feminine, ethnic) otherness as ever resurgent from repression. For if the parents' death puts an end to the symbolically resounding name "Aurélia Steiner" in the camp, it resuscitates elsewhere: "The words Aurélia Steiner no longer rang out in the camp. They were taken up again elsewhere, in other stages [étages], in other zones of the world" (Aur, p. 159). Further, directly addressing her parents in the present tense, the narrating daughter revokes the death sentence on another level, like in *Aurélia*-Melbourne.

Evocations of the murders in the camp run counterpoint to descriptions of the sea exploding in furious reaction, "invading" the narrator's town (Aur, p. 150). The ocean's revolt, with which Aurélia identifies, figures the anger of the Other. Through syntactic and lexical homology, identification of Aurelia with the sea is reinforced. "Elle, la mer" alternates with "elle, Aurélia Steiner." After the sea calms, Aurélia "lies on the depth of the sea" and as its "warmth" rocks her, she talks to it as though it were the child from the camp. Ambiguity affecting the antecedents of the pronoun "elle" and the direct object pronoun "la" allow Aurélia to position herself as child and as resuscitated mother: "I went to lie down on the depth of the sea. [. . .] Little girl. Love. Little girl. I called it/her [je l'ai appelée] various names, Aurélia, Aurélia Steiner [. . .] You, child, the sea" (Aur, pp. 154–155). The sea rocks Aurélia, who in turn soothes it with maternal words, and both become child and mother interchangeably. As Aurélia tells her story, the story is also being told to her: "I sang. I spoke to it/her, I sang, and I heard the story" (Aur, p. 156).

In *Aurélia*-Vancouver, a woman gives voice(s) to herself as daughter, mother and lover. Early in the text, she evokes itinerant sailors with whom she makes love. Nameless like the father, out(side) laws, the sailors call out as he does the name of a loved woman, a self named woman. *Aurélia*-Vancouver ends with a love scene which correlates "ignorance," love and a non-dominating use of discourse. Aurélia answers a sailor's query about her origins with a declaration of ignorance: "He asks me where I'm from. I say I don't know" (Aur, p. 161). This whiting-out creates a blank immediately materialized in yet another symbolic white rectangle, here a blank sheet of paper. Aurélia writes her name on it and hands it to the sailor: "I tell him: 'I'm going to give you a name. You will pronounce it, you won't know why, yet I ask you to do it' [. . .] I tell him the name: Aurélia Steiner. I write it on a blank page and I give it to him" (Aur, pp. 161–162).

The male characters' anonymity does not signify social exclusion; it deconstructs exclusion itself. And the full female name individuates less than it symbolizes.[55] Taking the same name as her mother, hearing it passionately pronounced, Aurélia associates the sailor(s) and herself with the imagined double scene of death and love, in which the latter triumphs in the person of the surviving child writing now. As Aurélia and the sailor begin to make love, her eyes are "closed on the white rectangle of death." Just as in *Aurélia*-Melbourne, a woman calls for a man who can see and love an other, a different, female subject. "I give them [the sailors] my fresh body, and they take it. [. . .] You could have been one of them except that you would have seen me" (Aur, p. 144). The sailor in the final passage looks at Aurélia, but his gaze veers towards visions of possession. To his announced wish to stay with her, she replies that she "belongs to no one definite," yet that she "is not free" (Aur, p. 165). She is not free to "belong," and therefore rejects the sailor's desire for possession just as Aurélia-Melbourne rejects the white cat. In her writing, she "lives" the kind of reciprocal love barred by dominant structures: "You are that which will not take place and which, as such, is experienced [se vit]" (Aur, p. 157).

Written in the third person until the last pages when "I" directly addresses "you," *Aurélia*-Paris resembles less a straightforward epistle than a text sent along with a accompanying note. Within the third-person narrative, two female characters invent together the absent, imagined story of origins. Aurélia Steiner is a seven-year-old Jewish child left with a neighbor by her mother moments before she and the father were deported by the German police. The neighbor, an elderly woman, knows nothing about the family. Another central white rectangle, this time a white patch sewn on Aurélia's clothing, symbolizes "ignorance:" "Except for that small, white cotton rectangle sewn inside your dress,' says the lady, 'we know nothing, neither you nor I. On the white rectangle there were the letters A.S. and a date of birth'" (Aur, pp. 178–179).

The child repeatedly asks the elder woman to tell her her story: how her mother used the excuse of an errand in order to persuade this neighbor to take her. When, like Madeleine, the lady drowsily halts the narrative despite requests to "tell me" (Aur, p. 194), Aurélia switches roles and prompts her. Based on details so scant they amount to nearly complete "ignorance," this collaboration frees imagination. The little girl tells her story in her own voice, filling the blank "page" of the rectangle, a metaphor Duras confirmed:

"It [the rectangle] is also a page, a scene."[56] Thus the three *Aurélia Steiner* texts have similar structures *en abyme*. The "signer" writes her identities in texts in which the protagonist "writes" *her* identities and those of her parents.

On the blank "page" the little girl "writes" invented scenes of royal origins, elevating her love to the legendary. "My mother was Queen of the Jews,' says the child. 'Queen of Jerusalem and Samaria. Then white men came and took her away" (Aur, p. 185). This mythologizing foregrounds the symbolic quality in the identity between the mother's and daughter's names. Again a child's voluntary identification with her mother signifies the return of the oppressed-repressed-suppressed: "'My mother,' says Aurélia, 'she called herself Aurélia Steiner. [. . .] Steiner, Aurélia,' says Aurélia. 'Like me'" (Aur, p. 198). And again, inscription of a nameless father in the story of parentage disassociates him from patriarchal (and fascist) law: "My father, I don't know who he was, probably a traveler, he came from Syria" (Aur, p. 186).

The lady and the little girl discard roles of authority and seniority. Neither adult nor child hides her fear, and each appeals to the other for information and help. (The older woman turns to the child for her thoughts on the destination of the allied bombers flying overhead, and the child turns to her for fuel for her stories.) Significantly, the lady teaches the child to write. This constitutes a prospective reference to the text's "author" and reinforces the triple onomastic identification between the child, the mother and the "signer." Because of the older woman's gift of writing, the little girl can grow into a writing woman, who will write herself in open letters of dialogue with a loved, loving, and plural "you."

In *Le Camion*, the hitch-hiking lady "tells her story to whomever is there. Every evening she tells her story for the first time" (Cam, p. 64). And each time it is different. This kind of "inaccurate" repetition, agent of (inter) textuality, founds Aurélia Steiner's writing and rewriting of her origins, loves, and identities in the three texts. From text to text elements recur: the cat, the roses, the imagined lover in the first and third *Aurélia*s, the blank rectangle common to all three, Jewishness and concentration camps. Duras links the *Aurélia Steiner*s in various ways to the other texts in the volume, *Le Navire Night*, *Césarée* and *Les Mains négatives*. Imagined by the little girl in *Aurélia*-Paris, the story of a Jewish Queen kidnapped by Europeans recalls *Césarée*. In *Les Mains Négatives*, a solitary man calls out his love to an unknown, absent lover, forming a sort of

photographic negative of *Aurélia*-Melbourne. The act of calling
(writing) constitutes the strongest intertextual connection in the
volume, as Marguerite Duras remarks: "In the book *Aurélia Steiner*,
one can see the progression of each text leading to the other. The call
in the night of *Le Navire Night*. Next, the call through geography.
Then in the caves and then across time."[57] The callers in all these
texts call out to anonymity itself. Duras discusses this with respect
to "ignorance" in the introduction to *Le Navire Night*:

> The person who reveals herself in the abyss claims no identity.
> She claims only this: to be equal. Equal to he who will answer
> her. To everyone. A fabulous clearing out happens as soon as
> one dares to speak, or rather as soon as one manages to speak.
> For as soon as we call, we become, we are already the same.
> As whom? As what? As that of which we know nothing. [. . .]
> When we write, when we call, already we are the same. (Nav,
> p. 12)

In addition to numerous avatars in films, plays and texts partially
repeated in other volumes, Aurélia Steiner resurfaces once again in
L'Eté 80. A "letter" in "Duras'" voice to an anonymous, unknown
"you" frames references to "Aurélia's" letters: "A year ago, I sent
you Aurélia Steiner's letters."[58] Duras and Aurélia call passionately
to lovers invented and "experienced" in their writing. "I wrote [to]
you here, from Melbourne, Vancouver, Paris. [. . .] Tonight I see you
again, you whom I did not know [. . .] This room could have been
the place where we would have loved each other, it is therefore that
place, of our love. [. . .] I sent you Aurélia Steiner's letters, hers, written by me. [. . .]" (Eté, p. 63). A far cry from the common metaphor of
Woman as missive sent from man to man, a closed, empty envelope
whose lack of an address represents her status as public property
for any man. Claudine Herrmann analyzes the symbol in Breton
and Barbey d'Aurevilly with respect to the silencing of women: "[it
figures] feminine attributes such as man pictures them; it is first of
all an *empty envelope without an address*, in other words a message men
address to one another, whose content is unimportant (preferably
empty), and whose addressee is equally indifferent since there is
no address."[59] In societies where men hold power and prevent
women from sending messages, "the sealed letter without an
address constitutes a remarkable metaphor of Woman."[60] Duras'
female letter writers unseal their lips and break out of the closed

circuit of deindividuation and commodification. Calling themselves into existence, they create other models of exchange.

Fiction, "Ignorance" and the Photographic Image in L'Amant

> "'La condition préalable à l'image, c'est la vue,' disait Janouch à Kafka. Et Kafka répondait: 'On photographie des choses. pour se les chasser de l'esprit. Mes histoires sont une façon de fermer les yeux.'"
>
> Roland Barthes

> "Le seul sujet du livre [L'Amant] c'est l'écriture. L'écriture, c'est moi, Donc moi, c'est le livre."
>
> Duras

Although much critical comment has been made about Duras' cinematic innovations on the one hand and about sight as a theme in her books on the other, her thematization of the relation between visual absence, discourse and textual production has rarely been analyzed. Nor has this been connected to intertextuality between genres. When Duras disconnects the sound track from the screen images in many of her films, this dislocation de-emphasizes the visual in favor of the verbal. Directed towards the invisible and the unknown, unstuck from concrete objectal representations, the gaze becomes a verbal instrument productive of open-ended imagination and textuality.

Often Duras' films play on several levels of visual absence. In "India Song" and "La Femme du Gange," we recall, invisible speakers "narrate" a story not enacted on the screen, which simply shows people dancing and lying down ("India Song") or walking ("La Femme du Gange"). We hear the speakers "see," since we know they are looking only because they say so, and we know what they are "seeing" – the story – only because they tell it. That what they are reconstituting is, most probably, a text, places the visual at an even further remove. Verbal embroidering on an absent textual referent replaces visual evidence both for the speakers and the spectators. Imagination is produced primarily through language. Duras' cinema tends towards screen images more and more neutral in the sense of not portraying the story. The spectator is steered away from the traditional visual cinematic experience, more towards the text. This type of focus on the verbal over the visual [61] occurs in many of Duras' films, with various interesting structural variations.

"I'm not going to make the film, I'm going to tell it," resolved Duras for "Le Camion."[62] The meagerness of the visual aids, so to speak, directs attention to what one hears more than to what one sees. We see only a truck, a desolate suburban landscape, and sometimes Duras and Depardieu, who do nothing but read aloud, on and off screen, the text of a possible film from manuscripts they hold in their hands. They speak in what a "stage direction" in the published text calls "a dark room, or reading room" (Cam, p. 11), a conflation confirming the linguistic nature of the images being "developed" in this verbal laboratory.

Emptied of direct action and speech, the screen or stage functions like an "echo chamber": "The image or the stage [. . .] will play the role of an echo chamber. The voices, passing through this space, should reach the spectator with the same weight [portée] as her/his voice of 'internal reading'" (Ind, "stage direction" p. 57). What reverberates are words, shared by the speaking readers and the spectators, readers in a way as well, in their own dark room: "But what is *their* [the public's] dark room? [. . .] It is that other space. The stage is only an antechamber, clear consciousness."[63]

Duras has repeatedly expressed the precedence she accords the verbal over the visual in her cinematic and theatrical production: "Talking in the theater after a rehearsal of the play *La Musica*, she says she makes films between books in order to keep writing,"[64] and: "In my movies the text comes before everything, before both the image and the actors. The object filmed is the text . . . First there are the words and then the actors."[65] Filming *Agatha*, was perhaps futile because

. . . it's so obvious in the image, there is such adequation, unity [. . .] between the image and the text, that making it was perhaps not worth the effort. The text would have said it just as well. Because the text says everything. [. . .] The film is an accident, a sort of consequence of no great importance [. . .] [*Agatha*] is a listening proposition, a reading proposition. They are there, for one and one half hours, they read seventy pages. That's all. [. . .] [I made the film] for the reading of the voice, not for the voice, for the reading of the text.[66]

Son Nom de Venise dans Calcutta désert and *Aurélia Steiner* show no human figures at all. Spoken words evoke the absent characters while unpeopled images fill the screen. With *Le Navire Night*, Duras wanted "to try to make a film without images."[67] During a lengthy segment of *L'Homme Atlantique*, the screen remains entirely blank. The narrating voice, identified as that of a woman writer and film maker abandoned by a man, tells the absence of her lover and "films" it as such, filling the void with her *words*. She defines her cinematic undertaking as primarily verbal, actually predicated on visual absence. She relates how, after her lover left, she cleaned her house, ridding it of all "signs."[68] This cleared a space, a metaphorical blank page on which she could *write*: "Everything was cleaned of life, exempt, emptied of signs, and then I told myself: "I am going to begin writing, to cure myself of the lie of an ending love. [. . .] And then I began to write" (Hom, pp. 17–18). Filming, the visual medium, came second, after the written text: "You remained in the state of having left. And I made a film of your absence" (Hom, p. 22).

Considered eminently cinematic, these techniques hark back nevertheless to schemas present in Duras' novels almost forty years ago. In *Le Marin de Gibraltar* (1952) textuality emanates from a visual void. The woman's stories about her vanished lover provide the impetus for the relation between her and the narrator, for the text we read, and for the novel the narrator plans to write. When the protagonists of *Moderato Cantabile* (1958) meet at the café and attempt to "perceive" the relationship leading to the crime of passion they did not see, it is as though they train their "vision" on a blank screen which they fill with words, their own projected images conjointly "narrated." Their voices have fundamentally the same function as those in Duras' later films. In *Le Ravissement de Lol V. Stein*, Lol's desire to see her own absence in the couple which excludes her leads her to project it phantasmically, creating a "cinema of Lol V. Stein" (Rav, p. 55). Contrary to Kristeva's contention, Lol does not spy on the lovemaking with the desire to take Tatiana's place.[69] Further, voyeurism is not her objective. She glimpses the lovers only from the waist up, and only when they come to the window. This fulfills the purpose of verification, of their presence and Lol's absence. The hotel window figures primarily a blank screen for her phantasy of "that non-existent, invisible, spectacle" (Rav, p. 73). Her "film," we recall, is silent, for the male narrator replaces her empty images with his words.

Thus these texts full of "cinematic" structures already disconnect the verbal and the visual within the written form itself. Narrators and protagonists project words on a space cleared to make room for them, and textuality exists as a function of a thematized visual blank. If Duras' texts pass so easily from one genre to another, it is in great part because of the inherent transportability of these blank "screens," which enables the author to focus on the verbal even in visual media: "Question: 'How do you combine literature, theater, and movies?' Duras: 'The secret is discovering that they are similar media.'"[70]

While *L'Amant* does not announce its inter-genres nature in the manner initiated with *India Song*, whose subtitle is "text, theater, film," it pointedly claims a correlation with the medium of photography. The first-person narrator informs us that she has articulated her text around two photographs which she "shows," or, to use the appropriate metaphor, "develops" before the reader, directly addressed as "you." Repeatedly referred to simply as "the image," the first "picture" figures "Duras," the ostensible speaking "I," at age fifteen, as she imagines she appeared to a young Chinese man who saw her on a ferry boat in Indochina. "Duras" presents it piecemeal, in several narrative "takes," and invokes it with photographic terminology. However, she quickly asserts that the picture was never taken. As such, a non-existent photograph becomes an agent of literature, the "absolute" of a memory not confined to a single representation. Memory of a "real" event – the river crossing – merges with imagination in a literary projection of what the writer *says* the snapshot would have reflected had it been made. Because the image was never "removed" [enlevée] from time, made concrete and invariable, its very "blankness" acts as a literary catalyst, the text's non-visual, verbalized support, its "author":

> It could have existed, a photograph could have been taken like any other, elsewhere, in other circumstances. But it wasn't. [. . .] That is why this image – and things could not have been otherwise – does not exist. It was omitted. It was forgotten. It was not detached, removed from the total [la somme]. It is to this lack of having been made that it owes its power, that of representing an absolute, precisely of being its author.[71]

Duras confided to an interviewer that she had originally intended to entitle her text *The Absolute Image*.[72] One notes the connection in the quoted passage between an absolute and its "representation" by something that does not exist. Otherwise stated, there can be no adequate representation; the open field of literature emanates from "absolute," irreducible referential absence. If the absolute image existed, it would preclude others, and inhibit imagination. Its absence, like that of God for Duras, constitutes the principle of creativity, and forms an explicit theme in this text. Although *L'Amant*'s opening has notes of devastation (her "destroyed face" (Am, p. 10) and her alcoholism, which "filled the position God never had," including that of "killing her" – Am, p. 15), the story is essentially one of creativity, in particular the self-making of a woman and of a woman writer whom we watch in the process of creating out of that very initial non-presence.

Duras situates the unsnapped but verbally pictured photograph on the same level as other things the book "figures," such as the boat, the countryside, and the country itself. Since everything has receded equally into the past, the same literary status applies: everything resuscitates via written images: "That image, that unphotographed absolute photograph, entered into the book. [. . .] That central image, as well as that ferry boat which doubtless no longer exists, that countryside, that country also, destroyed . . . but it [the image] will have been and will remain indicated [signalée]; its existence, its *retinian* permanence will have been placed there, in that book."[73]

But it will have been "placed there" with words. Whatever the genre, Duras treats vision as a verbal phenomenon: to see means to imagine with words. And to write or utter those words constitutes a favored mode of intersubjectivity. Duras recognizes verbally communicated imagination as the agent of shared experience, from its beginnings in childhood play. In *L'Amant*, the contrast between words and visual images (here photographs), in its relation to intersubjectivity, forms a thematic as well as structural component of the text. The narrating author explains that as long as she simply "sees" the "absolute image" she remains alone: "I often think of that image which I am still alone in seeing, and of which I have never spoken" (Am, p. 9). Appearing on the opening page, this first reference to a central but unsnapped photograph announces that the author is about to end her solitude by writing. Writing the image makes it verbally visible to the "you" continually addressed, to the readers, who will now "envision" it with the author as they read.

Further, the non being of the "absolute image" allows "Duras" to write memory in terms of desire, when she steps back to "look" at her young self. What she remembers of her appearance combines with her preferred imaginary vision of herself to compose the image. From among all "real" photographs or images of herself, the unreal, "absolute image" is not only the one that "pleases and enchants" her, it is the one in which she "recognizes herself" (Am, p. 9). This work of memory and imagination and of imaginary memory emanating from a necessarily absent source throws into relief processes at work in autobiography in general. In literature, of which autobiography is a part, the selected, imagined past *is* the past. While describing the clothing she recalls wearing on the boat, for example, "Duras" expresses uncertainty as to which shoes she had on. Then she imagines a possibility which immediately becomes fictional fact: "That day I must be wearing that famous pair of gold lamé high heels. I see nothing else that I could wear that day so I am wearing them" (Am, pp. 18–19). When, after relating the cutting of her long hair in Paris at age twenty-three, "Duras" returns to "the image," she invites the reader to join her in "seeing" the long hair, which she "still" has: "On the ferry, look at me, I still have it" (Am, p. 24).

The use of the present tense resituates the temporal relation to textuality. For Duras, imagination and the imagination inherent in memory take place in the present, and the reader's experience takes place now, while reading. This is emphasized when "Duras" completes the description of the gold shoes with a sentence whose conjoined clauses recount both "then" and "now" in a simultaneous present of imagination, desire, and memory: "I go to the lycée in evening shoes decorated with little sparkling patterns. That is my will. I can only stand myself with that pair of shoes, and still now I want myself like that [je me veux comme ca]" (Am, p. 19). Thus the text functions in the deictic register. Pointing to her literary pictures, "Duras" urges the reader to "look" at them with her, here and now.

Like the first image, with which it interacts contrapuntally, the second photograph has a name: "the photo of despair" (Am, p. 41). According to the narrating author, however, this second main picture actually did exist. Taken in Hanoi, it showed "Duras" with her brothers and her mother, who indeed felt perpetual despair at their poverty. Yet this photograph's material reality does not account for its textual productivity. Beyond the fact that it too remains perforce absent in a purely written text, and that the only proof of its existence rests in the "author"'s written word, the memory it represents had to fade from her "eyes" in order for her to write. Its visual referential power had to be neutralized in order for it not to inhibit the flow of textuality by imposing a finite, documentary image. The "author" can only write the picture because of the gulf between photographs and memory. Despite the photo's ostensible existence, she has "forgotten" her mother's looks, and this visual mnemonic absence forms the precondition of "Duras'" ability to write about her so copiously: "For memories also it is too late. [. . .] I've left them. [her mother and brothers] I no longer have the perfume of her skin in my head, nor in my eyes the color of her eyes [. . .] It's over. I don't remember any longer. That is why I write so easily about her now, so long, so stretched out, she has become fluent writing" (Am, p. 38).

"Ecriture courante," translated here as fluent writing, is a pun on "eau courante," running water, and on "parler couramment," to speak fluently. The liquid connotation of flowing writing applies most aptly to Duras' symbolic universe, in which water has so great a part. Additionally, "courant" means common. Faded visual memory enables the author to transform the singularity of experience by communicating it through language. Common to all readers and directly related to imagination, of which it is a vehicle, language communalizes.

Sensate experience, then, does not produce involuntary memory as it did for Proust. Voluntary verbal efforts produce an imaginary "memory" on the one hand, and involuntary forgetting of real photograph-memory spurs imagination on the other. After that, what incites memory and textuality in *L'Amant* is writing itself. By dint of an intrinsically metonymical power, the word on the page catalyzes simultaneously memory and the literary process. On several occasions, "Duras" explicitly attributes her recollection of certain details to the fact that she has just *written* a passage about things connected to them. For example, while describing the tension between her older brother and her lover during the dinners which bring them together in the Chinese restaurant, she suddenly "remembers" the former's facial expression, which appears, metonymically summoned forth by the words immediately preceding: "Speaking about it [her brother's hostility] now makes me rediscover the hypocrisy of his face, the distracted air of someone looking in another direction" (Am, p. 67).

Later, metonymy functions so to speak in absentia, in the cleaning episode, a rare happy scene during which the family and several neighbors participate in hosing down the house. Only upon writing does the author "see" that "everyone" did not include her older brother. The "sight" of her written memory conjures up the memory of his absence: "I remember, at the very moment I write, that our older brother was not at Vinhlong when we washed down the house" (Am, p. 77). Fictional or not, this recovered memory blends with the text's other levels. In a final example, the written statement of shaky memory attracts its own corrective. At the beginning of the brief story of a young man who committed suicide by jumping off a ship, Duras notes that she does not really know any longer whether the event occurred during the voyage she has just evoked or at some other time. A few lines later, as though invoked suggestively by writing itself, "memory" awakens: "No, writing it now, she doesn't see the boat but another place, where she heard the story" (Am, p. 137). The "correct" version turns out to be remembrance not of a witnessed event but of a text, as is so often the case for Duras' narrators.

It would be misleading to posit opposition between the two central images in *L'Amant*. Although a river crossing is involved which entails a passage to sexual initiation at once symbolic and concrete, it signals no definitive departure from one place to another. One must not neglect the fact that the rite of passage takes place on a ferry, which, rather than transporting one to a permanent destination, shuttles back and forth. The ferry has neither port of origin nor end port. Moreover, the alternation between the two "ports," the two "photographic" scenes, connects them, producing metonymical links. Rather than institute dichotomy between her lover and her family, "Duras" associates them. One "port" interprets the other, which it resembles: "I am still in that family, that is where I live to the exclusion of any other place. [. . .] The hours that I spend in the bachelor flat in Cholen [with the lover] make that place appear in a fresh, new light. It is an irrespirable place, close to death, a place of violence, of pain, of despair, of dishonor. And such is Cholen. On the other side of the river" (Am, p. 93). The sexual love affair coordinates with "Duras'" erotic feelings towards her two brothers, whose "shadows pass through the bedroom" where she and the Chinese man make love (Am, p. 122). Orchestrated so that they bring the two "ports" together, the dinner scenes evince a polarity maintained not by Duras but by the others involved. To be sure, she perceives an essential difference between herself and her mother (her family[74]), when her own sexual experience leads her to realize that her mother has probably never known sexual pleasure, and she "leaves" her in that sense: "The sons knew it already. The daughter, not yet. They will never speak about the mother together, about this knowledge they have and which separates them from her, about this decisive, final knowledge, of the childhood [enfance] of the mother. The mother has never known sexual pleasure" (Am, p. 50).

But if there is separation, it distances "Duras" equally from her family and from her lover. She knows that she has not left her mother for the lover. Nor will she leave her lover for her family. She learns that she will never consign herself, either symbolically or concretely, to one or the other of the river banks: "I told him [the lover] to regret nothing. I reminded him of what he had said, that I would leave everywhere, that I could not control my behavior" (Am, pp. 102–103). But it is not for other lovers, or to return to her family that she will betray him, it is for writing.[75] The mother understands this desire of her daughter: "I answered that what I wanted above anything else was to write, nothing else, nothing. Jealous, she is. No answer, a brief glance quickly turned away, the small unforgettable shrug of her shoulders. I will be the first to leave [. . .] She knew it" (Am, p. 31).

Yet she "leaves" only to return to them, to shuttle back and forth on the ferry boat of her writing, which these two "images," of family and sexual love, have always informed. She takes up permanent quarters on a figure of impermanence: a vehicle riding on water, that central Durassian symbol of the constant flow of feminine creativity and sexuality. The Mekong "carries everything" with it. Generous, full, "the river flows quietly [sourdement]; it makes no noise, blood in the body" (Am, p. 30). In the hazy sunlight "the river banks have disappeared" and "everything remains suspended" for the moment, as does this magnificent metaphorical description placed between two declarations of the young girl's intention to write, each of which corresponds to one of the central "photographs." With its promise to overflow, the river figures the writer herself, a young girl on the brink of affirming her own vocation to overflow, ink on the page, fluids from the body. Just prior to this passage, Duras takes up the picture of herself at fifteen, adding brush strokes to her physical portrait, describing her body, her breasts, her make-up and provocative attire. Lest the reader miss the profoundly literary message, Duras concludes the description with a summary of its meaning: "Fifteen and a half years old. The body is slender, almost puny, breasts still those of a child, make-up pale pink and red. And then that outfit. That could make people laugh but no one does. I see very well that everything is there. Everything is there and nothing is played out yet, I see it in the eyes, everything is already in the eyes. I want to write" (Am, p. 29). Thus *L'Amant* is also, and perhaps primarily, the story of an artistic vocation.

Several other "pictures" are written into *L'Amant*, such as that of the author's son (Am, p. 21), a second one of her mother (Am, p. 118) and flash descriptions of Marie-Claude Carpenter (Am, p. 79) and Betty Fernandez (Am, p. 82), two wartime acquaintances whose "portraits" suddenly interrupt the text, as though "Duras" had just happened upon them in a drawer where they had inadvertently been mixed in with the batch of "pictures" from Indochina. Or as though she had turned a page in an album and found them. The entire text is composed of brief scenes, or verbal snapshots thrown into relief by blank spaces: a photo album consisting solely of captions. Duras had originally planned to publish a collection of photographs accompanied by a brief text depicting the unphotographed boat scene: "The text of *L'Amant* was at first called *The Absolute Image*. It was to thread through an album of photographs of my films and of me."[76]

True to her *weltanschauung,* Duras abandons the structure of a picture book, whose main message would have been one of that documentary truth Roland Barthes declared to be the essence of photography, proof that "that really was."[77] Instead, she opts for a non-visual, poetic "that is, in my imagination and now in the reader's." The flowing, musical temporality of Duras' poetic prose replaces photography's visual and temporal stasis. Duras describes the writing of *L'Amant* in musical terms. Akin to a sort of literary "Pictures at an Exposition," the text unfolds in the temporal mode of the present, in contrast to photography's past tense. Just as in musical composition, juxtaposition constitutes the unifying principle, and Duras recognized its role: "I wrote it measure by measure, beat by beat, without ever trying to find a more or less profound correspondence between the beats. I let this correspondence work unconsciously. [. . .] When I re-read it, I notice it. There is constant, incessant metonymy in *L'Amant*."[78] As in every instance where other artistic media are involved, Duras uses them to elucidate literary techniques. Here she equates music, or the sounds and rhythms of words, with writing: "All composition is musical. In every instance, it is this adjustment to the book that is musical. If one does not do that, one can always make other books, those whose subject is not writing."[79] Verbal music, then, composes the "captions" which make up this non-visual photo album.

In French the word for caption and for legend is the same: "légende," as if, by adapting an older word to the modern context of photographic images in texts of all kinds, the French language implicitly recognized the fictive, even mythical quality of commentary in captions. Contemporary thought distanced all language from objective fact or truth when it accepted the implications of Saussure's contention, later elaborated on by Benveniste, that the relation between the linguistic sign and its referent is arbitrary. This implicitly attributes an inherently fictional nature to language itself. Barthes, who agrees with this position, contrasts language to photography, whose relation to its referent he declares factual, albeit signified in the past tense: " . . . in Photography, I can never deny that *the thing was there*,"[80] and " . . . language is by nature fictional [. . .] but photography [. . .] is authentification itself."[81] Couching the viewer's attitude in phenomenological terms, he maintains that "one must link photography to a pure spectator consciousness, not to a fictional consciousness."[82] At other times, he marshalls linguistic concepts to make the same distinction, calling the factual essence of photographs denotative and the fictional essence of language connotative.

Discussing the relation of text to photographic images, Barthes notes that despite their connotative nature, captions usually try to pass themselves off as denotative, as the factual explanation of what photographs represent. Therefore, the presence of the two together tends to undermine the captions' fictional status. Whenever a photograph is present, the denotative element predominates, even if the caption belies the image.[83] One may conclude that in literature this remains true, so that in books containing photographic illustrations a hybrid structure is produced in which the balance tips towards the factual register.

By excluding photographs from *L'Amant*, Duras avoids this sort of ambivalent relation between captions and their visual, referential support, and the attendant vacillation between the documentary and the literary. Indeed, she uses the absence of pictures to reverse the habitual relation between caption and photographs, to situate both in the "fictional" realm of language. Instead of the image eliciting the caption, the caption produces the non-material, verbally evoked "visual" image: "Betty Fernandez. Another foreigner. As soon as the name is pronounced, here she is, walking down a Paris street, she's nearsighted [. . .]" (Am, p. 82). In the wake of verbal invocation and visual absence, once again associative metonymy sparks textuality. Thus disconnected, Duras' "captions" are free to present the relativized idiolect of her personal (but public, because literary) mythology,[84] which she invites readers to share.

Virginia Woolf found non-linear, non-chronological rhythms typical of women's autobiographies.[85] Quite early in *L'Amant*, "Duras" cautions against considering it the straightforward story or history of her life: "The [his]story of my life does not exist. That does not exist. There is never a center. No path, no line. There are vast spaces where one leads people to think there was someone; it is not true, there was no one" (Am, p. 14). During *L'Amant*'s fabulous burst of commercial success, due partially to curiosity about the author's life, Duras reiterated what the text itself constantly thematizes and demonstrates: the correlation between "ignorance" (visual and temporal absence), memory and fiction:

> People think that life unfolds like a road between two limits, beginning and end. Like a book one would write, that life is chronology. That is false. While one is living an event, one is ignorant of it. It is through memory, afterwards, that one thinks one knows what happened. Whereas the visible part that remains is superfluous, appearance [. . .] The history of your life, or my life, does not exist, or else it is a lexical question. The novel of my life, of our lives, yes, but not the history. It is the imaginary's resumption of time that returns the breath to life.[86]

Mostly, the authorial "I" talking about her life in *L'Amant* is double. "I" refers to Duras now as a young girl growing up in French Indochina, now as the contemporary, older writer, with only occasional evocations of periods in between. Typically, "ignorance" permeates both levels of the text. On the past, autobiographical level, nothing justifies belief that *L'Amant* delivers "the" truth about Duras' youth. New "facts" do seemingly "correct" details found in earlier texts. For example, *L'Amant* apprises us that Duras had two brothers rather than the single one her readers knew from *Un Barrage contre le Pacifique*, *Agatha*, and *L'Eden Cinéma*: "I often speak of my brothers as a unit," she writes (Am, p. 71). Contrary to the version in *Un Barrage contre le Pacifique*, Duras' mother, we "learn," died in France, not in Indochina, etc. Characters from Duras' texts, such as Anne-Marie Stretter and the beggar, turn out to be "real." Nevertheless, if *L'Amant* is not subtitled "novel," nor is it labeled "autobiography." The intratextual admonition against taking it for

Duras' true life story and the express failures of memory which inform the text tend to undermine the factuality of the information offered. The "solution" is avoided, and truth remains open, plural, fictionalized.

When "I" is the author as writer living now, explicit explanations concerning her books, and subtle anaphorical allusions graspable only by attentive Duras readers, combine to make of this level of the text what I call an "authorbiography": A Rousselian "How I Wrote Certain of my Books." But no titles, no in-depth analyses are supplied. Only "I" guarantees "truth" in a domain where nothing is incontrovertibly verifiable. Shattering the illusions of fact seekers, "Duras" expressly asserts forgetfulness about her own texts, creating on this level as well a productive "ignorance":

> In the stories in my books relating to my childhood, I suddenly don't know any more what I avoided saying, what I said; I believe I told the love we had for our mother but I don't know if I told the hatred we had for her as well and the love we had for each other also, and the hatred also, in that common [his]story [. . .] which still escapes my understanding, which is still inaccessible to me, hidden in the depths of my flesh, blind like a newborn on the first day. I am still there, before those possessed children, at the same distance from the mystery. I have never written when I thought I was writing, I have never loved when I thought I loved, I have never done anything but wait before the closed door. (Am, pp. 34–35)

Thus the writer deconstructs traditional autobiography and (first-person) literary history – authorbiography. A book of two-tiered memoirs – of life and of texts – issues from the subversion of memory in both domains, and blurs the lines between them. Comparing *L'Amant* to her other books, "Duras" declares: "What I am doing here is different, and the same" (Am, p. 14.). Instead of effecting closure via documentation, photographic or verbal, *L'Amant* plays with the author's and the reader's memories of Duras' texts and of her "life" in ways which merely open the door to further textuality. As Duras remarked: "When the book is closed, no story is finished. Not that of the lover, not that of the brother, not that of the skies, the voyages, the departures. It is the book that is finished."[87] Indeed, seven years later *L'Amant de la Chine du Nord* appeared, reshuffling the deck, changing some cards, adding others, scrambling the order

of *L'Amant*. This time existential rather than pictorial absence is
cited as the textual catalyst: the alleged "discovery" in 1990 that
the lover had died years before, spurred (re)writing.[88] The text is
"spoken" by a "very young" female voice (Am-Ch, p. 17), pointedly
differentiated from that of the young protagonist, who "is not the
one speaking" (Am-Ch, p. 18). New characters are introduced,
information contradicts that of the former book (the brother-sister
incest, the girl's age, the physical strength of the Chinese lover, the
mother's knowledge of the affair, etc.); yet express references to the
text as an aesthetic product rather than as fact inhibit reception of it
as a closer approximation to "the" truth.[89]

Consequently, one must not distinguish too hastily between the
seemingly more autobiographical *L'Amant* or *L'Amant de la Chine du
Nord* and Duras' seemingly less autobiographical other works.

One must accept each text as one more planet circulating with
many others in non-chronological, dis-orderly "ignorance" around
ever absent, "blank" centers.

3

Sleeping Beauties: Discourse, Gender, Genre in the "Erotic" Texts

Husserl-Kapit: "Your feminine characters are lucid; they are aware of everything. Your men are unaware of everything."
Duras: "No, they are unaware of women."

"C'est à votre incompréhension que je m'addresse toujours."

Marguerite Duras

"Let the priests tremble – we're going to show them our sexts!"

Hélène Cixous

"Je connais, j'affirme, je veux la différence de mon sexe. C'est différent que je t'apppelle, c'est différente que tu me cherches . . . je n'aime que dans la perspective de la différence."

Annie Leclerc

INTRODUCTION

While several of Duras' texts contain sexual scenes, I separate *La Maladie de la mort* and *L'Homme assis dans le couloir* for purposes of discussion because they focus exclusively on sexual encounters and offer in distilled form images of erotico-pornographic relations as defined and experienced in patriarchal society. I conflate the terms or use them interchangeably because, conceptualized in the dominant symbolic order, the erotic and the pornographic are on a continuum in which the line between them tends to blur ethically and materially. Regardless of aesthetic distinctions, which rest on debatable grounds, the discursive system in question correlates sexuality with violence.[1] Duras' work throws these processes into relief. In *La Maladie de la mort* and *L'Homme assis dans le couloir*, this is achieved through further exploration of narrative modalities that inscribe discursive and implicit narrative plurality, though less through referential absence than through a certain overabundance of presence in conjunction with a displaced, yet essential matrix of narrative "ignorance."

A narrating "I" tells each story, with respect to which it is explicitly co-present. This internal "I" speaks about the couple and, more or less directly, to one of the participants. By inscribing the speaking viewer, Duras deconstructs the peephole quality of traditional erotic texts, structured in compliance with conventions that make the reader feel privy to scenes of which, ostensibly unbeknownst to the performing couple, he (sic) is a secret voyeur. "For example," she explains about *L'Homme assis dans le couloir*, "I have stated that the third person is the one speaking. Usually, in all erotic texts, it is as though there were no witness. There is someone who is looking, who is seeing, and someone who is speaking. That is certain. The one speaking is the third person and that is recent."[2]

This insertion of the narrator has profound consequences. Basic assumptions are shaken and questions are raised concerning the relation of gender to genre (erotico-pornographic literature) and (sexual) discourse generally. One cannot bracket the femaleness of the signer. When Duras' "third person" topples the edifice of objectivity, it does so in terms of gender, exposing conventional erotic literature's univocity and the bad faith of its universalism.

Traditional erotic texts, written most usually by men, address an implicitly male community of readers, which they regale with scenes and a discourse reflecting and perpetuating the socio-symbolic structures and ideology of patriarchal society. If women read them, they are expected to identify with the victim. In Marini's discussion of these texts' relation to standard pornography, she reminds us: "Our position as female reader is absolutely designated: it mimes and announces the one we have to occupy in the sexual act. The master pornographer initiates us, through violence and in the name of the law, into the truth of our pleasure: a pleasure taken in identification with the victim, or, in the extreme, [à la rigueur] defence against the horror through identification with the aggressor [. . .]"[3] Duras' female signature and insistent narrative "I" disrupt this pattern and elicit the following questions: to whom is the text addressed, what is the attitude of the speaker/author towards her text, what messages is she sending? That the texts produce these questions is in itself significant and subversive.

LA MALADIE DE LA MORT

The plot is extremely spare: a man pays a woman to place herself at his disposal sexually for several nights. In *La Maladie de la mort*, the "I," not a participant in the framed scenes, describes them directly to the male protagonist, the "you." I read this "I" the way I do Duras' ubiquitous "stage directions" and interventions – as "Duras'" voice asserting her presence *qua* author through the adoption of an intratextual, non-omniscient position from which, as speaker, she presents scenes she is "staging" on the page. Speculating in the afterword about a possible theatrical production of the work, Duras envisages a male "sayer" who would read the text aloud on stage, while a woman would say the female protagonist's role from memory (Mal, pp. 59–61). Later she discarded the project: "I thought about it for three months, especially for the theater – But I believe I am going to give up the idea. I believe that in *La Maladie de la mort* I am the one speaking. I do not give up the floor to anyone."[4]

Through use of the first and second persons and the conditional mood, the "author" positions herself as a hypothetical stage director-observer describing what "would" occur. The "ignorance" inherent in that stance is further conveyed through expressions of uncertainty and expressly subjective opinion previously mentioned but which bear requoting: "Perhaps you take a pleasure in her that you never knew before, I don't know. I also don't know if you perceive the muted, far away grumbling of her orgasm [. . .] I don't believe so" (Mal, p. 15). Or, speculation: "The next day, suddenly, you would perhaps notice her absence in the room. The next day perhaps you would feel a desire to see her again, there [. . .] Perhaps you would look for her outside your room, on beaches, café terraces, in the streets" (Mal, p. 55).

What the narrating "I" is staging is a man in the act of staging "the" erotic scene as prescribed by dominant symbolic structures. On the very first page, the text strongly suggests its paradigmatic character. The man, "you," would have "found" the woman anywhere:

everywhere at once, in a hotel, in a street, in a train, in a bar, in a book, in a film, in yourself, in you [vous], in you [toi], a random effect of your penis erect in the night, which is calling out for someplace to put itself, someplace to unburden itself of the tears filling it. You might have paid her. (Mal, p. 7)

In addition to generality, this beginning reveals the interconnectedness between the concrete, factual, "objective" (hotel, street, train, bar), the cultural in the narrow sense (book, film), the male personal imaginary (in you), and the economic (the payment).

Produced by dominant symbolic structures, "woman" is circulated in all these registers, a created commodity which can be "found," "chanced" upon anywhere. This Anywoman, then, could be – is – sought and bought by Anyman, an inherent replaceability further stressed by the characters' anonymity as well as by the conditional, verb tense of the conceivable. The text's narrative structure also exposes dominant society's reification of "woman." From the linguistic point of view, in much of *La Maladie de la mort*, the "third person" is not the narrator but the bought woman. The objectifying third person pronoun, predicative of non-personhood and non-voice, is used consistently and exclusively for her. (The exceptions, when she says "I," will be treated shortly.) Unlike in dominant erotic texts, which, indeed, this one deconstructs, "the" erotic is not presented as divorced from the social. Duras' text bares the culturally dictated contract regulating most male-female relations at the same time it bares the protagonists' bodies, which act in conformity with those dictates. Let us look at that contract.

Stating the terms, the man makes payment contingent on the woman's total submission to what amounts to her suppression. For she must lie there silent. "You say that she would have to be silent like the wives of her ancestors; yield to you completely, to your will, be totally submissive to you like peasant women in barns after the harvest when, exhausted, asleep, they let men come to them – so that, little by little, you could get used to that form that would wed yours, that would be at your mercy like women of religion are with God . . . " (Mal, pp. 10–11). One notes the demand for historical continuity, which provides diachronic contextualization for the scene. Synchronically, male economic supremacy structures gender relations ranging from prostitution to marriage. In its brevity and economic forthrightness, the contract proposed here is strikingly similar to prostitution. Consequently, the explicit assertion that the young woman is not a prostitute (Mal, p. 23) deconstructs the bad woman (public woman)/good woman (private woman) binarism, which it transforms from a dichotomy into a continuum. This further underscores the woman's position as paradigmatic.

Woman's contracted silence must steep her in a muteness physical as well as verbal. Not only may she not express herself verbally, she must also silence her body. The man forbids her to give voice to her sexual pleasure (much less to her desires): "Another evening, unwittingly, you give her an orgasm and she cries out. You tell her not to cry out. She says she won't cry out any more" (Mal, p. 14). After another orgasm: "She opens her eyes, she says, 'How wonderful.' You put your hand over her mouth so she will be silent, you tell her such things aren't said. She closes her eyes, she says she won't say it any more" (Mal, p. 15). As suggested by the initial image of exhausted peasant women taken by men in their sleep, a "sleeping beauty" utterly at the disposal of "a prince" forms the ideal representation of imposed feminine muteness and stillness, availability and self-effacement. The silenced woman "closes her eyes," promising not to say "it" – her own sexuality. Like the wives of her ancestors, she spends most of the time asleep, while he uses her at will. At his demand, she simulates lifelessness, and he "makes" her as he wishes. He controls her movement, her speech, "creates" her, names her and unnames her, suppressing her identity. He selects a name for her but forgets it, since even an identity conferred by him proves too much for him: "When she sleeps you have forgotten the color of her eyes, as well as the name you gave her the first night" (Mal, pp. 24–25).

Thus goes the normative erotic scene. The man has the money, the control. Only he will be the speaker, the doer, the one who sees, the one in command. The woman will be the one seen, the one to whom things are done and said, the one who may rarely speak, and only if she echoes and reinforces male desire, only if she reflects male imagery. She may not speak her body, her self. In addition to staging this standard scene, *La Maladie de la mort* discloses how it is conveyed and perpetuated in the symbolic register through erotic literature. Otherwise stated, it shows how the genre treats gender. Duras accomplishes this by miming the traditional erotic text – but with a major difference. And that difference is voice. While the text focuses on the dominance of the male voice within the couple, the man is not the text's speaker. Herein lies the narrating "I"'s pertinence, in its structural presence, its subjective form, its gender. The other eye seeing, the other voice telling, the other memory remembering produces another rendering of dominant erotic literature most particularly because the other involved here is dominant society's designated Other, a woman.

Her sheer authorial-narrative presence subverts the dominant male-female contract by stating it, and exposes the usually tacit, and tacitly male, reader-author-hero complicity. Although the narrating "I" addresses only the man directly, she speaks for and with the woman, something which also affects any pact between the author and readers. Instead of a purportedly neutral voice claiming the transparency of a window while actually speaking from a masculinist point of view, we have a female voice, from a radically other perspective, relating to us and to the man what the man does and sees and says. This exposes the violence involved.

In addition to telling what he does, she says what he can not do. The woman he has reified, bought, and silenced escapes his grasp. As the speaker informs him, he can not see her, know her, or have her. Lying there naked and asleep, "exposed to being seen by you," (Mal, p. 33) she is nevertheless invisible to him: "You see nothing. You would like to see everything of a woman, as much as that can be done. You do not see that that is impossible for you" (Mal, p. 39). Denied self expression, "woman" becomes unknowable, sexually "mysterious" (the question "what does woman want?" usually arising after women have been prevented from answering it, or from formulating it for themselves): "She would always be ready, consenting or not. On that precise point you would never know anything. She is more mysterious than all the external facts known to you until then" (Mal, p. 19) and: "You would never know anything, not you or anyone, ever, about how she sees, how she thinks about the world and about you, your body, your mind [. . .] She doesn't know herself. She wouldn't know how to tell you . . . " (Mal, p. 19). Caught in the solipsism of his univocity, the man will extrapolate: "Because you know nothing about her, you would say she knows nothing of you. You would leave matters there" (Mal, p. 20). Finally, unable to see or know her, he will lose her without ever having had her: "So, still, you have been able to experience this love the only way possible for you, by losing it before it happened" (Mal, p. 57). Refusing to be had, the woman leaves and does not return.

Told in a different voice, "the" scenario becomes another scenario. The one who wakes the sleeping beauty is not a prince who will confine her to a space he rules, it is the female author, whose "kiss" endows the woman not only with movement but with speech. A fundamental shift occurs, structurally and diegetically. Discourse changes position, pluralizes. The silent-silenced woman who "doesn't know" (Mal, p. 19) is modified, first into one who knows, but still in silence, unaware of her own knowing: "she doesn't know she knows" (Mal, p. 20). But as soon as she is allowed to articulate her thoughts, she both knows what she thinks and how to say it. The first personal question the man addresses to her furnishes the opportunity. Upon learning she is not a prostitute, he asks why she accepted the contract. In a voice still drowsy, this newly awakened sleeping beauty makes a reply which contrasts her knowledge of his inner dynamics to his inability to know her, giving the lie to his above – mentioned assumption:

> She answers in a voice still sleepy, almost inaudible: 'Because as soon as you spoke to me I saw that you were afflicted with the malady of death. During the first days. I didn't know how to name that malady. And then I could.' [. . .] You ask her: 'In what way is the malady of death fatal?' She answers: 'In that the one stricken with it doesn't know he is a carrier of it, of death. And also in that he would have died without ever having lived, without any consciousness of dying to any life. (Mal, pp. 23–24)

The woman names the "illness" "death" only after experiencing its deadliness, after being verbally and physically silenced, and after ascertaining the man's blindness to difference, to that which he has silenced and repressed: "'You must be very beautiful.' She says: 'I am here, look, I am here before you.' You say: 'I see nothing.'" (Mal, pp. 21–22). The incapacity to embrace difference, to love, which is the malady of death works in two directions, "killing" (suppressing) the Other, and deadening the killer: "She asks: 'You have never loved a woman?' You say no, never. She asks: 'You have never desired a woman?' You say no, never. She asks: 'Not once, not for an instant?' You say no, never. She says: 'Never? Never?' You repeat: 'Never.' She smiles, she says: 'How curious – a dead man'" (Mal, pp. 34–35).
The woman's reaction does not signal a reversal of roles. When discourse changes hands, discourse changes, reflecting the radically different perspective of the different speaker. In *La Maladie de la mort*, the woman speaks first and foremost in order to reject the very basis

of dominant discourse: the equating of love with knowledge defined as possession of a reified object, something the man expresses at the text's opening. When he proposes the contract, she asks him what he wants (a question never put to her). "You [the man] say you want to try, to attempt it, to attempt to *know that*, get used to *that*, that body, those breasts [. . .] You say you want to try [. . .] She asks: 'Try what?' You say, 'To love [. . .] to sleep on her spread sex, there where you do not *know*' [. . .] She smiles, she asks: 'Do you also want me?' You say: 'Yes, I'm not acquainted with that yet. I want to penetrate *there* also. And as violently as I'm used to doing.'" (Mal, pp. 8–10 – emphasis added). The use of impersonal forms in response to the woman's "do you also want me" is especially telling.

The female protagonist rejects precisely this elimination of otherness and with it the dominant epistemelogical conceptualizing that spawns it: "She says: 'I would never want to know the way you know, with that certainty coming from death, that irremediable monotony, exactly equal to itself each day of your life, each night, with that deadly function of the lack of loving'" (Mal, p. 50). With her newly awakened voice, the woman deconstructs dominant discourse, to which she will no longer submit.[5] The traditional erotic scenario collapses because the woman ceases to play the mute part. When it does, the man stops appealing to her as a prostitute paid to give up her own voice and respond erotically and verbally on his terms. Switching to the binary opposite, he attempts to place her in a maternal role; he begs her to listen to the story of his childhood. But this reverse side of his discursive coin fares as badly as the first. The woman does not respond with the words he anticipates. She elects not to receive his story, which she rejects both in terms of history and textuality: "She smiles, she says she has heard and also read that [his]story [histoire] many times, everywhere, in many books" (Mal, pp. 51–52).

These words near the end of the text echo those at its beginning, and reiterate the connection between history and textuality. Because the history of his story (of patriarchal domination) entails the silencing of her story (of women's history and speech), because it has functioned by invading, conquering, suppressing all other stories in order to place itself "everywhere," and monopolize culture, the woman no longer accepts it. The long-silenced female, a "form suspect for centuries" (does woman become suspect as a function of the very silence imposed on her?), the woman suffering from an "immemorial fatigue," (Mal, p. 24) a "monumental fatigue" (Mal,

p. 51) no longer consents to act like the "wives of her ancestors" continually violated in their sleep (Mal, p. 10).

The repeated allusions to history and the man's despair situate the text at a juncture where patriarchal culture has reached an impasse, and where women's resistance has become more successful. Indeed, the female protagonist in *La Maladie de la mort* starts from a position of strength based on an implied community to which she can return. She accepts – temporarily – the contract because the man seems anomalous to her, an exception rather than the rule(r). She knows he can not "impose death" (Mal, p. 48) on her. Although she identifies him as a type whose "malady of death" she easily recognizes, the text suggests that that type is no longer monolithically dominant. That its edifice is on the brink of collapse. That the woman has alternatives, knows other forms of love. That she is not bound by permanent financial dependency, that when she leaves, she has somewhere to go. That she has voice.

The female protagonist has mimed the woman's role in dominant erotic acts just as Duras has imitated dominant erotic texts. With the same difference: voice. With the same result: imitation goes from parody to revolt, because of the empowerment attendant on access to discourse. Again, what permits this shift in *La Maladie de la mort* is the way the text shifts shifters. The traditionally extra-diegetic third person author/narrator has changed into an internally active first person narrator/author who says "I." Linguists have shown that shifters' "referents can only be determined with respect to actual interlocutors."[6] The ability to say "I" carries with it the ability to confer subjectivity on others through the "I–You" relation in dialogue and/or through the creation of texts. Superficially, the narrator seems to adhere to the traditional discursive-erotic schema, since she addresses only the male protagonist as "you" and refers to the woman only in the third person. But we have seen that this simulated complicity becomes subversive through Duras' use of shifters. Again, the man is not the speaker of the text. His "I" bestows not subjectivity but objectivity on the woman he speaks not with but at, and blocks both verbal and physical intercourse. He says "I" not to create texts but to repeat a centuries-old text which locks him in subjective solipsism: "You continue to speak, alone in the world like you want to be" (Mal, p. 49).

In contrast, the narrating "I" creates a text the subtext of which is the communication of subjectivity. This text gives subjectivity to the "her" by giving her voice. The shifters continue to shift, "she" says

"I"; the text's linguistically designated third person becomes a first person and asserts her subjectivity. From the moment the female protagonist gains access to discourse, the two women's voices relay each other. On their different textual levels, they each denounce their oppression directly to the paradigmatic figure of their oppressor, and in that very act announce its end. After showing "you" the effect his discourse has had historically, they inform him that the speaker of that discourse has now become its victim. The carrier of the "malady of death" is succumbing to his own disease, which he can no longer inflict on them.

This play of internal shifters also affects the determination of the referent of the external shifter presupposed by any text: the "you" of the reader. One can no longer assume its singularity or uniformity. *La Maladie de la mort* subverts traditional erotic literature's convention of presupposed male readership, complicitous with a (male) author and (male) hero. Indeed, to this text in which traditional erotic literature is deconstructed by the woman writer and by the heroine, reader response has correlated strongly with gender. Whatever the discrepancies in their individual interpretations, most women critics have analyzed it from the point of view of the woman and the female narrator, whereas most male critics have read it from the point of view of the man.[7] A strikingly clear demonstration of the fact that gender has pertinence to the reader-listener as doer as well as to the writer-speaker as doer. This implicit denunciation, and, in this text, this demise of the universality of the reading "you," a correlate of the text's narrative structure, is not the least of its accomplishments.

L'HOMME ASSIS DANS LE COULOIR

"Les héroïnes érotiques sont muettes."

Claudine Herrmann

In *L'Homme assis dans le couloir*, "Duras'" combination of a certain discursive neutrality with insistent subjective presence in her narrative position produces a disturbingly ambiguous stance. In the erotico-pornographic encounter that is this text, the woman goes beyond submission, beyond acquiescence; she desires, even requests her own violent reification. Readers have expressed dismay that a woman writer as politicized as Marguerite Duras would write a text apparently in perfect accord with dominant ideology, according to which, as Marini puts it: "[. . .] peace between the sexes demands that we [women] not only consent to our humiliation, to our suffering, to our submission – of which our being put to death is at once the emblem and the guarantee – but even more, to their eroticization."[8] The question of congruence, of whether or not *L'Homme assis dans le couloir* conforms completely to the tradition of dominant erotic literature, is crucial.

As the text opens, the man, seated in a corridor, looks at the woman lying prostrate on a stony path in the hot sun, naked except for a dress ripped open (by him?) in the front.[9] Her head has fallen limply onto her arm, and her eyes remain closed most of the time. This "definitive image" (H-as, p. 10), inert, headless, "sleeping" (H-as, p. 10), then moves. As the man's eyes bore into her (H-as, p. 11), she spreads her legs, "mutilating herself of her length" (H-as, p. 12). The sun becomes so hot that she screams, calls out to the man, who comes and stands over her. With her eyes still closed, she directs her open legs towards him so that he sees her vaginal secretions (H-as, p. 15).

Once she is exposed, her body fully "caught in his shadow" (H-as, p. 25), he urinates on her, the stream "crashing down" first on her lips, her teeth which she offers up, eyes and hair, down her body, until with an extra spurt it mixes with the sperm of his orgasm as it crashes into the "heat" of her sex. (H-as, p. 16). The woman's eyes open slightly, but remain unseeing (H-as, p. 16). Next, the man kicks her down the path, where she lies with her face against the ground (H-as, p. 17). He rolls her back and forth on the stones, puts his foot on her chest, says he loves her, and begins to press down. The woman's half-opened eyes close again as the pressure increases, crushing her (H-as, p. 18). He stops only when her repeated screams warn that he is about to kill her. The man returns to the corridor and collapses back into his armchair, while the woman, still screaming, rolls over. Thrashing about, she cries and weeps, calling for him in what might or might not be an orgasmic frenzy. So ends the first scene.

Now the woman approaches the man, and together they stare at his penis. Tenderly she begins to perform fellatio, guiding him over and over to orgasm (H-as, p. 27). She stops the moment his pleasure approaches pain. She then kisses him again "there where the fetid odor reigns" (H-as, p. 30), until he pushes her away, throws her down, lies on top of her, and penetrates her, while she weeps (H-as, p. 31). End of scene two.

The final scene begins after they have each had an orgasm (H-as, p. 31). They lie apart, the woman still weeping. Pulling her to him with his leg, the man says he would like to stop loving her, and that he will kill her one day" (H-as, pp. 31–32). As if cued, she announces her desire to be hit "hard, like just before in the heart," and that "she would like to die" (H-as, p. 33). He beats her while she puts her face "more at his hand's disposal," "makes it more material" (H-as, p. 34). Under the blows raining on her whole body, her face, "emptied of all expression," "moves around on the neck at [his] will like a dead thing" (H-as, pp. 34–35). This too produces screams and fear, culminating in a silence that submerges them both (H-as, p. 35). The scene and the text end with the woman covered, again, by the man. He lies atop her and weeps. Nothing can be seen of her except her "immobility" (H-as, p. 36). We do not know whether she is dead or alive.

Thus the bare essentials of this text offer standard pornographic fare, with the woman an abject, masochistic object and the man a sadistic subject in a sexuality which associates the erotic and violence so closely that they merge. But in literature, there are no bare essentials, plot being clothed in the discourse presenting it. In this text there are important rents in the fabric, caused by the structural presence of the internal narrating "I" and by certain of her remarks. These gaps create a distance which exposes porno-erotic language and activity as such. But it works more ambiguously than in *La Maladie de la mort*. *L'Homme assis dans le couloir* does not thematize and critique dominant erotic discourse explicitly. Moreover, the characters themselves hardly speak at all. It is the narrator who does. Whether or not she does descriptively or prescriptively constitutes the problem.

To begin with, the diegesis appears dressed in dominant symbolic clothing. The very geography splits into traditional masculine-feminine metaphorical distribution. Near the woman, a garden "falls in a brutal declivity" (H-as, p. 14) towards a plain dominated by the crest of a hill (H-as, p. 8). The suggested (masculine) hardness and violence contrast with their (feminine) opposite: the "nudity of the plain (H-as, p. 22) lying flat and exposed like the woman, the soft, "undulating" countryside "without trees" (H-as, pp. 7, 10, etc.), and especially the nearby but invisible sea. On each side of the masculine-feminine divide, homologous binarisms accumulate: hard vs. soft, light vs. dark, distinct vs. indistinct form. Like the man's eyes, the sun (a masculine noun in French and a privileged metaphor of male specularity) bores into the woman's dark private parts with nearly unendurable "force" (H-as, p. 13). Definite, visible, "male" forms stand in opposition to the indefinite, invisible, "female" sea, an "indecisive space" (H-as, p. 7), an "indefinite immensity" (H-as, pp. 11, 33) beyond the horizon. The ever present haze (H-as, pp. 18, 22) renders it even more indistinct, and the "purple fog" (H-as, pp. 33, 35) ("a mauve immensity" – H-as, p. 22) further figures femininity (the female sex organ) as a shapeless, huge spread.

These binarisms commonly connote the masculine as positive and the feminine as negative, in the sense of deficiency. Rather than different subjects, we have male and minus-male, the female existing primarily as lack (of maleness, of the phallus). The formless, sightless woman opens her eyes only to see the phallus. Her sex is seen only as its "lack," symbolized as a dark, mushy, gaping hole/wound oozing disgustingly, in an "obscene, bestial pose" that makes her "ugly" (H-as, p. 12). A "vomiting, visceral mouth," her "quartered sex" (H-as, p. 15) exudes slimy liquids. The man's foot sinks into the mud ("s'y embourbe") (H-as, p. 18) of the swampy flesh (H-as, p. 19) of her "slovenly" (H-as, p. 18) "undone" body (H-as, p. 22). The woman is the abject. Constructed this way, Woman elicits violent reactions of rejection and suppression from *the* symbol of articulated, articulating form: the phallus and its bearer.

In *L'Homme assis dans le couloir*, the woman not only excites but invites these reactions. Internalizing her role so thoroughly that she reaches the very limits of alienation, she enacts it physically and verbally. Striking the pose which "mutilates" her of legs and head, she presents herself as lack (of phallus-logos-sex-head). She lies there asking for it in both senses, and the double entendre illustrates the meshing of the erotic with the violent. Woman as lack also functions as woman as mirror. She conforms to representations according to which woman longs to fill her "void" with "it," jealously covets "it," "hungers" for "it." Transposing the vagina = mouth metaphor, she takes "it" into her real mouth (which has real teeth). Correlatively, Woman mirrors male subjectivity, reflecting male desire exclusively. She wants what he wants: his pleasure. And she gives it to him, repeatedly.

Although her teeth are real, they remain neutralized, like Woman, through the preemptive coup of a founding stricture against female violence, a law as powerful as the "originating" (law of the) phallus itself. Actually, it is the law of the phallus, which prohibits anything not itself. The passage bears quoting: "Her mouth would have been filled by it [the penis]. Its sweetness [douceur] is such that tears come to her eyes. [. . .] Nothing equals in power that sweetness if not the categorical interdiction against harming it. Interdicted. [interdite]" (H-as, pp. 26–27). Etymologically, the French "interdire" (to interdict) comes from "dire – entre": those in possession of discursive power (of the power to legislate) meet "to say among themselves; to invoke a law against" something, thus to prohibit.[10] The feminine adjectival form "interdite" applies to the woman. Along with any attack against the "Phallus," woman *qua* woman is interdicted. In common parlance, someone who is "interdit(e)" is rendered speechless, "can not answer."[11] Mouth and mind phallically invested (literally and figuratively, for the penis fills both: "she devours it in her mind, nourishes herself with it, gorges herself on it in her mind" – H-as, p. 27), (the) Woman has no space left for her own speech. The adjectival form "interdite" is a past participle. Women have always already been silenced by the founding patriarchal cultural interdiction.The only speech permitted is one complicitous with the dominant symbolic order. In *L'Homme assis dans le couloir,* just as with her body and gestures the woman mirrors masculinist sexuality-subjectivity, with her words she echoes it. Compared to his, her very few utterances confirm her lack of, and his possession of, a subjectivity culturally conferred by the phallus alone. Her first words name him, call for "it" as she lies spread-eagled in the sun (H-as, p. 14). After he says "I love you" (H-as, p. 18) he crushes her chest. But after she pronounces the same words, she caresses him (H-as, p. 23). Face buried in his genital area, she talks while kissing his penis. When he expresses his intention to kill her, she responds, as though programmed, with her request to be beaten. Thus words and acts are articulated entirely within univocal, masculinist discursive-sexual schemas.

The negation of the woman's subjectivity structures whatever pleasure occurs for her. The symbolic and nearly real murder during the chest-crushing episode precipitates her first orgasm – if indeed one reads the scene's end as orgasmic rather than as a description of near death throes. (The possibility of a double reading again underscores the association of the erotic with female death.) Just prior her second orgasm, she effects her own erasure, burying her face "in the darkness of the man's body" (H-as, p. 30), after which he penetrates her, and lies motionless on her, effacing her body with his. This presumably triggers the orgasm not staged, but evoked after a blank space. What might be taken for a reversal of male = active female = passive roles when the woman begins to initiate things, actually confirms traditional distribution. The woman remains in her prescribed position as the opposite of male subjectivity, an abysmal, repugnant lack of self, active only on his behalf, enacting her negation with him.

The disruptive aspect of *L'Homme assis dans le couloir* intervenes with the one who does speak. Like in *La Maladie de la mort*, a narrating "third person" speaks in the first person. Again an explicitly present "I" stages "the" erotic scene, setting it immediately in the theatrical imaginary through use of the past conditional tense, which regularly precedes the present in the "acting out." Statements of "ignorance" obviate the omniscient stance, limiting "Duras'" authorial power: "I see beauty floating, undecided, around the edges of the [woman's] face, but I am unable to make it merge with it, to make it become peculiar to it" (H-as, pp. 12–13); expressing uncertainty: "Through her eyelids she probably perceives the darkening of the light" (H-as, pp. 14–15); restricting vision and knowledge of the "I," an internal, situated observer: "That is what I see of her" (H-as, p. 9); "I see nothing of her but her immobility. I am ignorant [je l'ignore], I know nothing, I do not know whether she is sleeping" (H-as, p. 36). Invoking herself on nearly every page, the speaker subverts the standard voyeuristic pact by constantly calling attention to the fact that in "the" erotic scene, someone, usually behind the scenes, is pulling the strings. Here the one doing the pulling and showing that pulling, the "someone [outside the couple] who is looking, who is seeing, [. . .] who is speaking,"[12] staging everything, is a woman, "Duras." She stresses this theatricality so insistently that the reader can hardly ignore the directorial, authorial function of narration. As Duras so often reminds her readers: "My voice, you must hear it when you read."[13] Marini, who concentrates on tone more than on structure, alludes to the subversive possibilities of such tampering with traditional suspension of disbelief: "If Marguerite Duras succeeds in shaking some of the foundations of the pornographic genre, it is at once by stressing its theatrical character in order to destroy its pretension of faithful mimesis of an indisputable reality, through repeated commentaries [en déroulant les commentaires] and, finally, by playing on the equivocalness of the relation between story and discourse [récit et discours]."[14]

In *L'Homme assis dans le couloir*, then, breaches in dominant eroticism result from the tension between the lack of an unambiguous intratextual critique, narrative or thematic, of a scene that adheres strictly to the dominant script on the one hand, and structural interferences on the other. On the latter level, shifts in narrative position, point of view, and address further destabilize things, and affect the reader's position as well. Throughout the text, "I" alternates with the traditional third person or with the pronoun "on," on whose referential flexibility Duras plays. The presence of these pronouns disturbs the assumptions subtending their absence in standard erotic literature: objectivity, universality, or, otherwise stated, the prescriptive element in the descriptive.

The narrative interpositions consist mostly of observations using the verb "to see," a deconstructive device because it emphasizes the spectator's presence and raises the question of the spectator's position and gender. For example, before any introjection of the first person, "on" appears in the first pages, speaking from the perspective of a non gender-specific, watching "we." Inclusive of reader and speaker, alternating with the third person, this "on" seems to perpetuate standard voyeuristic complicity, with the woman as object of vision on the same plane as other *things*: the landscape, her clothes, etc.

However, on the third page, the first introjection of "I" clouds the composition of the assumed, masculinist (if not male) communality, because of "I"'s gender and insistent self-inscription as someone seeing: "that is what I see of her" (H-as, p. 9). The source of vision narrows. Suddenly the narrator speaks in the singular, from her perspective alone, and to, not with, the reader, who becomes an implied "you." In another switch, "I" aligns with the woman's unseeing knowledge: "She knows that he is looking at her [. . .] She knows it with her eyes closed as I know it, I who am looking" (H-as, p. 9). The form "I see" or an equivalent reappears more frequently in the text than any other narrative intervention, but not fixed to a single point of view. While remaining within a non-omniscient yet not narrowly subjective stance, "I"'s directionality varies so greatly and at times so rapidly that it inevitably elicits questions of with whom, for whom, and to whom the narrating author is speaking and/or seeing. Although (because?) these questions can not always be easily answered, their very existence is subversive of dominant erotic literature, which presupposes unproblematic positioning.

The text contains two particularly significant narrative shifts. After a two page interval written in the third person, during which the speaker changes to a more detached stance, she returns to that

"I": "I speak to her and I tell her what the man is doing. I also tell her what is happening to her. *That she see, this is what I desire*" (H-as, pp. 16–17 – emphasis added). Duras places this extraordinary intervention between two episodes, told in the third person, of degradation and violence inflicted on the non-resisting woman: the man urinating on her and the man kicking her and crushing her heart.

With respect to the first, these remarks invite a doubling back typical of Duras' work. What we read gets retrospectively recast from an additional angle when "I" announces she is recounting the proceedings to the woman involved as well as to the reader. This delayed, sudden disclosure deconstructs the conventional notion of privacy in literature, specifically in erotic literature, where it is most strongly assumed and where it has particular significance. The expansion also functions prospectively, affecting the next scene and everything that follows, producing at least a double reading. Whatever the other narrative positionings, we can consider the entire text framed within this female structuring: "Duras" speaking simultaneously to the female protagonist and to the reader. This subsumes even passages where "on" speaks in collusion with third person forms with or from the dominant perspective. Once again Duras sabotages the implicit universalist closure of "on," the objectivity of the third person, and the customary extrapolation from the latter to the former.

If Duras never imparts voice to the female protagonist, it is clearly stated that she does want to give vision to this woman who, blinded by alienation, can not see on her own. The text makes numerous allusions to her closed eyes or absent glance. The shift produced by the switch to the first person occurs in optical as well as vocal terms, altering the visual field and thematizing it. "I" speaks to "her" so that she will "see" "what is happening to her," so that, looking into the discursive mirror held up to her by the the narrator, the woman will specularize herself, see the spectacle of her blind, silent submission, see "the" erotic scene as spectacle, as a spectacle of violence perpetrated on women, and her role in it.

Yet the expected subversive force of distancing does not seem operative for this female protagonist, who continues cooperating mutely and unseeingly. Moreover, the speaker's non-committal tone, the fact that Duras does not wake this sleeping beauty and that she uses the word "love" with respect to the man in a manner one can not with certainty label ironic,[15] lead one to question the author's intent. Does Duras wish the woman to see the scene as inevitable, natural, and continue (as she does) eroticizing her masochism and the man's sadism? Or is she portraying alienation at its extreme point so as ultimately to condemn it?

The subversive function does get activated on the level of the other "you," the reader. The reader is placed at a remove from which s/he witnesses "Duras'" description of the spectacle to the female actor. The thematization of this "showing" undermines identification between women readers and the masochistic female protagonist. Structurally separated from her, the female reader no longer occupies the traditional position. *Her* eyes having been opened by Duras' structural alteration; *she* questions intent, specularity, and the spectacle of dominant erotics and erotico-pornographic literature.

In this text, the first person gives voice to a female glance ("Duras'"). Women are encouraged to look. Thus a female voice manipulating the visual exposes what the reification of women as the object of male vision entails, and valorizes voice as the means to subvert it. It shows that what the paradigmatic erotic scene leads to is women's death, simulated or real. With her final sentences, "Duras" again invokes vision, this time to inform us that she can no longer see the woman, who is lying underneath the man, invisible, mute, unseeing, perhaps dead (H-as, p. 36). Just previously – and this is the second major narrative upheaval – we learn, also in terms of vision, that this putting to "death" has had more witnesses. In addition to the reader, the writer/speaker and the female protagonist, "other eyes," specifically identified as female, have been watching all along: "I see that other people are looking, other women, that other women now dead have looked in the same way at summer monsoons forming and unforming before rivers bordered by rice paddies, opposite vast and deep river mouths" (H-as, pp. 35–36).

This new dimension further stresses the female gender of the text's interlocutors at every level: the author/speaker, these women watching with her, the internal narratee and possibly the external narratee: the reader. The insistent feminine framing makes it particularly noteworthy that the text at no point addresses the male protagonist or anyone else designated as male. To be sure, within the erotic scene re-presented by *L'Homme assis dans le couloir*, only the man has subjectivity in vision, action and, implicitly, in the articulation of the symbolic structures organizing that scenario.

However, the other narrative levels specularize the man (as well as the woman and the entire scene), turning the male subject into the object of the vision of the internal, "now dead" female spectators, of the narrator and of the reader. The pattern of discursive agency shifts to female voices and glances.

With its allusion to the past, the introduction of the dead, observing women constitutes the only historically contextualizing element in a text otherwise so remarkably devoid of any situating notation that it has been treated as pure allegory.[16] But one must distinguish between, on the one hand, what is framed – "the" erotic scene, indeed constructed by dominant discourse as natural, timeless, universal and, on the other hand, the framing, which I read as intrinsically deconstructive of that notion. Still, interpretative ambiguity persists concerning Duras' intent, once again due to her vagueness of tone and the concision of her interventions. It is difficult to determine whether the reference to the dead women means to present history as mere repetition of an immutable structure (the dead women looking "in the same way") or as process changeable through praxis, which here undermines the structure it exposes. Uncertainty also affects the "who" of the implied comparison. Do the dead women look "in the same way" as the female protagonist, or as the author? What of the reader's glance? If but one of the three looks differently, then the text activates a notion of history which encourages contestation and transformation.

Considered from the distance afforded by these narrative and structural dislocations, the scene's congruence to the dominant model is so absolute that one may be tempted to read it as parody, for example when the man declares love only to prove it by crushing the woman's chest, and especially in the fellatio scene. There obsession with the penis reaches a degree of fetishization so extreme that whatever intentional equivocalness Duras may have had in the writing, I for one find it difficult to read it without irony.

The "crude, brutal form" (H-as, p. 23) of the Phallus-God inspires awe, caution, obedience. Almost a being with its own will, it is "planted in the man, around which he struggles" (H-as, p. 23). Both man and woman look at it reverently, not daring to touch it: "'on' hesitates to put 'on's' hand on it" (H-as, p. 25). (Note that this is the only "on" inclusive of the woman, the law of the Phallus-Godhead inspiring "universal" veneration.) Seat of power and of the word, it confers them on the phallically endowed man. And the woman

.– always wanting in this regard – obeys its interdiction against female power, speech and, importantly, against anger. While she performs fellatio: "Whereas the crime is in her mouth, she can only permit herself to lead it, to guide it to pleasure, teeth ready" (H-as, p. 27). Syntactic ambiguity introduces additional possible parodic overtones. Is the "crime" the woman's desire to harm "it", or is the "crime" the interdicting male speech and violence of "it" itself?

In another twist, Duras refers to the penis, *the* emblem of phallic power, solely with a feminine pronoun: "elle" – "she." Not only does no masculine word (le pénis) ever name the organ which props up the concept of masculinity, the antecedent of the feminine pronoun never appears either. Might one infer an ironic reference to Old Testament interdictions against naming the (patriarchal, phallic) God? Is there not additional irony in the fact that the term suggested by the feminine pronoun further evokes that wrathful, chastising God? The word for this additional, intradiegetic quasi-"third person" is "verge." Its polysemy includes both penis and a rod used for beatings. (According to the Littré dictionary, the latter meaning has been functional since the French translation of the old and new testaments.) Playing on the verb "to beat," Duras evokes the absent word's polysemy. Of a form "gross and brutal like his heart" (H-as, p. 23) 'it' ['elle'] beats, in jolts, to the rhythm of the heart" (H-as, p. 25). Then: "it's in the woman's hair now that it ['elle'] beats [. . .]" (H-as, p. 28). This prefigures the ultimate beating scene, in which the function transfers to the man's extended hand: "the hand beats, strikes" (H-as, p. 34). The woman frantically craves the instrument of all this beating and the beatings themselves.

For Yvonne Guers-Villate, the feminine pronoun re-presenting the penis subverts the correlation between active-passive and male-female sexual roles, and for Mary Lydon, it deconstructs sexual identity. Evoking the "other woman on the scene," ("Duras"), Lydon sees in the penis as "elle," "the pre-Oedipal desire of the daughter for the mother, whose desire is the mother's desire, in Lacan's formula."[17] But the text stresses the interdicton attached to the penis ("elle" or not), to both revolt against phallic law and to non-alienated female desire (for the mother or not). Given that the roles remain fixed, I read the text as less a subversion of sexual identity than as a denunciation of its imposition and function in sexual oppression. In contrast to the repulsive vagina, the over-valorized penis inspires desire, hunger, even in its foulest manifestations. Head buried between the man's legs, the "famished" woman "breathes lengthily the fetid odor" (H-as, p. 29): "there where the fetid odor reigns, she kisses, she licks" (H-as, p. 32). While "elle" designates the penis, the word "femininity" appears with respect to the man's anus, which the woman also licks: "Her tongue descends towards that other femininity" (H-as, p. 28) – his entire sexual apparatus being "what he does not know of himself" (H-as, p. 29). It is feminized as a function of the impossibility of knowledge in the Biblical sense: he can not physically reach it himself, and therefore it can only be "known" by an other. But, protected by Phallic Law, it remains incompletely feminized. If anything, the man ends up possessor of both sexes, the woman dispossessed of both, and pleasuring both of his.

Whether or not one reads *L'Homme assis dans le couloir* as a *Beauty and the Beast* parody, Beauty does not civilize the Beast, but instead succumbs to his bestiality. Sleeping Beauty does remain asleep. No transformation into a prince regenerates the brute. Duras' response to a question put to her in 1977 might help us in our interpretative quandary as to her intentionality in this text:

> "Q: 'How do you experience the woman question?'
> Duras: 'As the fundamental question Starting from that everything else is possible. Without that, nothing will be. [. . .] If we do not resolve – I'm speaking about you, men, and about us – the complete alienation [of women] in submission we will never get any farther than we are now.'[18]

In *L'Homme assis dans le couloir*, "the complete alienation and submission" of women in the dominant erotic plot is taken to the limit. Because it seems to hover between exposing and espousing, the text stops short of unambiguously "resolving" women's victimization and the issue of female complicity. Still, at the very least, it problematizes dominant eroticism, and its discursive strategies disrupt the structure of the standard erotic genre. Consequently, even this disquieting work can be received as contestation.

Some critics contend that Duras offers only negative images of women, that her female protagonists are passive, objects of the male gaze (Trista Selous), sick with an "anerotic" melancholy (Kristeva), have the role of "erotic object and masochistic victim but with the status of a subject" (Frappier-Mazur[19]), are desirous of an eroticized death (Kristeva, Barbara Freeman) and even, if unconsciously, of an eroticized nuclear destruction (Freeman).[20] Considered in this light, *L'Homme assis dans le couloir* could be taken as the extreme concretization and expansion of a thematic continuum in Duras' oeuvre. Several of her texts contain sado-masochistic episodes in which women submit to and/or desire male sexual violence. In *Moderato Cantabile*, interpreting the man's murder of the woman as a supreme act of love, Anne and Chauvin undertake to imitate it verbally. Maria tries to save the life of a man who killed his wife out of jealous passion in *Dix heures et demie du soir en été*. When Jacques Hold symbolically murders Tatiana during sex in *Le Ravissement de Lol V. Stein*, "possessing" her "mercilessly," she "offered no resistance, said nothing, refused nothing, thrilled by such possession" (Rav, p. 142). In *Le Vice-consul*, Charles Rossett phantasizes beating Anne-Marie Stretter in the face while she endures it willingly. In a number of texts sexual aggression against women is not enacted, yet surfaces in isolated remarks. In *Hiroshima mon amour*: the woman says, "You're killing me. You're doing me good" (Hir, p. 27). In *La Maladie de la mort*, that the man has never desired the death of a lover proves his inability to "love," prompting the woman to pronounce him "dead" himself. (Mal, p. 45). With the telephone lovers of *Le Navire night* "Their orgasm reaches [metaphoric] murder" (Nav, p. 83). Voice Two of *India Song* passes a test of love with a positive response to Voice two's query: "If I asked you to kill me would you accept?'" (Ind, p. 12). (Here the female-male roles divide a lesbian couple into "feminine" and "masculine."). Describing Hélène Lagonelle as a ripe victim unaware of her own sexuality, "Duras" adopts the masculine position in *L'Amant*: "Hélène Lagonelle makes one want to kill her, she elicits the marvellous dream of putting her to death with one's [or her][21] own hands" (Am, p. 91).

Staged or suggested, these erotic scenarios hark back to the symbolic legacy of the Judeo-Christian tradition, with its "sacrifice" (elimination) of women on the altar of monotheism. Elements of Durassian erotics seem to internalize the dominant culture's capitalist and Christian underpinnings, with its reification of women, ritual punishment for sex as sin (especially female sexuality) and its semiology of passion. The erotic often becomes a sacred rite complete with sacrificial victim: the woman. A slow, ceremonious repetitiveness combined with other stylistic devices (discussed more thoroughly in Chapter 5) lends a quasi-religious aura to these scenes. One thinks of the near litany quality of the passage just cited from *Hiroshima, mon amour*, of the "death rite" (M-C, p. 113) accompanied by ceremonial wine drinking in which Anne and Chauvin indulge, in

Moderato Cantabile, (something reminiscent of the ritualized drinking in *Dix heures et demie du soir en été*), or of the Hôtel des Bois scenes in *Le Ravissement de Lol V. Stein,* with their "sacrificial" putting to death of Tatiana.

Perhaps not coincidentally, *L'Homme assis dans le couloir* is the text in which religious overtones appear the most blatantly, but to such a degree that on this level as well one might suspect Duras of parodying dominant erotic literature, which is so anchored in transgression and/as sacrilege. I have discussed the episode of the kneeling woman adoring God the Phallus, obeying His divine decrees, chastised by Him. Syntagmatic and lexical manipulation intensifies the imbrication of the Christian text and the Western erotic text, the conflation of love, Passion, sacrifice of a self, death. The first page presents the woman prone "on a path of stones" (H-as, p. 7). The French syntagma "chemin de pierres" evokes the "chemin de la croix" – the way of the cross ("chemin" translates as way or path). The ensuing text consists of the woman's "stations of the cross." Moreover, "Duras" announces this with a biblical turn of phrase, telling the woman "what is happening to her [ce qu'il advient d'elle]" (H-as, p. 16). "Ce qu'il advient de" is a common Biblical discursive form in French. The awed woman, blinded by "faith," or Law, accepts the sacrifice of her self, desires to die of/for "love", is flagellated, "crucified."

Crimes of passion have inspired several of Duras' texts. This adds another dimension to her complex, ultimately contradictory conception of passion. On the one hand, in accord with a tradition dating at least from *Tristan et Iseult* and continuing through the surrealists' "amour fou" (mad love), it is an external force which happens *to* one, an irresistible cataclysm beyond will or responsibility, and for the consequences of which one can not be blamed. Passion removes one from history, into an a-political, a-moral realm, replacing God but not the sacred, and which becomes associated with the forces of nature. This contrasts sharply with Duras' personal history of political activism and the political consciousness informing all her texts on other levels. But she has maintained that the two domains do not intersect or conflict, that they coexist:

> More reasons why I have written, why I write for newspapers [. . .] partake of the same irresistible impulse that brought me to the French resistance or the Algerian, anti-government, anti-militarist, anti-electoral ones, etc., and also brought me, like

you, like everyone, to denounce the intolerableness of injustice of whatever kind, suffered by a whole people or a single individual, and which has also directed me towards love when it becomes mad, when it abandons prudence and loses itself where it can, towards crime, dishonor, indignity, and where judicial imbecility and society permit themselves to judge – that – nature, like they would judge storms, fire.[22]

Duras' short story "Le Boa" grants the immunity of "nature" to passionate criminality and sexuality. "Fatal" forces, they must not be defiled by the "commercial," a factor the ignorance of which led to mistaken youthful ideas about bordellos as "temples" where "sacred" anonymous nudity would free animal passions with women in charge.[23] Outside the purview of morality, passion is anti-social: "In any given society, love is always a scandal."[24] To judge it is unjust. But passion itself is a crime, the sin of preferring one individual to humanity as a whole: "passion: one loves a definite person and it's like a curse. We have no right to love one person as much as the world, the whole [le tout]. Passion is a criminal displacement of feeling."[25] This returns to the religious. Whereas in the Christian text Christ dies for love of all people, in Duras' texts, true to tradition, death punishes (the woman) for her love of an individual. If one hasn't experienced passion, if one hasn't desired death, one hasn't lived. (The woman tells the man in *La Maladie de la mort*: "The desire to be on the brink of killing a lover, of keeping him[26] for yourself, for you alone, to take him, to steal him against every law, against all moral exigency, you don't know that, you have never known that?' You say: 'Never.' She looks at you, she repeats: 'How curious: a dead man'" – Mal, p. 45). Yet therein lies the "crime." Passion betrays humanity in its very a-historicity and in its narcissism, of which sado-masochism partakes, and which is also a function of the desire for possession. The inherent contradiction in the will to possess leads to theft, reification, murder of the other in a desire for permanent private property, and to the arresting of history. Again, it is not indifferent that historically the woman's "desire" has been one of being possessed, being put to death – her crime being alienated masochism – and that the man's has been to possess and to kill (punish, repress, suppress) the woman. In the absence of God, a Durassian given, traditional religious structures become questionable. Historicization demystifies religious interdiction, the sin of sex, the metaphysicized transgression of preference. Contextualized within the master(ing) discourses of theology and capitalism, sin sinks into a criminality articulated by historical discursive patterns analyzable through critically different discursive strategies.

Duras confronts those dominant, traditional cultural formations in all her work, including *L'Homme assis dans le couloir*, which, one must not forget, is the only text whose plot conforms entirely to the traditional sexual scenario. Despite disclaimers about adjudicability, she knows that all writing moralizes, including the "objective" reporting of journalism: "Every journalist is a moralist. It is absolutely inevitable. A journalist is someone who looks at the world, its functioning, who watches very closely every day, who holds it up to view, who holds up the world, an event, to review [qui le donne à voir, qui le donne à revoir]".[27] This applies to Duras' other practise/praxis: storytelling, something as historical as journalism, as or more re-visioning, and unquestionably involved with the moral.

We have seen the importance of the speaking viewer in Duras' work. Extratextual comments implying equivalence between passion and nature notwithstanding, Duras knows that, like the rites of religion, the rites of passion are cultural. When she writes them, the play of structure, voice, and style contextualizes and historicizes the mechanisms of dominant erotic ritual, exposing the misogyny inherent in its symbolic representations, in its distribution of roles and punishment.

To restrict interpretation to the diegetic level for an oeuvre where structural and narrative articulations have such explicit significance may result in conclusions quite at odds with what I consider the major thrust of Duras' work. Minimizing, even denying Duras' exploration of form, Kristeva, for example, collapses the different levels of author, narrator, character and Duras' style itself. Psychoanalyzing them together, she diagnoses a "malady of grief," a sickly melancholia, an a-political internalization of history which connects to an archaic love-hate and loss of the mother, a love of death which precludes feminine "jouissance" and steeps women in a blankness of signification – an illness not only incurable but "contagious,"[28] so that "Duras' books should not be put into the hands of oversensitive readers."[29] "If there be a formal search [recherche], it is subordinate to confrontation with the silence of horror in oneself and in the world."[30] Duras "texts domesticate the malady of death, they fuse with it, are on the same level with it, without either distance or perspective."[31] Kristeva suggests that Duras can not extricate herself from the mad melancholy that is the consequence of the forces of mass destruction unleashed in World War II. In a curiously traditionalist view of literature, she bemoans the lack of catharsis in Duras, whom she contrasts with "Mallarmé and Joyce [who] were believers and aesthetes":[32] "Lacking recovery or God, having neither value nor beauty [sic] other than illness itself seized at the place of its essential rupture, never has art had so little cathartic appeal."[33] Duras "follows ill being step by step, almost in clinical fashion, without ever getting the better of it."[34] With Duras, "there is no purification in store for us at the conclusion of these novels written on the brink of illness, no promise of a beyond, not even the enchanting beauty of style or irony that might provide a bonus of pleasure in addition to the revealed [sic] evil."[35] Thus afflicted with a "melancholia" which is the "secret mainstring" of her "rhetoric",[36] Duras is refused any mediating artistic agency. For her female characters, the erotic is contaminated by death, which they "love" and contain within themselves. Duras' is "the literature or our illness," and leads to "a blankness of meaning."[37]

Kristeva's inattentiveness to narration elides the often explicitly denunciatory nature of Duras' work and the subversive effects of the very formal concerns she denies the author. Other critics are more sensitive to contestatory, positive, feminist aspects. Jean Pierrot sees women's enactment of the absolute right to sexual freedom as a recurrent theme in Duras, for whom love "establishes true communication."[38] Among readers who engage psychoanalytical parameters, Lydon and Guers-Villate find feminist possibilities on the level of the signifier in the erotic texts.[39] Marini uncovers in Duras' language and thematics generally a strong challenge to dominant psychoanalytical and social structures, and Willis finds potential in Duras' non-essentializing, non-static "writing on the body," her "perpetual 'calling' of language to the body, of the body to language," in which she locates "the 'feminine' voice of Duras' texts."[40] These perspectives might coordinate with what I consider the deepest level of textual genesis, which raises questions of textual production with relation to voice and access to discourse, preoccupations omnipresent in the oeuvre and contextualized with relation to history, class, race and gender.

In Duras' work diegetic concessions to the dominant dictum that passion can only lead to death (of the woman) are quite limited. The few texts that conform to it portray it at the very least as an impasse for both partners. Moreover, other textual levels in Duras, and others of her works denounce and undermine that dynamic, as I show throughout this study. Several go much farther, offsetting isolated expressions of it by proposing alternative structures of non-dominating love, erotics and discourse as articulated by non-alienated female figures. Selous ignores those of Duras' female characters and narrators who are not simply objects of someone else's gaze and desire, but rather subjects of their own gaze, and more importantly, of their own discourse and desires.[41] Among such heroines we recall Aurélia Steiner, Anna in *Le Marin de Gibraltar*, Madeleine in *Savannah Bay*, Alissa in *Détruire, dit-elle*, Agatha, the narrator and the protagonist in *L'Amant*, and the woman in *Hiroshima mon amour*.[42] The verbal nod to dominant erotics in the latter two texts is contravened by depictions of love scenes devoid of violence and domination. Leah Hewitt's sensitive study of *L'Amant* grasps Duras' message of female empowerment outside relations of sexual domination: the text frees the woman from the status of object of a reifying masculine gaze while avoiding the trap of simple role reversal. Hewitt demonstrates how, with the introduction of "active feminine desire," the denigration entailed in classically defined prostitution gets replaced by female agency, by the undoing of fixed roles and by a circulation of familial and sexual identities which include positive feminine identifications.[43] In accord with this, I read, for example, in the wish to "give" Hélène Lagonelle to the lover a desire to give the lover and pleasure to Lagonelle (plus knowledge and agency: Lagonelle is temporarily unaware of the "fabulous power" of her breasts – Am, p. 91) as well as the protagonist's desire for her, and identification with her.[44]

As noted earlier, Duras' work correlates the possibility of women articulating love scenarios in which both sexes participate as subjects, to discursive, sexual and economic freedom. Her liberated heroines are financially independent, occasionally through inherited wealth (Anna), but mostly through work involving self expression. They are actresses (Madeleine, the woman in *Hiroshima mon amour*), revolutionaries (Alissa), writers (Aurélia, the woman in *L'Amant*, the woman in *L'Homme atlantique*). They embody a different equation, which associates love, language and living with literature and the political. This informs Duras' work on the profoundest levels: from inscribed possibility to denunciation, implicit or explicit, of its repression and, always, in the pervasive presence of "Duras'" voice. Duras has formulated these interrelations: "Question: 'You have said: "When I write I do not die."[45] Would you add: When I write I love?' Duras: 'Yes. There is an equivalence there. Yes, one can close the syllogism: when I love I do not die.'"[46] Beyond Duras' contradictions and struggle with her own and women's alienation, then, her texts give voice to a call for different sexual structures articulated with different social structures.

Part II
Towards a Poetics of Duras' Prose

4

Elements of a Style

"Il faut nous défaire de l'illusion d'avoir possédé en disant."

Maurice Merleau-Ponty

" [. . .] la fiction, qui est une action, a une efficacité. Le désir qui la produit, rendra possible ce qu'il désire."

Hélène Cixous

INTRODUCTION

That Marguerite Duras has produced "one of the most recognizable styles of contemporary literature"[1] has often been noted. Something more rarely scrutinized is the "how" of her achievement. I caution that the following presentation of some of Duras' discursive strategies does not constitute an exhaustive inventory. Rather, it offers examples of recurrent structures, techniques, and metalinguistic themes characteristic of her work. I do not conduct a traditional stylistic enquiry. Dominique Noguez's article[2] is valuable for its meticulous survey of certain rhetorical figures characteristic of Duras' writing. Yet the description of traditional figures of speech can not render many of the most significant particularities of a prose full of configurations "not to be found in Fontanier's or any other repertory of tropes," as Christiane Makward objects in critique of Noguez,[3] because it presupposes the very unitary discourse Duras deconstructs. It subsumes her writing within the classical structures of language posited as genderless and universal, which has historically meant male, and misses her pointedly gendered critique and rearticulation.

Duras' work indicates the use to which women's silence can be put. Makward notes: "[. . .] for Marguerite Duras there is an absolute revalorization of silence [. . .] Silence is *militant*, feminine passivity is the greatest force of the movement, 'inaugural of a feminine politics'."[4] Redefined, "silence" and "passivity" become integrated into political activity and into speech . In *Les Parleuses* Duras states: "passive refusal, in sum the refusal to answer, is a colossal force [. . .] it is the force of women."[5] She explains: "But it is *aware* passivity. [. . .] When I talk about the passivity which could be inaugural of a feminine political activity as a response to class society in its present form, I'm talking about a passivity completely informed about itself, completely."[6] And: "It would be a force [. . .] and I believe women could counter with it. [. . .] I believe they [women] would act if they had speech."[7] Susan Husserl-Kapit sees the affirmation of silence as the basis of Duras' project: "What Duras wants is for women to emerge from silence *not* by rejecting it but by acknowledging it as their strength, expressing it artistically and politically, and finally by affirming it as a superior principle, making *this* the standard by which everything, including masculinity, is judged."[8]

Silence in Duras functions as a strategy of resistance both "passive" and active. Germaine Brée observes: "The established syntax, the admitted forms of culture erase one discourse in order to impose another; for her part, Marguerite Duras sets out to erase that false order."[9] But this process does not obliterate meaning itself, as Selous suggests.[10] Duras' enterprise is not a nihilistic one resulting in meaningless muteness. Within Duras' texts, actively signifying silences manipulated by the author/narrator, by her female narrators and by many female and some male protagonists, contrast sharply to the deadening muteness to which characters such as Lol V. Stein and the Indochinese beggar succumb, and which others such as the woman in *La Maladie de la Mort* and Claire Lannes, for example, strenuously resist. Implicit in most of Duras' texts, the "destroy" in the title *Détruire, dit-elle* (*Destroy, She Says*) designates an initial step, to be followed or preferably accompanied by the institution of other discursive articulations. Dislocating, refusing unitary language, encoding different meanings and structures challenge what Dale Spender calls the dominant "monopoly on the production of names [and] monopoly on reality."[11]

To be sure, one can not wipe the slate entirely clean, for one is born into history and language. Duras knows that she neither starts from a cultural zero nor produces one. What she does do is demystify and reject dominant, unitary language, and construct something else in its stead.

LISTENING

"Xavière Gauthier: 'S'il [le rôle d'Alissa dans le film *Détruire, dit-elle*] était joué par un homme, il ne perdrait pas quelque chose?'
Duras: 'Oui, il perdrait l'écoute, en tout cas . . . '"

"J'aime quiconque entendra que je crie."

MargueriteDuras

Dominant culture casts woman not simply as language's object, but also as giver of silent approval, as listener. Exploring certain modalities of listening, Duras recasts it as an integral part of discourse. The silence that is listening no longer acts as the opposite of speech.

Of the two female protagonists in *Le Vice-consul*, the beggar occupies the first position and Anne-Marie Stretter the second. The latter's very seductiveness to her "lovers" is a function of her role as a listener whose mediation screens the horrors of India and colonialism. In contrast to white diplomatic society, Anne-Marie Stretter opens herself to Calcutta through a connection at once physical and symbolic. She walks bareheaded in the sun the others flee, bathes in the water, and weeps. Her tears are the emblem of contact "made through pain, Anne-Marie Stretter's tears, tangibly, organically."[12] When she weeps silently, "traversed"[13] by the ambient misery, the men recognize this sign of her projection into Calcutta, turn away and await her "return" to them. She knows she suffers in their stead: "'[. . .] someone has to weep; it is as though it were me'" (V-C, p. 198) and they know her sorrow protects them from confrontation with the city's suffering and affords relief: "sometimes she falls into profound despondency. Some have spoken about that; one doesn't know the nature of it but it is restful for he who sees it; it refreshes [. . .]" (V-C, p. 109).

Her receptivity is further symbolized by her unlocked residences, a detail which enabled Michael Richard, attracted by the sound of her piano playing, to enter the embassy and meet her. Her music furnishes another shelter: "Before I met Anne-Marie, says Michael Richard, I heard her play in Calcutta, at night [. . .] I had come to Calcutta as a tourist, I couldn't bear it, at all; I wanted to leave the first day, and . . . it was because of her, because of that music that I heard, that I stayed – that I was able to stay in Calcutta"

(V-C, p. 187). The soothing European melodies she plays mute the disquieting noises of grinding poverty so often evoked: "Again Calcutta softly screams" (V-C, p. 158) "Again Calcutta grinds and creaks" (V-C, p. 160) etc. She alone allows herself to be penetrated by those sounds. In the widest sense, Anne-Marie Stretter listens to Calcutta in the "lovers'" place. They beg her to play, and hear her music instead of the world around them, and instead of her. The maternal aspects of her role are evident. She protects the men and calms them at night with the equivalent of a lullaby.

The insulation Anne-Marie Stretter provides secures "the lovers'" discourse from an external position, for she listens to Calcutta more than to them. Because listening entails participation, her refusal to do it when they discuss Morgan's text about the beggar implicitly condemns their reifying discourse. Not listening, it will be remembered from my analyses in Part I, constitutes actively resistant silence in that scene.

Anne-Marie Stretter's conversation with the Vice-Consul illustrates the participatory nature of listening. His most significant traits are radical incapacity for communication and the correlative violence of his occasional incursions into the world, the most extreme being the shooting of lepers in Lahore. Comparing men's and women's historical reactions to "suffering" (la douleur), Duras factors in the question of a certain use of language:

> Suffering, for men, until now, throughout the ages, history, has always found its outlet, its solution. It turned into anger, into external acts, like war, crimes, the exclusion of women in Moslem countries, in China, the burying alive of adulterous women with their lover, or their disfigurement. [. . .] We alone never had any other recourse but to be mute. [. . .] Man can not bear suffering, he gets rid of it, he has to remove himself from it, he throws it out of himself in consecrated, ancestral manifestations, which are his recognized transfers: battle, screams, the deployment of discourse, cruelty.[14]

She contrasts Anne-Marie Stretter to the Vice-Consul accordingly:

> [. . .] in Anne-Marie Stretter's pain and in the Vice-Consul's anger. It flows in her . . . it is like a river that has traversed her, as though traversed by that river of pain . . . and he is, on the contrary, like a machine of death, he is full of fire, or

explosives . . . he has to get rid of it, it has to explode, to be expressed on the outside [. . .] whereas Anne-Marie Stretter's insertion in India is physical [charnelle]. It is internal.[15]

When the Vice-Consul dances with Anne-Marie Stretter at the reception he acquires a temporary capacity for dialogue: "He listens to no one, everybody knows it, except her, the Ambassadress" (V-C, p. 130). Suddenly receptive to another, he modifies his pace for her: "The Vice-Consul must have perceived that she is hot, that he is dancing like they do in Paris [. . .] The Vice-Consul, who notices nothing, notices that: he murmurs an apology and slows down" (V-C, p. 122). Yet this attentiveness is brief and misleading, like the harmony his facial features assume while he dances: "Deceptive appearance of the silhouette and face with regular features" (V-C, p. 123). Gradually it becomes clear that he seeks not an interlocutor but a listener: "Yes, I would like to be heard by you, by you, tonight" (V-C, p. 126). He demands comprehension, explaining "that he can say nothing about Lahore, nothing, and that you [Stretter] must understand him" (V-C, p. 126). The demand edges towards coercion: "I would like you to say that you perceive the inevitable side of Lahore. Answer me" (V-C, p. 127), which places the episode under the sign of the violence so characteristic of him.

For her part, Anne-Marie Stretter consents to hear, that is, as Maurice Merleau-Ponty defines comprehension, to "accompany [the Vice-Consul] in silence," opening herself to his discourse until she "perceives" his point of view, and "speaks his language."[16] With the act of listening, Anne-Marie Stretter lets herself be "undone" and "remade" by his speech. Merleau-Ponty affirms: "there is speech, (and, finally, personality) only for an 'I' which carries in it this germ of depersonalization. Speaking and understanding presuppose not only thought, but, more essentially, and as the foundation for thought, the power to let oneself be un-made and re-made by an other who is present, by several possible others, and, presumably, by everyone."[17]

Because what the Vice-Consul wants Anne-Marie Stretter to hear and understand are acts of murder, the depersonalization she must undergo entails abandonment of her open empathetic approach to the world, which the text explicitly connects to her womanhood. "'It is very difficult to perceive it [Lahore] completely' – she smiles 'I am a woman . . .'" (V-C, p. 127). Nevertheless she acquiesces, and goes from partial comprehension ("I see a little, only a little" – V-C,

p. 127), to incipient identification with his "I" ("Help yourself with the idea that one ['on' – he] is a clown waking up.[. . .]' 'That is to say,' she says, 'I'm not thinking anything.' 'That's it'" – V-C, p. 127). Finally, he coerces her into complete understanding: "I would like you to say that you perceive the inevitable side of Lahore. Answer me.' She doesn't answer. 'It is very important that you perceive it, even for an instant.' [. . .] 'I perceive the inevitable side of Lahore,' she says" (V-C, pp. 127–128).

An active part of speech, listening produces identification through reciprocity: "[. . .] in the exercise of speech, I become the one to whom I listen,"[18] writes Merleau-Ponty. In Duras this extends to the physical: Anne-Marie Stretter begins to resemble the Vice-Consul in her demeanor ("People say: Look how she appears hard at times . . . " V-C, p. 125) and in her gaze ("People notice in both their eyes a common expression, an attention to the same thing perhaps?" V-C, p. 127).[19]

Thus the performative nature of listening has worked in both directions. At first, during the Vice-Consul's fleeting attentiveness to Anne-Marie Stretter, he resembles her; his body becomes more fluid and his voice more melodious. Then he takes her into his "world," where she must resemble him. Yet that this scene of communication remains largely one-sided is further confirmed by the Vice-Consul's next request: "Do you think there is something we can do, both of us, for me?" to which Anne-Marie Stretter replies "No, there is nothing" (V-C, p. 128) and the conversation ends. Her negative response and subsequent refusal to see him attest to her awareness of his essential incapacity to listen to an Other. Given the nature of listening, to receive the Vice-Consul would necessitate repeating the dehumanization-defeminization she underwent in order to hear him, and invite a contagion that would change her radically. For she can not at the same time serve as the "lovers'" sheltering mediator and identify with absolute violence: "'You see,' she says [to Charles Rossett], 'if I forced myself to see him, Michael Richard would not forgive me, nor would anyone else, actually . . . I can not be she who is here with you except by . . . wasting my time like this . . . ' 'That is all there is here,' says Michael Richard, laughing, 'Anne-Marie, nothing else'" (V-C, p. 194).

So she resumes listening to Calcutta, alone. Precisely for this reason, she remains discursively isolated, "wasting her time," because no one listens to her. The "lovers," for whom her usefulness consists in enabling them to turn a deaf ear to India and, by extension, to her, are radically unavailable as listeners, as are the other male characters. The other white women have apparently been subsumed in the "on" of the diplomatic community, something the text suggests by designating them only as diplomats' wives. To be sure, Anne-Marie Stretter communes silently with the beggar. Yet the latter's muteness and madness prevent dialogue. That Anne-Marie Stretter suffers, rejects, revolts alone (at no point in the text do we see her attempt to make contact with Indian women, for example) condemns her to isolation, political and personal. Duras situates whatever "liberation" Anne-Marie Stretter achieves on a limited, individual plane: "I don't say she is a liberated woman, I say that she is on a very sure road to liberation, a very personal, individual road to liberation [. . .] it is a matter of a universal despair, which connects very closely to a profound political despair, and which is experienced as such, calmly. [. . .] She becomes Calcutta. There is a double slippage, Calcutta towards the form of Anne-Marie Stretter and Anne-Marie Stretter towards the form of Calcutta."[20]

She does disturb the white diplomats. Through her invitation of the Vice-Consul to the reception, she confronts them with his "embarrassing presence" (V-C, p. 97), mirror of their complicity with the violence of colonialism, figured by his murders and their cover-up ("is killing lepers or dogs really killing?" – V-C, p. 94).[21] Yet diegetically her efforts have few durable effects. Society may not be able to assimilate her transgressive behavior, but by not listening to her it reduces her to the incidental and functions with but temporary discomfort with her. At most she is a thorn in the side of the colonial discursive order, and her remark about the fleeting effect of the Vice-Consul's disturbance applies equally to herself: "For half an hour they will feel ill at ease. Then they will talk about India" (V-C p. 145). Further, the text implies that she herself will remove that thorn by committing suicide.[22]

The text discloses the connections between the discursive, the political and the sexual in the isolation to which Anne-Marie Stretter seems to succumb. Discursive and political in that she has no audience. Sexual for the same reason. For if, as François Péraldi asserts, Anne-Marie Stretter represents feminine "jouissance,"[23] then what he calls male dread of it makes "the lovers" avoid it. She fascinates them because of her ambiguous position between two societies. Figured by the beggar, women of color are "obscene," repulsive to the white men, too foreign, too "inferior," too close to "nature" (Richard says: "I see her among [. . .] other young girls

[. . .] I see them seated [. . .] obscene, their bodies uncovered . . . "
– V-C, p. 180). The men replace them as objects of desire with a
European woman whose origins – Anne-Marie Stretter is half Italian
– carry connotations of sensuality associated with Southern Europe,
and make her a less threatening erotic figure. But the distinction is
not as operative as it would appear. If her class, race, education
and position place her among the colonials, diminishing desire, her
connections to Calcutta (the tanned skin, the associative links with
the beggar, her openness) and her rumored promiscuity neutralize
the very desire they incite. Ultimately assimilated to Woman, with
the contradictions inherent in that concept, Anne-Marie Stretter is at
once the pampered white reading woman[24] – boring wife material –
and the forbidden/forbidding darker, supposedly promiscuous and
therefore desired *and* denigrated and feared female. Frightened or
repulsed, the "lovers" do not act on their desires. Devoid of lovemaking scenes, the text contains only aborted or perverted attempts:
Rossett's kiss which goes no further, his fantasized beating of her,
the Vice-Consul caressing her bicycle. Her relationship with Michael
Richard seems reduced to the remnants of an earlier passion.

For Eleanor Skoller, Anne-Marie Stretter "is the seat of love [. . .]
in a debased version of a tradition [. . .] of courtly love."[25] The
recipient of fealty has, in Lacan's words, "the discourse of the
master."[26] However, Anne-Marie Stretter refuses master discourses
and discourses of mastery, and the men accomplish no chivalrous
feats. Not unlike the Vice-Consul, who casts Stretter as one of "those
women who seem to sleep in the waters of kindness [. . .], towards
whom all waves of all kinds of pain go [. . .]" (V-C, p. 120), the
"lovers" remain in the realm of impotent, oedipal fantasy, limiting
her to the protective, comprehending, listening maternal role.

If diegetically doomed, the extradiegetic discursive model Anne-
Marie Stretter provides does find a listener in the reader, and
therefore has the possibility of social impact. The succeeding sections
explore the ways in which she and others of Duras' female protagonists alter dominant discursive structures and propose a radically
different use of language.

Initially, the discursive-sexual politics in *La Maladie de la Mort*
recall those of *Le Vice-consul*, but things end quite differently. So
long as the female protagonist in the former listens to dominant
discourse, she resembles what it projects. Obedient to the injunctions
of silence and passivity, she lies mute and motionless, miming the
objectification of women like the dozing Anne-Marie Stretter in

Le Vice-consul's literary conversation scene. Later, her refusal to listen any longer to the male protagonist compares to Stretter's termination of relations with the Vice-Consul. Because he continues to speak "alone in the world, like you [he] wants to be" (Mal, p. 49), "she doesn't listen, she sleeps" (Mal, p. 50).[27] The woman emerges from silence to denounce the man's bad faith: "You think you are weeping because you don't love. You are weeping because you are not imposing death" (Mal, p. 48), rejects the maternal role and his attempts to force it on her by screaming, and leaves. The context of this leaving constitutes the crucial difference between the two female figures. Discursively isolated, trapped in the contradictions between acceptance of "contracts" (financial dependence in marriage, the agreement to shield the "lovers"), rejection of colonial discourse and listening to Calcutta, Anne-Marie Stretter falls victim to the externally imposed "malady of death." With no one to talk to, she has nowhere to go. In contrast, La *Maladie de la Mort* not only implies that the female protagonist returns to a community not stricken with his illness, it includes a "listener" in the text, the narrator, who hears and seconds her.

Many of Duras' texts foreground the pernicious effects on women of their exclusion from dialogue. Structured around this very issue, *L'Amante anglaise* makes it clear that Claire Lannes commits murder for want of an interlocutor. Isolated in a small town where existing structures go unquestioned, where her husband ignores her "ravings" and the other person sharing her house is her deaf mute cousin who works as their servant, she has no one to hear her. She kills her cousin.

Locked in silence, Marie-Thérèse Bousquet incarnates Woman as dumb domestic, reduced to mindless muteness. Far from objecting, she cheerily internalizes dominant representations. Claire finds it intolerable that her cousin never opens her mouth to speak, but only to eat the "meat in sauce" she continually serves, and with which Claire equates her, calling her "an enormous mass of deaf meat" (A-A, p. 177). She is "on the other side" not because of a physical handicap which in itself would not preclude communication, but because she embraces what it symbolizes: "but if she had been normal she would have been the queen of the other side [. . .] She devoured them with her eyes when they passed by on the sidewalk and on their way to mass. They smiled at her, so you see. At me, never, no one smiled" (A-A, p. 177).

The murder is a complex gesture which can be viewed as a two directional displacement. On the one hand, Claire strikes down a collaborator rather than a full member of dominant society. On the other, she kills a symbol of her own discursive exclusion (a metaphor heightened by the metonymy of the familial relation) – instead of committing suicide. Deprived of discourse since no one enters into dialogue with her, Claire lives in a solitude her cousin mirrors, but one more shattering because of her awareness of it and struggle against it. Even the murder partakes of Claire's resistance, for it is also an abortive attempt at the writing-calling achieved by Aurélia Steiner. Asked whether she remembers writing the name Alfonso (a Portugese wood cutter to whom she feels attracted) on the wall of the cellar where she killed her cousin, Claire replies: "No. Perhaps I wanted to call him for help? And since I couldn't cry out, that would have awakened my husband, I wrote? [. . .] I have, on occasion, written in order to call, knowing that it was useless" (A-A, p. 178). Her appeals fail because nothing encourages this uneducated, working class wife to address her "letters" to a wider audience: "'I could have written letters about him [her first lover] but to whom?' 'To him?' [asks the interrogator] 'No, he wouldn't have understood. No, I ought to have sent them to anyone at all. But anyone at all is not easy to find. Yet that is what I should have done: sent them to someone who knew neither him nor me, so that it would have been completely understood'" (A-A, pp. 159–160). "Letters" sent to anyone/everyone are precisely what Aurélia Steiner succeeds in sending. In other words, she becomes a writer. Unable to express herself in art, her communicative attempts judged irreceivable, Claire inhabits an untenable impasse which finally explodes.

Before resorting to murder in order to make her desperation heard, Claire had attempted other forms of calling. Like her speech, they were quickly quelled by her husband and cousin: "So, then, I've had it, you understand [. . .] So I open the window and I break plates so that they will hear me and come to unburden me of myself" (A-A, p. 172). Significantly, she breaks the objects that bear the meat in sauce so symbolically revolting to her.

Although Claire's crime will ultimately ensure her permanent silence in prison or an asylum, at first it enables her to break it. Murdering the image of female muteness is a symbolic and real putting to death of her own silence. For now, people listen to her. She quickly understands that by not providing the answer they seek, the whereabouts of the head of her victim, she can continue to speak. Having dis-articulated Bousquet's body (she cut off the limbs at their joints, "articulations" in French, disposed of them separately, and hid the head), she now articulates her own existence, albeit within the confines of a jail. Claire cannily keeps the blank spot blank so that she may continue to be articulate. A modern Scheherazade, she captivates her male captor(s) through a perpetual textuality which frustrates the desire for closure. As with her predecessor, this permits her to live in a tenuous limbo, but which affords a certain limited empowerment. Reversing women's traditional situation of required silence, these female prisoners speak continuously in order to distract their male jailors from their projected end.

As long as Claire Lannes does not reveal her secret she can live, that is, speak, a conflation she makes explicitly: "So only that word, among all others, would count? And you think I'm going to let that word be taken from me? So that all the others get buried alive and me with them in the asylum?" (A-A, p. 192). That the absence of the head forms the condition of possibility of Claire's discursive agency can be interpreted in relation to Freud's elaboration of the male castration complex. The concept of decapitation as a displaced castration symbol helps explain the fascinated persistence of the captors' desire to know the head's whereabouts. But beyond this masculine perspective, Duras' novel gives voice to a feminine text. Claire has disposed of the head, the cultural symbol of the over-bearing phallus-logos silencing women. The absence of the signifier (and the hidden referent) for that head-logos-phallus is precisely what opens a space for other, women's words to be disinterred, and to at least defer their reburial. So Claire's is a woman's "secret": dominant culture's obsession with its own castration castrates the Other, of discourse.

If, unlike Scheherazade, Claire remains doomed, she too subverts discursive power relations. The earlier heroine delays her death sentence and wins life for her and other women by manipulating language in ways which pleasure her male master while at the same time "civilizing" him. Listening to Scheherazade, King Schariar gradually mitigates his prejudices against women and grants them life. Aware she has already (been) lost in the nexus of male castration anxiety, Claire turns discourse to her own pleasure, to express herself. She focuses on her own stories, the intense love affair she once had, and her marriage, both told in a woman's terms, with the hope that the interrogator will hear a discourse of (sexual) difference. Knowing that she will ultimately be enclosed in yet another living tomb, Claire tries to delay her "execution" through an ever broken promise of providing the closure she withholds. After the interrogator confirms that he would leave if she did so, she makes a final plea to be heard, with which the novel ends: "'If I told you where the head is would you still speak with me?' 'No.'" (A-A, p. 193). "'If I were you, I would listen. Listen to me" (A-A, p. 195).

In the interrogating would-be writer, Claire does find someone to "unburden her of herself," in both senses. She finally delivers her discourse, but at the same time completes the symbolic and actual murder-suicide. Yet once again, beyond a woman's tragic personal end, her call is heard by the reader: Duras sends Claire's letter for her by writing and publishing *L'Amante anglaise,* by making of it an appeal for a rearticulation of discursive practise in general.

The hitch-hiking lady of *Le Camion* is another foiled potential woman writer who soliloquizes about herself to a man, and whose speech gets dismissed as mere ravings. An unreflecting member of the communist party, the truck driver automatically pronounces "reactionary" or insane any discourse straying from the dictated line, especially one issuing from an older woman (Cam, pp. 47–48). Mostly, he ignores her: "He doesn't ask himself who she is. He asks nothing . . . He has nothing to do with a middle aged woman. His habits are [. . .] discriminatory: a middle aged woman is not something interesting" (Cam, p. 37).

The lady expresses ironic awareness of these repressive tactics, which she nevertheless internalizes to a degree: "I must tell you that I am always in a sort of mental confusion. [. . .] Oh, all you have to do is not listen to me, actually. That is what people around me say: 'One can very well not listen to her'" (Cam, p. 52). Her wanderings are rather hopeless searches for an interlocutor, profoundly akin to Claire Lannes' appeals. She too equates her writing with crying out and futility: "My head is full of dizziness and cries. [. . .] So, sometimes, for instance, I write. Pages, you see. Or else I sleep" (Cam, pp. 35–36). Society officially silences her through periodic incarceration in asylums, and the driver's reaction is identical to that of the system he opposes. Himself partisan of a rigid order, he can not abide this threat of "disorder." Like Claire, then, the lady is condemned to speak essentially to herself. This contrasts to the narrative frame, which depicts a successful woman artist being heard by a famous male actor and shows how this collaborative listening produces textuality.

In *L'Homme atlantique,* the novice actor has a difficult time in his apprenticeship of listening. The first half of the text consists of "Duras" teaching him to "forget" his constructed social identity ("You will forget. That it is you, you will forget" – Hom, p. 7). After that he must learn the basic words "look," "listen," "think," "see," "move," in a scenario not written according to dominant definitions.

Part I examines how the parasitic listening of Duras' male narrators with artistic aspirations represses women's speech. Exploiting the pretext of the woman's madness deprives her of her discourse and "justifies" its appropriation by the male writer. (Cf. The writing narrators of *Le Ravissement de Lol V. Stein* and *Le Marin de Gibraltar*, Morgan in *Le Vice-consul*, the interrogating writer of *L'Amante anglaise*). Used as a silencing device by other male figures as well, this traditional ploy functions performatively, effecting discursive – social isolation, which can result in the woman's madness and/or suicidal despair.

In the texts featuring mutual listening between men and women, it is noteworthy that the male characters usually belong to some category of Otherness. They are working class in *Le Square* and *Moderato Cantabile*,[28] Jewish (an intra-European Other) in *Détruire, dit-elle* (in which two Jewish men listen to and love a woman, Alissa, who directs the proceedings), Asian (the Oriental Other) in *Hiroshima mon amour* and *L'Amant*. De Beauvoir was among the first to perceive connections between the status of women and the feminization of the Other.[29] Sander Gilman describes the Christian discursive move to feminize Jews in Europe through semiotic association with categories of the impure.[30] Rana Kabbani demonstrates the symbolic force of feminization as eroticization or devirilization of the Oriental colonized.[31] While exposing the historical consequences of such strategies, Duras reverses the negative connotations they produce. She reconceptualizes "femininity" as positively marked receptivity. Precisely because they are not "virile" (a word Duras equates with *macho*), her sympathetic male heroes can listen – and love.

The Chinese man in *L'Amant* is a case in point. For the French colonials in Indochina, any Asian's racial otherness signifies inferiority to any white regardless of class, and "Duras" pointedly mentions the racism of her poor white family towards her rich Chinese lover. But the text deconstructs that negative feminization by overemphasizing the man's "femininity," making it an attractive part of his physicality. His body is soft, hairless, weak, "without virility other than that of his genitals" (Am-p. 49). He approaches the young girl with a ("feminine") timidity correlated socially to his racial difference. Kristeva implicitly accuses Duras of racism, taxing the book with "exotic eroticism."[32] However, in addition to eliding the effects of the text's structural distancing, she disregards an essential diegetic element. If the Chinese man is exotic – a word more à propos would be "forbidden" – to the young girl, she is equally forbidden to him.[33] Fabulously wealthy, he is her economic superior. Her family's disdain causes him discomfort, but more than its rejection, he fears legal sanctions if his liaison with an underaged white girl gets discovered. Above all, he fears being disinherited by his father for consorting with what, with Chinese racism, the latter considers *their* racial inferior: the trashy white girl.

Far from being exoticized (there are no allusions, for example, to Oriental eyes or hair),[34] metaphorically he becomes familial, paternally washing her, merging with her absent father and desired brothers. Additionally, Duras includes him in the category of foreign exploiters of the indigenous Vietnamese, the provenance of his inherited wealth being tenements owned by his father. All this contributes to the subversion of fixed classifications of race, class, and gender, so that the text portrays love between two subjects, marginal and "feminized" in different, actually complementary ways. Cognizant of the violent binarisms militating against as well as structuring their affair, they listen to each other and love unsentimentally. She tells him of her family, he tells her of his, and their very silence is a silence of communication.

In *Hiroshima mon amour*, physical lovemaking dialogues with the lovers' discussion of the impossibility of talking about the bombing of Hiroshima, and with their conversation about the woman's affair with a German soldier in wartime France. The text stages the performative nature of listening in a context of mutual love, so that both participants' identities are affected. Hearing the desire in the man's "you are like a thousand women together," the woman accepts it: "It does not displease me to be a thousand women together for you" (Hir, p. 28). Listening passionately to the woman's story of past passion, the man temporarily "becomes" the soldier she had loved: "'When you are in the basement, am I dead?' Her: 'You are dead'" (Hir, p. 71). In contrast with Hold's theft of Lol's story, here the man's position compares to that of an analyst. When the woman "acts out" memory of extreme passion and painful loss, he consents to a "transference" which helps her bring the trauma from repression through mourning. But the analogy ends there, for what makes the "transference" possible is not analysis or exact reproduction of the past, something the text openly critiques,[35] but the listening of non-simulated, non-commodified love. Reciprocal receptivity to each one's past (she "hears" his wider "trauma" of Hiroshima) confirms the present passion between two conversing subjects.

In *Véra Baxter*, being heard by a man saves the eponymous heroine from suicide and opens a possible love relation. Although nothing indicates conventionally defined Otherness in The Stranger, his anonymity and the absence of identifying notations (profession, etc.) place him outside dominant structures. He responds to Véra's intuition that he too once entertained thoughts of suicide with: "That is a possible identity which perhaps I will keep for you" (Ver, p. 107). Again, attentiveness produces identification. As he begins to understand the death of Véra's love for her husband: "It's strange . . . this pain . . . when you were telling me . . . there.' He turns slightly, places his hand on his heart [. . .] 'As if I had just lost you myself'" (Ver, p. 97). Listening again signals love: "They look at each other. A common fear. Perhaps fear of love" (Ver, p. 107).

Conversation sometimes *is* the love relation, as in *Moderato Cantabile*. Agatha and her brother obey the incest tabou in *Agatha*, replacing physical love-making with dialogue. The lovers in *Le Navire Night* "enact" their passion over the telephone. Under the woman's direction, they listen so closely to each other that they "see" themselves through the other's eyes: "The woman: 'I am looking at myself with your eyes.' He says he sees" (Nav, p. 27).

Verbal "physical" love relations between women occur twice in Duras' oeuvre. Elizabeth Alione listens to Alissa's subversive message of unrestricted love in *Détruire, dit-elle*. That she "hears" Alissa's declaration of desire for her[36] as well as for the two male protagonists constitutes incipient receptivity. Elisabeth does not make love with Alissa, but she responds physically on another plane, with fits of vomiting, symbolic, like for Anne in *Moderato Cantabile*, of a nascent rejection of imposed structures and values. As the female voices in *India Song* imagine/remember and listen to the tale they tell one another, the past story permeates and intensifies their present passion. But they listen differently, producing non-symmetrical results. Voice One listens so intently to the story of Anne-Marie Stretter that she risks projecting too completely into it, "becoming" the suicidal woman: "the difference between their respective passions [. . .] Voice Two's dread of the incessant vertigo of Voice One with respect to the resuscitated story. [. . .] the danger, to which Voice One is exposed, of 'losing' herself in the story of *India Song* [. . .] And of leaving her own life" (Ind, p. 12).

One finds other modalities of woman-to-woman listening in Duras. If and how one hears the beggar forms a sort of Litmus test of good or bad faith in *Le Vice-consul.* I have shown that despite her omnipresence, stressed through numerous "authorial" allusions, the white colonials ignore her and Peter Morgan objectifies her for reasons similar to theirs, whereas Anne-Marie Stretter communes silently with her. The beggar seems to comprehend this, for she follows Stretter whenever she leaves Calcutta for her island villa. When Rossett ventures out of the protected circle and happens upon the beggar in uncharted, "female" territory beyond the confines fenced in for the whites, the scene becomes a parody of the castration complex which blinds and deafens men to sexual difference and women's speech. The beggar emerges from the Ganges river mouth covered with mud, and holds out a fish she has caught. When Rossett does not accept the offering, she bites off the head and eats it while he, paralyzed with fear, gapes at this slimy Venus-Medusa (V-C. p. 205). His uncomprehending, panicked flight makes of this passage the text's most spectacular exposure of what Marini calls "the hegemony of phallic symbolization."[37] In the person of the beggar, in whom the Otherness of gender, race and class coalesce, the real castration represented here is that of women, who, as Irigaray notes, are "connoted as castrated, notably and above all castrated of words."[38]

My narrative analyses of *Savannah Bay* and *Aurélia Steiner-Paris* describe powerful models of female communication which deconstruct prevalent concepts of subjectivity, identity, and language itself. Receptive listening equips a younger woman and an older one to hear each other. This reciprocity dissipates the consecrated age/youth dichotomy, and these women entertain relationships free of domination.

In *Nathalie Granger*, Isabelle Granger and her female friend communicate through an attentiveness which Duras considers the most radical form of entente: "[. . .] absolute communication-communion in silence . . . " (Nat, appendix, pp. 68–69). Silences and words signify equally. In the telephone scene, for example, a "stage direction" informs us that "the friend [. . .] listens [. . .] to Isabelle Granger's silence" (Nat, p. 20). The story takes place in a house, that culturally constructed "female space" to which so many women have been removed. We see how the women turn to their own purposes the space to which they are confined. From within their outside position, they subvert the social which excludes them. When Isabelle destroys her mail (the newspaper, the electric bill and her daughter's report card), she silences the printed emissaries of the discourse of the society that silences her and denies her participation. She accomplishes this act in silence (Nat, p. 77), accompanied by her friend's smiling approval (Nat, p. 78).

If Duras stresses gender so much in this text, it is because listening is the pejorated "blank" of discourse to which women have been relegated. Therefore, its rearticulation by women as a dynamic force has socio-historical specificity. Listening between women constructs solidarity. Empowered by it, the two women can go further. Isabelle gradually comes to the decision not to send her daughter away to school, implicitly understanding her child's violent behavior in that institution as a revolt. This socially anonymous woman ("Isabelle Granger – but does she still have a name?") (Nat, p. 87), married and incarcerated in her husband's house, manages within extremely circumscribed circumstances to subvert the very invisibility, muteness, and social non-existence meant to be her lot. In the encounter with the traveling salesman, an unhappy agent of alienating capitalism, listening and not listening, silence and words combine in successful resistance.[39]

BLANKS

"Evocation et invocation! [. . .] Avec des riens, avec du vide, Marguerite Duras, comme un peintre chinois, réinvente des paysages où tout est absence et vie."

Marc Abru

"[We must] deliberately emphasize these *blanks* of discourse which recall the places of her [woman's] exclusion, spaces which, with their *silent plasticity*, ensure the articulation and coherent expansion of established forms. [we must] reinscribe them as *gaps*, [. . .] as *ellipses* and *eclipses* that deconstruct the logical grids of the reader/writer [. . .] Disrupt syntax [. . . .]"

Luce Iriguray

In addition to referential absence and the thematization of listening, Duras' work stages silence on the page. Beginning with

Moderato Cantabile, one of the most characteristic features of her prose is its verbal restraint. "To write, for Marguerite Duras," observes Marini, "is first to make silence [faire le silence] and empty space; to kill ready made discourse."[40] Duras reorders language, something Merleau-Ponty considered an essential feature of great writing: "All great prose is also a recreation of the signifying instrument, henceforth manipulated according to a new syntax."[41] Beyond "killing ready made discourse," Duras' "new syntax" includes silence as a component of speech, of which it is also the foundation.

Blank spaces form structural elements in this "syntax." Duras' paragraphs are brief, some only two or three lines long, many only one, and they often end well before the right hand margin. Thus a great deal of blank space appears on the page. These visual silences are performative in ways similar to the narrative "blank screens" described in Part I. Duras has consistently explored their possibilities: "I was experimenting with the blank in the [signifying] chain [. . .]."[42] She connects this to her refusal to adhere to dominant syntax: "These are blanks [. . .] that impose themselves. [. . .] blanks that appear due perhaps to a violent rejection of syntax . . . "[43] Duras' blank spaces have a variety of functions. To begin with, they throw into relief the written words they surround, attracting one's attention to utterance as such, as well as to the silence of the blanks.

In *Le Vice-consul*, when "the lovers" hover over the reclining Anne-Marie Stretter while her eyes fill with tears, signalling her "departure" to commune with India, Rossett calls her back:

> She looks at the storm through the open window, still stretched out amidst their gazes. Charles Rossett holds back from calling. Whom? Her, doubtless. What is this desire?
>
> He calls her.
>
> I weep without a reason I could tell you [. . .] (V-C, p. 198).

Separating "He calls her" from the preceding paragraph, in which it belongs according to standard structure, dramatizes Rossett's need to call Anne-Marie Stretter. That we do not learn the words which compose his call[44] directs reader attention to the act of calling.

Duras "writes" her blank spaces as readable signs: "Sometimes it is the place of a sentence to come that offers itself, sometimes nothing, scarcely a place, a form, but open, to be taken. But everything must be read, the empty place also [. . .]."[45] "Animating" these "empty places," Duras accomplishes what Irigaray calls for: "Why not have remembered instead those 'images' made for children, pictographs in which some hunter or hunted and the dramatic relations between them would have to be found *between* the branches, between the trees . . . . Spacings which organize the scene, blanks which subtend its structuring, and which, however, will not be read as blanks. Not read at all? Not seen at all? Frozen in the forgotten while waiting to be animated."[46]

The following examples from *Le Vice-consul* illustrate a variety of contents in the blanks. Anne-Marie Stretter rests in the island villa:

> It seems that Charles Rossett reaches out his hand towards her, that this hand finds itself caught, brought onto her face, which it blinds.
>
> The trembling of the eyelids had ceased. She was sleeping by the time they had left. (V-C, p. 198)

The large space contains several levels of signification. Metonymically filled by the preceding word "blinds," it figures interrupted vision (Stretter's face is covered: she can neither see nor be seen), and *is* a blind spot. The retrospective metonymy of the subsequent verbal forms confers density of action to the blank space. Before it, we find the present tense; afterwords, the verb "to cease" is in the pluperfect, and "to sleep" in the imperfect. Much occurred, then, in the "blank" time – space in between: Anne-Marie Stretter fell asleep and the men left the room. Time is conveyed spatially as well as verbally, and the rhythmic pause created by the blank space further contributes to the intensity of what is silent as well as of what is spoken.

Ill at ease during an encounter with the Vice-Consul at the reception, Charles Rossett withdraws:

> Charles Rossett, who tries to laugh, can't do it, and moves away.
>
> Charles Rossett has once again asked Anne-Marie Stretter to dance. (V-C, p. 120).

Again a word which gives pause triggers the ensuing blank space. After the words "moves away," utterance vanishes with the character, leaving the reader in the same solitary silence as the Vice-Consul. Far from being empty, it materializes his situation and indicates the temporal space during which Rossett walks over to Anne-Marie Stretter and invites her to dance. Once again a past verbal tense points retrospectively to acts completed within the preceding blank space. In each instance the text reverts immediately afterwards to the present.

Throughout *Le Vice-consul* lexical expressions of leaving, waiting, covering someone's face, sleeping, withdrawing one's attention, etc., motivate blank spaces, which function illustratively and temporally as well as on other levels of signification.

Anne-Marie Stretter lies on a gravel path leading to the sea:

> [. . .] she lies down on the path, her head on the palm of her hand [. . .] she gathers some gravel and tosses it away. Then she no longer throws any gravel, she unfolds her arm, places her face on that stretched out arm and stays there. (V-C, pp. 199–200)

The vocabulary depicting the character's gradual immobilization prepares the ensuing blank space, which covers nearly one and a half pages (200–201). Intra- and intertextually, as I have suggested, this blank signifies Stretter's permanent absence. She does not reappear in *Le Vice-consul* other than in Rossett's imagination, and thus does indeed remain "there" – in a pose implying some kind of metonymical death/merging with the sea. The word "stay" literally stays the text and Anne-Marie Stretter's movement in it.

Le Vice-consul ends with a final evocative blank when the Vice-Consul announces that he has nothing left to say:

> 'Nothing else, you have nothing else to tell me, Monsieur?' [asks the Director of the European Circle]
> 'Nothing, no, Director'.
>
> (V-C p. 212)

The text ceases after this performative remark.

The orchestration of blank spaces forms a constant in Duras' oeuvre. For example, several blank pages precede each of the eight subdivisions of *Dix heures et demie du soir en été*. Nearly all of them follow expressions of waiting, during which silent, "blank" action occurs. Page 37, for instance, ends with the words: "She waits for Judith to fall asleep. She waits a long time." Three blank pages ensue, which "materialize" both the waiting and the falling asleep. Blank pages again figure sleep after page 114, the last words on which are: "They sleep a deep sleep." The written text begins again on page 117, when Maria awakens as someone calls her name.

Taken together, this sort of verbal announcement and its enactment in the form of blank space, might be considered a composite speech act, speech being taken in the wider sense as inclusive of silence (the blank space). This happens often in *Le Ravissement de Lol V. Stein*, with blanks of sleep, and waiting (Rav, pp. 40, 57, 66, 211, etc.). When Lol's fiancé leaves the dance with Anne-Marie Stretter, Lol falls down in a faint ("évanouie" Rav, p. 22). The French "s'évanouir" means both to faint and to vanish. With the word "évanouie," Lol does indeed disappear existentially, and for good, first into unconsciousness, then into neurosis, finally into psychosis. The text vanishes with her into a blank (Rav, pp. 22–23), the image of Lol's absence in the faint.

Certain blanks in *Le Camion* "picture" a silent "seeing" evoked through a form of invitation. The lady tells the driver to look at the political emptiness left by the absence of God (this also critiques his quasi-religious faith in the French communist party):

> She says: it's man's new political situation.
> He asks
> Concerning God?
> She says:
> Yes:
> Concerning emptiness.
> Look.

> (Cam, p. 23) [A blank space follows]

Duras has often confirmed her conscious choice of blanks, for example, concerning *L'Amant*: "I was asked to put 'novel.' I said I could do that and then I didn't. I preferred the dryness of the blank. Whether or not one says 'novel' basically concerns the readers. Reading is the novel."[47] Her statement that the white/blank rectangles in the *Aurélia Steiners* figure not emptiness but a page[48] to be/being written on connects thematically evoked blanks to those of narrative "ignorance" as well as to the ones just described.

Thus, contrary to Selous' contention, Duras' blanks are not impasses demonstrating "an impossibility of articulation",[49] and her whole oeuvre does not tend toward a situation in which "the only way out is sex, death, madness," i.e. the "destruction of meaning" as the simplistic binary opposite of the order in place.[50] The thrust of Duras' work on narrative structure and language subverts the very binarisms Selous accuses her of "proposing": "language/rules/meanings" vs "silence/scream/chaos."[51] I have shown and will continue to show throughout this book Duras' practice/praxis of critiquing the premises of dominant symbolic structures while at the same time articulating other discursive avenues.

HESITATION, REPRESENTATION AND INDICATIVE LANGUAGE

"Quelle lueur! a dit l'abbé – quelles lueurs, les femmes quelque fois tirent des simplicités de leurs impressions et des incertitudes de leur langage!"

Paul Valéry

Duras' organization of textual elements produces what might be called a discourse of hesitation. In this context, blanks become pauses conveying an unsureness also figured by other graphical signs and by lexical units. Another manifestation of "ignorance," discursive uncertainty elicits reactions concomitant with the speaker's approach to language.

The unitary language sustaining colonialism maintains itself through a stance of certainty which informs the white community in *Le Vice-consul*. Although some of the male characters do not fully embrace this disposition, their inability to construct another discourse prevents them from challenging it. Discursively disarmed, they unwillingly lose assurance. Blank spaces, suspension points, question marks, questions remaining unanswered and expressions of vacillation such as "I think," "it seems to me," "perhaps," abound in the speech of all the characters in the text. The series of dots in the Ambassador's remarks about the Vice-Consul, for example, manifest the discomfort with which he discovers his inability to define an act he can not categorize, and which threatens the colonial order. The expressions of conviction he does employ betray his efforts to reassure himself. Failing to do so, he ends with an anxious, unanswered query: "Here [concerning the shootings] there is no adverse party, is there, it is a . . . state of things . . it's obvious and Lahore, Lahore . . . what does that mean?" (V-c, p. 42).

Charles Rossett's failure to conceptualize the chaotic suffering in Calcutta ("and you, would you have preferred something else to . . . this?" – V-C, p. 102) leave him in a state of discursive frustration, as do his unrewarded efforts to fit Anne-Marie Stretter into "comprehensible" structures: "She is so . . . secret, I know nothing, thus, this morning [. . .] when she came to walk me to the gate, suddenly she wept . . . without any visible reason . . . she did not say why . . . everything in her behavior must be like that, I think . . . " (V-C, p. 171). The inadequacy of Rossett's conventional logic is figured by the collapse of its linearity: "That reading, those nights spent in the delta villa, the straight line breaks, disappears in a shadow in which there is expended or expressed something whose name does not come to one's mind. What is hidden by that shadow that accompanies the light in which Anne-Marie Stretter always appears?" (V-C, pp. 108–109). These two attempts and his debacle with the beggar are related. Calcutta's inarticulate, disorderly qualities set it on the side of what commonly connotes the feminine. Immersed in the omnipresent, oxymoronic crepuscular light emblematic of the city, Anne-Marie Stretter, figure of femininity, is explicitly linked both to it (she is dubbed "the woman of Calcutta" – V-C, p. 93 – and "the queen of Calcutta" – V-C, p. 202) and to the beggar, that other Other, female symbol of its suffering. Rossett remains paralyzed by his inability to grasp what his discursive frame represses.

Michael Richard greets difficulties of verbal rationalization with anger: "The Vice-Consul of Lahore, I am sure that we must forget him. There is nothing to say about the reasons for this forgetting. There is nothing to do but suppress our memory of him. Or else . . . 'he clenches his fists – ' . . . we will be in great danger of . . . at least of . . . " (V-C, p. 193). "Man," writes Duras, "when he can not name things, is in perdition, is in misery, is disoriented. Man is sick from talking; woman, no."[52] Part of this disarray is contingent on a deep association between the logos, virility, and domination. Accordingly, hesitation signifies weakness, the dominated, femininity. Duras' fiction at once critiques the mechanisms producing the pejorative connotations attached to hesitation (or any form of silence), and redefines it within a different conception of language. In Anne-Marie Stretter, Duras presents a woman at ease speaking a positively marked discourse of hesitation. Her use of it constitutes a model for a different discursive relationship to the world. Like most of Duras' female protagonists and a few of her male ones, Stretter knows and embraces uncertainty, dis-order, ambiguity, otherwise stated, "ignorance," and speaks from these "feminine" areas.

Anne-Marie Stretter repeatedly counsels against trying to fit the unspeakable into logical categories of representational discourse. Before the temporary reciprocity with the Vice-Consul can be established, she must play the role of guide. The Vice-Consul disdains colonial discourse, yet neither knows nor seeks any other. His verbal incursions consist of aggressive sarcasm directed at the diplomats, drunken monologues delivered to the director of the European Circle and renting, destructive shrieks. Because of the imperative desire to express himself to the listener/mother Anne-Marie Stretter, he manages to take his cue from a discursive example she provides to ease his way. In a speech whose hesitations express the impossibility of conveying the experience of India through the representations of unitary language, Stretter warns him against reductionism. Pointedly not searching for such words, she constructs a discourse of other words, pauses, questions, and blanks:

> 'We were in Peking the last time. [. . .] They will tell you . . . like they told us, that Calcutta is very difficult, that, for example, this extraordinary heat, one never gets used to it, don't listen to any of it . . . in Peking it was the same . . . everyone would talk . . . one heard nothing but opinions . . . everything they said was, how to tell you, the most precise word to say that . . . '
> She does not look for the word. (V-C, pp. 123–124)

Marked by punctuational and lexical signs of hesitancy, the speech culminates in a pause which trails off into a blank space whose content – not looking for words – is further foregrounded by the narrative interjection. Prompting by the Vice-Consul in the form of a question elicits further explanation: " [the Vice-Consul:] 'The word to say it . . . ?' [Stretter] 'That is to say, the first word that would seem suitable, here as well, would prevent others from coming to you, so . . . '" (V-C, p. 124). During this moment of openness, the Vice-Consul projects sufficiently beyond himself to listen, to follow the other's verbal pointers and see what her words suggest. Although he quickly reverts back to imposing his violence on her, he does momentarily understand what is being communicated: that to name literally unspeakable suffering within dominant structures is to objectify it, limit, and distance one from it: "He says: 'You were in Peking too.' 'Yes, I was there.' 'I think I've understood. Don't look [for the word]'" (V-C, p. 124).

Naming it would, to borrow a telling formulation from *Moderato Cantabile*, "reduce it to speech." (In that novel's piano lesson scene, the teacher gives up trying to get a recalcitrant young pupil to talk. She refrains from forcing him: "The lady was astonished by so much obstinacy. Her anger gave way, and she despaired at counting for so little in the eyes of this child, whom, however, with a simple gesture she could have reduced to speech" – M-C, p. 12.) Anne-Marie Stretter shuns the discursive politics of a representation which defines and classifies in order to control or repress: "To speak about it very quickly, at all costs, to think about it at all costs, very quickly, in order to be done with it, would prevent [one] from saying something else, something completely different, much more remote, that might also have been said, why not, right?" (V-C, p. 124).

Yet, far from producing or advocating muteness, this combines with an affirmative use of hesitation, silence, and verbal and non-verbal signs, to create what might be called a truly "indicative" language: one which points towards, indicates that which is not sayable. Duras' recreated signifying instrument functions in the deictic register. I have discussed her abundant use of deictics, which range from "here," "now," "here is/are", the present or future tense, the conditional mood, to a host of other forms, including punctuation (dashes and suspension points). To clarify what I mean by indicative language, I alter the concept of deixis slightly, extending it to include any verbal or noverbal pointing. Umberto Eco's description of the shifter "this" modifies the classical stance (" . . . a shifter like /this/ [. . .] receives its semiotic character from the presence of the actual object,") into a definition which *excludes* physical connection with the referent and considers closeness *as a signified content.* /This/ does not acquire a meaning because something is close to it; on the contrary it signifies that *there must be something close to it.*"[53] I would submit that what Marguerite Duras' indicative language indicates needn't be present or close. Durassian deixis includes any kind of pointing towards something near or far, usually absent. Part I shows how her narrative deixis points to non present, mobile and malleable referents. On the level of discourse *per se*, her indicative language either directs towards something designated as not classically representable, or becomes a self-reflective pointing to the absence of certain words. In their very sparseness, Duras' words light the way towards what is unsaid but imagined: "[. . .] I make incomplete sentences, I put words down [. . .] Afterwards, when I re-read my words, I put them together with sentences, I make a sort of syntax, but a poor, even a labored syntax, you see. That doesn't matter. The words are there like beacons. They light up what I want to say."[54]

The Vice-Consul succeeds in speaking "indicatively" himself only after Anne-Marie Stretter challenges his discursive sidetracking. "[Stretter] 'Why are you talking to me about leprosy?' [Vice-Consul] 'Because I have the impression that if I tried to tell you what I would like to succeed in telling you, everything would crumble into dust . . . ' [. . .] 'the words to tell you, you, the words . . . from me . . . to tell you, they don't exist . . . [. . .]'" (V-C, p. 125). Many passages in *Le Vice-consul* have as their subject Anne-Marie Stretter's rejection of positivistic language. When Rossett begs for an explanation of her weeping, she replies, "I weep for no reason I could *tell* you" (V-C, p. 198 – emphasis added). About living in Calcutta she remarks, "You know, almost nothing is possible, that is all that one can *say* [. . .]" (V-C, p. 109 – emphasis added).

In *Le Marin de Gibraltar*, Anna "indicates" the sailor's significance through a discourse of hesitation:

'In your American novel,' she tells me [the male narrator], 'if you speak of this encounter, you must say that it has been very important for me. That it has enabled me to grasp, to understand . . . a little of what that affair meant, that is to say the meaning that he [the sailor] could have, he in any case, and even the meaning he had had for me . . . and that it is since this has happened that I believe that it might be in the realm of the possible to meet him again, to meet anyone, any time. And that I believe also that I must devote myself to looking for him like others devote themselves to . . . ' (Mar, pp. 217–218)

The final suspension points figure the catalyzing blank of the absence of the sailor or any "original" referent, and of discourse adequate to render it.

Throughout her oeuvre Duras critiques unitary language and

replaces it with indicative discourse. Intervening *qua* author, she thematizes verbal pointing and non-representation in a "stage direction" in *La Femme du Gange* "They pass. Together. Alone. Without a word. Without a glance. [. . .] Herd-like deambulation. Serene organic transhumance towards (word missing)" (Fem, p. 131). Together, the deictic "towards," the parentheses, the lexically "named" verbal absence, at once point self-referentially to the discursive practice at hand and open several signifying options for what is indicated. Leaving the blank spot blank activates an irreducible multiplicity of silent meanings.

The beginning of *Hiroshima mon amour* makes explicit the futility and bad faith of traditional representational strategies: "What do they talk about? About Hiroshima, precisely. [. . .] [It is] Impossible to talk about Hiroshima. The *knowledge of Hiroshima* being *a priori* posited as an exemplary trap for the mind" (Hir, p. 2). Language directs our imagination towards what is beyond words: "Him: 'You have seen *nothing* in Hiroshima. Nothing.' Her: 'I have seen *everything*. Everything . . .'" Symmetrical repetition of "nothing" and "everything" continues until they become equivalent in their expressive double pointing, negatively, to the inadequacy of representational language, and positively but not definitively to Hiroshima projected into the imagination.

Noguez notes that the "everything" in this passage "suffices to designate the impossibility of enumerating, relating in detail [. . .]," and connects this to "a sort of impossibility of saying, a primal, total ignorance which haunts the [Duras'] oeuvre [. . .]."[55] But because he obeys almost totally the injunction of traditional stylistics against interpretation, he neglects the intentionality of Duras' "style." Therefore, he reads in it defeat in a discursive struggle to "say," rather an other type of language manipulation. Because Noguez treats language as a genderless, objective entity, his analysis occludes the social specificity of Duras' traditional tropes and ignores "tropes" not conventionally defined. If the catastrophe of Hiroshima can not, must not be mimetically represented, it can be and is indicated, through another discourse, which combines pointing words and silence. Duras' "indicative" language has political and poetic signification.

Denying Duras both a stylistic and a political project, Kristeva conflates these "deficiencies" as signs of Duras' "malady of grief." She pronounces her prose "lacking in acoustic charm," "painful," an "awkward" "discourse of dulled pain" with "a stilted, artificial, and sickly grandiloquence."[56] In her reading of *Hiroshima mon amour*, Kristeva ascribes to the heroine "the postwar version of love," which vacillates between being "a love crippled by death [and] a love of death," "a love that was made impossible [and] a necrophilic passion for death," a "my love is a Hiroshima, [and] I love Hiroshima for its suffering is my Eros,"[57] whereas at no point is that suffering eroticized. Disregarding the explicit political message of the thematized rejection of representation, Kristeva accuses Duras of absorbing the political into the (a-political) personal (the latter being only death-loving melancholy) so that "the private domain [. . .] depreciates the public domain [. . .] As a result, public life becomes seriously severed from reality whereas private life [. . .] is emphasized to the point of filling the whole of the real and invalidating any other concern."[58] This despite Duras' statement of intention in the synopsis: "And that is one of the major goals of the film, to be done with the description of the horror through horror [documentaries], for that has been done by the Japanese themselves, but to have that horror re-emerge from its ashes by inscribing it in a love which will necessarily be particular [. . .]" (Hir, p. 3). The personal love story will "triumph over HIROSHIMA" making the text/film "a sort of false documentary which will be far more probing of the lesson of HIROSHIMA than a commissioned documentary" (Hir, p. 4). Beyond the text's efficacy in this regard, Kristeva also ignores the allusions to history (through the personal) as well as the heroine's explicit political statements, such as: "I desire to have no more country. I will teach my children [. . .] intelligence and the love of other people's countries [. . .]" (Hir, p. 114).[59]

The narrator of *Le Ravissement de Lol V. Stein* speculates that Lol's silence has resulted from her inability to find a word to express her replacement, her unspeakable absence in an impossible triangle, "un-nameable for want of a word" (Rav, p. 54). But nothing in Lol's reported behavior supports his assumption that "she believed, for a split second, that that word could exist" (Rav, p. 54). She became silent because of her instantaneous comprehension of a situation which deprived her of speech because it entailed her disappearance. The passage merits quoting for its "indication" of that word in its very un-sayability.

For want of its existence, she is silent. It would have been an absence-word, a hole-word, hollowed at its center by a hole, by that hole in which all the other words would have been buried. One would not have been able to say it, but one would have been able to make it resonate. Immense, endless, an empty gong, [. . .] that word, which doesn't exist, is there nevertheless: it awaits you around the corner from language, it defies you – it has never been used – to pick it up, to make it surge forth from its kingdom pierced all over with holes, through which the sea flows out, the sand, the eternity of the of the ball in the cinema of Lol V. Stein (Rav, pp. 54–55).

The narrator can make the non-existent word "resonate" because he has at his disposal others he can manipulate in order to point towards it. Lol's silence indicates her own as well as the word's absence. Like the beggar in *Le Vice-consul*, Lol's person silently signifies a void. Both are punished with existential death, i.e. muteness, for specifically feminine infractions: the beggar for transgressing the strictures of peasant society by becoming pregnant out of wedlock (a crime for which only the woman incurs sanctions), Lol for transgressing the rules regulating the lives of idle young women of the bourgeoisie, for not continuing to please her man. Duras' imagery evokes original sin, which also assigns culpability primarily to the female. We have two instances of a Fall, and the French "tomber" (to fall) is used markedly in each. The beggar "falls pregnant," as the standard French expression "tomber enceinte" phrases it. Duras ironically concretizes the metaphor : "She was driven away because she fell pregnant, from a tree, very high, [. . .] she fell pregnant" (V-C, p. 20). Lol: "fell down on the floor in a faint" when the couple left the ball. (Rav, p. 22). To each is meted out the punishment of banishment from an Eden of love (maternal for the beggar, romantic for Lol), identity (the beggar must literally lose her self[60] in order to leave her land and people, and Lol's identity, like that of many middle-class women, hinged on her relationship to a man), language (far from the country where her language is spoken, the beggar falls dumb, as does Lol when expelled from the idiolect of love) and, consequently, from sanity. Their ensuing muteness is a far cry from the rich, productive silences practised by others of Duras' female protagonists.

If in her cinematic and theatrical production Duras gives precedence to words in the dialectical relationship between the verbal and the visual, one must interpret with caution assertions of hers such as "books do not satiate, close nothing,"[61] and "the text says everything."[62] It should now be evident that not just any word "contains a thousand images."[63] The speech Duras' texts critique corresponds to the type of visual representation her cinema eliminates. Just as she subverts the adequation of image to word in visual media, in the verbal one she deconstructs the adequation of word to referent, or to a ready-made signified. Duras' texts "say everything" a text can say by ostentatiously not saying everything. In the cinematic medium, the rejection of mimesis can take the form of images dislocated from the sound track or simply omitted. (Makward aptly calls the blank screen sequence in the film *L'Homme atlantique* an "optical silence"[64]). In the books, it takes the form of narrative "ignorance" and non-representational discourse.

In both domains, the author develops an "indicative language" which points, mostly verbally, to non present referents. "That is the paradox I show in my cinema," explains Duras, "that impossibility: I show what is not representable [. . .]."[65] Concerning her texts, as Jean Baroncelli observes, she "suggests the unsayable."[66] Off stage, off screen space correlates to space off the page. Figuring differently according to the medium involved, the character of the beggar illustrates this. She remains anonymous yet is "visible" in *Le Vice-consul*. In the film "India Song," one hears her sing but she never appears on screen. Naming her in the former or showing her in the latter would have conformed to traditional concepts of representation and reduced her to the anecdotal.[67] The idea that if voice and image translate each other their co-presence destroys imagination and textuality is basic to Duras. At one point the off voices' speech coincides with the images in the film *La Femme du Gange*: "There is a spot where the film of the voices touches the film of the image [. . .] Yes, there is a shock. They touch each other, and it is fatal. It is fatal, the voices disappear."[68]

For the couple in *Le Navire Night*, whose love predicates visual absence, seeing each other is ruled out. More precisely, the woman does see the man, but the reverse would destroy the love and the story, perhaps because vision would trigger a masculine desire for "possession." Orpheus like, the man must not turn around when the woman follows him: "They both know it: if he turns around and sees who [it is], the [love] story dies, struck by lightning" (Nav, p. 76). Not the object of a text, but co-producer and director, this Eurydice has taught her Orpheus that in order for their love (their words) to continue, they must both remain in the dark, on the Night Ship (Le Navire Night), sailing "on the sea of black ink" (Nav, p. 32).

When the man does figuratively turn around, the story immediately halts. The woman sends him photographs of someone – perhaps herself. He looks at them, and "the story stops with the photographs. [. . .] The Night Ship is at a standstill on the sea. There is no longer any route possible. No more itinerary. Desire is dead, killed by an image. He can no longer answer the telephone. He is afraid. From [looking at] the photographs, he would no longer recognize her voice" (Nav, pp. 51–52). Still, he passes the test, returns the pictures (Nav, p. 55) and forgets them. This sets the Night Ship back on course. The love story takes off again on its textual voyage: "He says: 'I have forgotten the photographs.' Things began again like before" (Nav, p. 58).

In *Hiroshima mon amour*, a certain recounting "reduces" the love affair with the German to a certain speech, becoming a betrayal: "I told our story. I betrayed you tonight with that stranger. I told our story. It was, you see, tellable [. . .] Look how I'm forgetting you . . . Look how I've forgotten you" (Hir, p. 90). However, because of the non-congruence between speech and image (in the text and the film) this effect remains limited to the protagonist. Both loves are "indicated" to the reader/spectator.

DOUBT, ERROR, QUESTIONS

"La certitude de connaître [est] la seule bêtise définitive."

Duras

Le Camion makes the supreme denunciation of uncritical militancy: "A militant is someone who does not doubt" (Cam, p. 42). In contrast to the truck driver's blind certainty, Anne-Marie Stretter concludes her speech to the Vice-Consul with the words: "I might be mistaken" (V-C, p. 124). Duras faults all unitary languages for their exclusion of ambiguity, which she connects to an historically evolved "feminine" discursive strategy and to her own conception of literature.: "They [women] are capable of ambiguity, of profound duality, in order to thwart the purity of the general rule [. . .] ambiguity is literature. There is no literature without ambiguity. A thing never has just one meaning."[69]

Doubt and uncertainty often take the form of questions circulating outside the characters' quoted speeches. The text rarely answers them, and their distribution inhibits clear attribution to a particular voice. When the "lovers" interrogate Anne-Marie Stretter in *Le Vice-consul*, an unanswered, perhaps even unuttered question demonstrates their inability to interpret her reactions. Its source is unspecified:

> [a "lover" asks] 'And what if the Vice-Consul of Lahore were only that, a man who is one of those who seek this woman by whose side they believe they should be able to forget?' Did she smile? (V-C, p. 159)

In the following passage from the beggar section, the suspended questions could have been "uttered" either by the white French lady, to whom she is trying to give her child, by Morgan as narrator/writer, or by "Duras": "The lady pushes her aside, as she yells something. The white child with the lady looks at the little girl [the beggar's baby] like she would look at what? But what? [. . .]" (V-C, p. 55).

Unsituated, unanswered, Duras' floating questions are what Jane Gallop calls "a truly feminist gesture, to end with questions, not to conclude, but to be open."[70] Part I demonstrates how this device undermines omniscient narration in many of the texts. To cite a few more examples:

Dix heures et demie du soir en été: "How to name this time opening up before Maria? This exactness in hope? This renewal of the air she breathes? This incandescence, this bursting of a love finally without an object?" (D-H, p. 146). This articulates the issue of adequate verbal representation in the interrogative and links aspects of Duras' indicative language I have separated for expository purposes. In conjunction with the lack of answers, the multiplicity of the questions indicates the very plurality of possibilities they suggest. Framing the "answers" as questions prevents closure. Consistent with Duras' manipulation of deictics on every textual level, the "this" beginning each sentence points to possibilities not fully present or representable.

Le Camion: "She says she has had children, a life, once, in an indeterminate time [. . .] A child she might perhaps have invented . . . Jewish? A Jewish child? Invented?" (Cam, pp. 57–58).

La Femme du Gange, "stage direction": "*the film of the voices* was not planned. It arrived once the film of the images was made, finished. It arrived from far away, from where?" (Fem, p. 103).

Aurélia Steiner: In this passage all the discursive constituents discussed so far in this chapter function together: graphical signs (suspension points), blank spaces, unanswered questions, unortho-dox syntax, unfinished sentences, and the thematic level (the call for listening and the theme of the "senselessness" of searching for a word to say the unsayable):

> "The cat. It's crying out . . .
> [. . .]
> Listen . . .
> Through tears, the cat . . .
> In the wind and hunger, it cries out. In the black cave . . .
> Listen . . .
> Its cries . . .   One would think they were moans . .
> [. . .]
> Listen . . .
> What? What would it say? Which word?
> What senseless designation?
> Inept?"

(Aur, pp. 130–131)

LIES

When afforded the opportunity to speak, Duras' female protagonists improvise numerous renditions of real or imagined stories, the original, "true" version of which they never seek to recuperate or stabilize. As shown in Part I, for her female narrators this constitutes *the* principle of creativity and founds signification on principles of multiplicity and narrative play. The male narrators resist "ignorance," cling to dominant conceptions of truth and treat their texts as tools for tailoring reality to them.

The women unable to accede to artistic expression also embroi-der discursively. If addressed to unsympathetic male characters, their fabrications are received not as intentional weavings of texts, but as threats to prevailing rules and values, discounted as lies and usurped or repressed. In *Le Camion*, each time the driver accuses the lady of lying, she "falls silent" (pp. 29, 56), and the text disappears with her, revealing the blank of imposed feminine muteness. Contact having ceased between the protagonists, the "speakers", Duras and Depardieu, step in to resuscitate textuality. In *Le Vice-consul*, the vehemence of Rossett's reluctance to envisage the possibility of

Anne-Marie Stretter lying demonstrates his refusal to relinquish the dominant concept of truth: "She isn't lying,' thinks Charles Rossett, 'no, not her, I desire that she not be lying [. . .] She isn't lying, she will not lie, Mme Stretter is telling the truth" (p. 129).

Yet the women's persistence in "lying," and the purposeful inconsistencies in their "lies" subvert the concept of objective, unitary truth on this "private" level just as parallel tactics do on the more easily admitted "public" level of fiction acknowledged as such. These women do not lie to dissimulate fact. They redefine truth within a discourse articulated on a foundation of non (self) presence, difference in the lexical and in the Derridean sense, and multiplicity. To restricted-restricting "truth" in the singular, they prefer the multi-faceted, unlimited "field" of lies evoked by Montaigne: "If, like the truth, a lie had but one face [. . .] we would accept as certain the opposite of what a liar would say. But the reverse of truth has a thousand faces and an infinite field."[71] "Lies" enable one to play a "field" not enclosed by fixed structures. I reiterate that in Duras, the play of signifiers is never divorced from political consciousness and engagement. Durassian play is always seriously directed, towards the construction of a different social-discursive order, and against the structures of domination.

If the male "narratee" listens receptively, these fictions usually produce love. The French woman in *Hiroshima mon amour* blends lies and truth while recounting her past passion to her new lover. Significantly, she is a professional actress, someone who perpetually tells and retells stories. Aware, like Madeleine, of the fictional components in all narration, she discourages simplistic distinctions between falsehood and truth: "[the man]: 'When you speak I wonder if you are lying or telling the truth' [the woman]: 'I am lying. And I am telling the truth'" (Hir, p. 41). This decentering of "truth" by refusing to distinguish it from its "opposite" correlates to the rejection of the documentary approach to truth as totalizable through representation in the text's opening scene. Because the new lover listens and participates in an other discourse, mutual love precipitates out of the couple's discursive and physical communication.

Lies are integral to the love affair in *Le Navire Night*. Foiling facile replacement of vision with words, the female protagonist fabricates contradictory portraits of herself and her activities. She describes herself as brunette (Nav, p. 24), blonde (Nav, p. 46), a factory worker, a medical student, and a traveller to China (Nav, p. 25).

She withholds her name, that most conventional classifying mark. As long as the "ignorance" of "lies" continues, the love affair can flourish. The text provides another model of a non-masculinist male lover, receptive to the opening made by "feminine" "lying." He listens to a different voice, accepts the condition of its possibility and collaborates in the construction of a non dominating erotic love.

However, this experiment provokes brutal reactions. Like in *Le Marin de Gibraltar*, *L'Amante anglaise*, *Le Ravissement de Lol V. Stein* and *Le Camion*, a woman's transgressions of discursive-behavioral codes gets translated within those codes as madness, in a move which classifies and suppresses that which, by not conforming, menaces the structured order. It is a typically patriarchal figure who makes that gesture. A doctor old enough to be the woman's father and who is about to marry her, interrupts the unruly discursive love affair. Standing in for the Lacanian "name of the father" (le nom du père), he says the "no of the father," (le non du père). In the symbolic system of bourgeois rationalism, the doctor and his word represent disinterested, authoritative truth.[72] Invoking the authority – and power – of medical discourse described by Foucault,[73] he pronounces the woman insane and interdicts the love affair:

> She tells him [the lover] that she is getting sicker and sicker.
> And has to die.
> Announces her marriage.
> Her husband is the surgeon who has been treating her for ten years. Does he remember? The one who has always known her, who saw her birth? Who has always treated her, protected her?
>
> Shortly thereafter someone calls him. A man. He says he is the future husband.
> He demands that their relations cease.
> He confirms the imminent death.
>
> He pronounces for the first time the word madness.
> For the first time the word is pronounced: madness.
> [a blank space follows] (Nav, pp. 88–89)

Only superficially paradoxical, Duras' choice of a surgeon to treat a woman ill with leukemia elicits suggestive questions: What is it that this ever watchful "father" is "protecting?" Given that surgeons cut, what is being excised here? This one cuts in on the telephone conversations to cut them off, to admonish the male lover to "cut it out," an operation the surgeon will perform symbolically on the woman by cutting her off from discourse and sexuality. As often happens with physical excision, the removal of the organ of female speech-sexuality by agents of order results in the silencing-death of the victim. This interpretation issues from Duras' favored technique of juxtaposition. The proximity of "future husband" to "demands that their relations cease" and to "imminent death" produces a relation which, in the characteristically Durassian absence of conjunctions, the reader constructs. The marriage hinges on "the imminent death" of free love-free discourse, of the woman.

She demonstrates her own understanding of this process through her linkage of death with marriage, expressed as the impending imperative in "has to die. Announces her marriage." By declaring the woman mad (another seeming inconsistency since a surgeon, not a psychiatrist, passes this judgment), the surgeon severs her from accepted rational discourse and cuts off the possibility of audience and appeal. Duras stresses the gravity of this fiat by repeating it in a way which evokes the finality of judicial sentencing. Thus the text shows the repercussions a powerless woman may suffer when her "lies" give the lie to the "law of the fathers": castration and murder, symbolic and/or concrete, of the woman, and, consequently, of any non-dominating relation between the sexes.

Whereas the imposition of silence entails a certain death, the opposite saves women's lives, as in *Suzannah Andler* and *Véra Baxter*. A present lover's listening in the former text and a potential lover's listening in the latter dissuade the respective heroines from suicide by re-opening vital discursive space, which they fill with prevarication. Fibbing being the women's salient personality trait, the texts themselves become tissues of lies. A "stage direction" in *Véra Baxter*, specifies: "The essential factor of the story has just been evoked: lying" (p. 15).

Pushed into an affair with another man whom their chronically unfaithful husband has bribed for that purpose, Suzannah and Véra fabricate blatantly false stories about everything in their lives. Disconcerted, the new man nevertheless listens. When Michel Cayre realizes, for example, that Suzannah has lied gratuitously about her whereabouts during the day, he becomes frightened.[74] Yet he continues listening until he hears what she is trying to communicate, and envisages spending "a summer with you in lying and in truth" (Suz, 70). In *Véra Baxter*, the Stranger replaces Michel Cayre. Informed by the latter of Véra's habitual lying, the Stranger at first tries to get her to tell the "truth": "I am only passing through your life . . . so if a . . . (hesitation) truth were said here tonight, it would not become anything . . . it would have no consequences" (Ver, p. 79). However, he quickly drops this approach, and listens and "lies" himself, in consequence of which he begins to fall in love with her. Thus these two texts further exemplify the correlation between listening and love.

Articulated in other discursive patterns, the women's prevarication does not constitute deception. To the contrary, Suzannah and Véra are women "stricken with fidelity" (Ver, p. 114), upper middle class housewives whose husbands do the deceiving. They do not lie in order to conceal adultery, a breach in the bourgeois sexual order which subterfuge merely perpetuates. Feminine transgression is certainly involved, but in a much more subversive mode. The women's lying is a strategy that exposes and sabotages the discursive structures of dominant ideology. In order to succeed, the lies must be perceived *qua* lies. Suzanna and Véra achieve this through the overabundance, seeming gratuitousness and obvious inconsistencies of their lies, tactics which first attract the intrigued listener's attention, then direct it away from the lies' content, towards their function. Being heard permits the women to rearrange language so that it conveys the muteness and isolation in which their situation of economic, psychological and discursive dependence within a masculinist structure had trapped them, and which had driven them to the brink of suicide.

Finally, *Véra Baxter* affords an example of two women lying to each other, both conscious of the type of "truth" being communicated. Monique Combes, a former lover of Véra's husband, "listens intensely" (Ver, p. 46) to Véra during their long conversation punctuated by silences indicative of the women's mutual understanding: "Monique Combes (painful smile). 'We lie a lot, you and I.' Véra Baxter. 'A lot, yes.' They smile at each other, look at each other. Silence." [a blank space then figures this silence] (Ver, p. 47).

NAMING SILENCE AND SPEECH

> "Elle [son histoire familiale] est le lieu au seuil de quoi le silence commence. Ce qui s'y passe c'est justement le silence, ce lent travail pour toute ma vie."
>
> Duras

Verbal sparsity characterizes most of Duras' indicative language. In texts containing relatively few words, a remarkable number of them denote silence, complementing lexically the modes of designation already reviewed. Through abundant use of the verb "se taire," Duras re-presents silence as an active gesture of signification, worthy of notation. "Se taire" translates as "to be silent," "to fall silent," "not to speak." Because English possesses no verbal equivalent, I include the French, to emphasize that the verbal form conveys silence as an act. In *Le Vice-consul*, for example: "People ignore the Vice-Consul and he accepts it. Standing, he is silent [il se taît]" (p. 107). The lady in *Le Camion* lists silence among her activities: "Note that [. . .] it can happen that I say more substantial things [. . .] It also can happen that I am silent [de me taire] for a long time . . . yes . . . To tell the truth, everything happens to me, you know, like to everyone, speaking, being silent. Or sad. Or gay" (Cam, pp. 52–53).

In *Le Vice-consul*, as the "lovers" discuss Morgan's book about the beggar, "Anne-Marie Stretter is silent [se taît]" (p. 180). "Duras" evokes Stretter's silence lexically eight times in the passage, in one-sentence paragraphs set off by blanks, which further foregrounds it as a purposeful strategy.[75] Silence is "named" as a tactical response disruptive of colonial indifference when Rossett imagines Anne-Marie Stretter's first reaction to the poverty of Asia: "She looks at what is before her [. . .] around her they are intimidated, they talk, always too much, too loud, fences in the distance, sentries in kaki uniforms who already guard her as they will all her life, they expect her to cry out her distress, to fall down before their eyes, but no, she is silent [elle se taît] . . . " (V-C, p. 166). Juxtaposed to "too much, too loud," the "fences" and "sentries" underscore the use of language as a separating screen. Stretter's silence both returns the image of this discursive operation and links her to the exploited-repressed. She defies the distancing of words and fences through strategic silence and gazing, which in Duras nearly always effect contact. Naming silence in this passage exposes the manipulation of vision and speech to separate and dominate. Heidegger's "to see is to have at a distance"[76] is replaced with to look/listen silently is to join with.

Duras deploys a variety of negative periphrases to "name" silence, such as "she does not answer," "she says nothing," "she does not seem interested," etc., and the noun "silence" itself occurs continually in her work. A passage in *Le Vice-consul* "indicates" Duras' sense of silence first grammatically, making it the subject of a verb of doing, then by saying what it is not: "Silence forms [se fait] [. . .] it is not the silence that precedes departures, nor the one that comes from people not having anything to say to one another" (p. 195).

In the texts structured like scripts, the function of many of the "stage directions" is to specify silence. In *Véra Baxter* we find: "She does not answer. Silence everywhere. Here and outside. Silence like an event" (Ver, p. 98). As the passage continues, "stage directions" stating Véra's silence alternate with the Stranger's remarks to her. This figures silence's role in what is indeed a dialogue. Blank spaces surrounding most of the notations adds visual impact.

In the traveling salesman scene in *Nathalie Granger*, the repeated allusions to two women's shared silence signify a refusal to listen so radical that it shatters the discourse of capitalist hard sell. After inviting the intruder to sit down (he entered without knocking), the women stare at him without a word. Their immobility physically echoes their muteness: "Silence. No reaction from the women. One would think they don't hear what he is saying" (Nat, p. 52). The same non response, noted regularly by the "stage direction" "silence," meets each pause in the man's mechanically repeated sales pitch, so that his words reverberate in a void which exposes the alienating discourse he has been forced to adopt. Gradually he progresses from surprise to panicked understanding of his own victimization.

The women's silence rejects not the salesman himself, but that imposed discourse. They recognize in this man "at the bottom of the ladder" of capitalist selling another societal other, one "required to degrade himself by imitating the speech of the bosses" in order to survive, unlike workers, who at least "have the right to be silent" (Nat, note pp. 51–52). Another note adds:

With the traveling salesman we are very far from the parental model, from the Man in Charge. It is the opposite. The man in the film, then, is a man other men would reject, but whom the women welcome . . . and in whom, precisely, they destroy his plagiarism of those men who would reject him, their discourse, which is, actually, theoretical in nature, since it is unilateral, even if it describes the merits of a washing machine. (p. 91)

Duras considers this use of silence to decompose dominant discourse an eminently "feminine" strategy, developed in the course of "immemorial oppression."[77] Had Isabelle Granger's husband been present, "[that] kind of essential silence – let us say: corporeal silence" and the scene itself "would not have existed" because "any man, I think, would have become impatient with the salesman, at best, that is if he had not instantly liquidated him as soon as he came into the house. Because a man *would have listened* to the traveling salesman's speech. And a man's gaze *has not yet found* [retrouvé] that submerging function, that burying of discourse in a place where it is nullified, falls silent, is suppressed – that a woman's gaze has" (Nat, note, pp. 89–90).

This "burying" instills "fear" in the salesman (Nat, p. 53) for, unlike the women, he has developed no alternate language or space in which to be. He holds desperately to the alienating social identity conferred by the discourse he parrots, offering business cards and photo I.D.s as proof. Strong in their articulated space and communicative mode, the women deny his reified identity at the same time they deny his discourse. To do this, they combine silent and verbal negation, declaring several times: "You are not a traveling salesman," (Nat, p. 54) which then alternates with the word "no," and silence ("named" in the "stage directions"), until "He begins again; the text comes in detached fragments. The text [the sales pitch], like him, is being destroyed" (Nat, p. 56). Affected by the women's indicated message, he reflects on his exploitation by society (Nat, p. 81), weeps (Nat, pp. 83–84), yet succumbs to fear of the radical dis-possession they exemplify, and flees the too threatening "women's house" (Nat, p. 87).

Just as words focus attention on silence *qua* silence, inversely, a certain silence foregrounds speech *qua* speech. One of Duras' favored devices is to refer to utterance while withholding its content. In *Le Vice-consul*, this is thematized in the allusion itself: "Sometimes certain evenings she [Anne-Marie Stretter] also does it, she speaks. With whom? About what?" (V-C, p. 123). In my discussion of blank spaces I cite a passage in which Charles Rossett calls Anne-Marie

Stretter. Stating the calling ("He calls her" – (V-C, p. 198) but not the words themselves emphasizes the act of speaking.

Instances of this device appear throughout Duras. Given her general verbal restraint, these "blank" announcements of speech present both speech and silence as events. In *Dix heures et demie du soir en été*, not divulging what is said throws into relief both talking and not listening: "Maria takes Judith's hand and speaks to her. Accustomed to this, Judith does not listen" (D-H, p. 18). In *Agatha*, the "stage direction" "silence" reinforces the content of an announced but unuttered scream: "Him (softness): 'Look at me . . . I am screaming . . . ' She: 'I am screaming with you.' Silence" (Ag, p. 19).

This can function similarly for an uttered but undisclosed proper name, as in *Moderato Cantabile*: "Then he gets up, takes a pebble, aims at one of the bay windows, turns around again, and, out loud, pronounces a name" (p. 97) or *Savannah Bay*: "This time he shouts her name. He is afraid, always afraid. He shouts the name of that woman who has definitively become a stranger to anyone other than him" (p. 51). The first example produces temporary anonymity grammatically through substitution of the indefinite article "a" for the possessive adjective "her." Because Anne Desbaresdes is otherwise consistently named in the text, this sudden dis-identification startles the reader into perceiving its purpose. Conversely, in *Savannah Bay*, using the precise possessive adjective "her" in a context of anonymity achieves the same result of focusing attention on the shouting rather than on the name.

Duras' virtuosity in "reinventing the signifying instrument" is especially striking in its technical inventiveness and variation. Even seemingly classical attribution of speech often functions non-traditionally. Its rarity and contrastive co-presence with unmarked sentences ascribed to no individual speaker and with the other techniques just described, endow it with unusual significance. As Noguez notes, Duras favors "theatrical" attribution, with "she/he says" preceding the cited remark, over the more conventionally novelistic "said she/he," which usually follows it.[78] More than identifying the source of utterance, Duras' notations of speech stage the act of speaking as such. In combination with the other aspects of her indicative language, utterance is presented as but one among many kinds of communicative activity. Thus Duras' rearticulated syntax recharges with meaning an otherwise nearly empty literary convention. To cite one particularly rich example, the following passage from *Le Vice-consul* illustrates Duras' decentering of utterance through a multiplicity of devices. In a context of variously signified and signifying silences, speech seems exceptional and is emphasized as such:

> [. . .] They [the "lovers"] remain there, they wait near her [Anne-Marie Stretter], she who has left [she had "departed" into tears] and who will return.
> Michael Richard turns around and calls her softly:
> 'Anne-Marie.'
> She gives a start.
> 'Oh, I sort of fell asleep.'
> She adds:
> 'You were there . . . '
> Michael Richard's face expresses suffering.
> 'Come,' he says.
> She comes towards him as if after a real absence, and places herself in his arms. Ah, you were there. [. . .]
>
> (V-C, p. 196)

The separation of cited words from the mostly prefatory notations of the acts of speaking and gesturing draws attention to all three. The periods and suspension points activate the surrounding blank spaces, pauses which indicate the ambient silence. Inserted after a statement of non-verbal signification ("Michael Richard's face expresses suffering") which would have sufficed to establish attribution for the word "come" (as the preceding "she gives a start" does for "Oh, I sort of fell asleep") the conventionally placed "he says" seems redundant. Yet it draws attention to the speech act summoning Anne-Marie Stretter back from the realm of her silent communion with Calcutta. She "answers" the call with the silent gesture of placing herself in Richard's arms. A repetition of the earlier, voiced, and clearly attributed "you were there," the second, unmarked "Ah, you were there," is impossible to situate. Nothing marks it as uttered or attributes it to anyone.

Just as linguistic communication comprises both speaking and not-speaking, non-verbal communication includes doing and not doing: not moving, not looking, etc., acts of gestural silence. On the one hand, for example, if in *Le Vice-consul* the beggar succeeds at last in giving her starving child away it is because the white woman finally looks at her. Realizing what the beggar wants, the woman turns away. But in a highly charged scene of non-verbal communication, the white woman's child stares at the beggar's baby. When the white woman "hears" the message of her own child's gaze, she accepts her. "She [. . .] looks only at the glance of her child. And yields" (V-C, pp. 56–57). On the other hand, when the Vice-Consul does not look at Anne-Marie Stretter, this is also portrayed as a conspicuous deed: "She passed very close by him and this time he did not look at her. It's striking . . . " (V-C, p. 105).

One repeatedly encounters sentences like the following from *Dix heures et demie du soir en été*: "They do not look at the woods" (D-H, p. 172). As the author explains: "[. . .] usually one sees something being done, or else one sees something being undone. One looks at the full [le plein]. Not the hollow. 'Does not see that people are looking at her,' that, for me, is something that is done as much as 'sees that people are looking at her'."[79]

The female protagonist in *La Maladie de la mort* combines verbal silence and corporeal, non-verbal "speech" to subvert dominant erotic discursive structures.[80] Forbidden to speak, she employs other means of expression, such as sleep, which she transforms into a complex strategy of resistance and subversion. With a rationalist-scientific attitude, the man attempts to disassociate (the female) body from mind in order to constitute the former as an object of knowledge. But this same objectification precludes knowledge, and the man's efforts to "know" the woman's body fail. He talks, looks, manipulates, penetrates at will, but: "You see nothing [. . .] You look at the closed form" (Mal, p. 39) and "You do not know what the sleep of the one in the bed contains" (Mal, p. 16).

What it contains and expresses is a critique. "She mocks [him] still while sleeping" (Mal, p. 51). Her sleep caricaturizes masculinist fantasies of reducing women to mute bodies, exposes the mind-body dichotomy which relegates women to the physical by denying them (access to) discourse, and proves that very binarism invalid. As physis the woman communicates constantly, her very body "talking" in her sleep. Her mind can not be separated from her body, and it is her body which expresses this: "You look again. The face is abandoned to sleep, it is mute, it is sleeping [. . .] But always the mind emerges at the body's surface, running over all of it, so that each of this body's parts bears witness by itself to the whole [. . .]" (Mal, pp. 26–27). The sleeping body reaches out to communicate:

"You see [. . .] the eyelids tremble as though the eyes wanted to see; and then the mouth opens as if the mouth wanted to talk [. . .]" (Mal, p. 39).

In another reversal, the sleep which parodies the desired death of woman affords the woman respite from that very death: "She goes back to sleep. You ask her why she sleeps, from what monumental fatigue she needs to rest. [. . .] She says that in that way she also rests from you, from death" (Mal, p. 51). The very prison to which he consigns her excludes him: "She is sleeping, naked, in her place in the bed. You do not understand how it is possible that she is unaware of your tears, that she is protected from you by herself [. . .]" (Mal, p. 28). Convinced by this demonstration of the ineffectiveness of repression, the man envisages a more final "solution": "You say to yourself that she should die. You say to yourself that if now, at this hour of the night she died, it would be easier [. . .]" – Mal, p. 30).

When awake, the woman also deploys non-verbal tactics, usually some combination of smiles, laughter, looking, not listening, and the silence of refusing to speak. Each manifestation of her subjectivity threatens an edifice constructed on its absence: "You discover that she is looking at you. You scream" (Mal, p. 25). (He can not bear her gaze because he conceptualizes seeing as objectification and possession. This contrasts to the mutual seeing between subjects in *Aurélia Steiner* and *Hiroshima mon amour*[81]). The woman's refusal to utter the man's name constitutes a rejection of his entire "language" and simultaneously confirms her subjectivity: "you tell her to pronounce a word [. . .] the one that says your name, you tell her that word, that name. She does not answer, so you scream again. And that is when she smiles. And that is when you know she is alive. [blank space] The smile disappears. She has not said the name" (Mal, p. 26). When the man does enjoin the woman to talk, she either declines, or deconstructs his speech, as I show in Chapter Three. Rather than second his naming, she names his malady, and explicitly refuses a system of naming founded on the exclusion of otherness.

5

Legends

"Le récit rituel ou épique est le plus souvent une forme d'expression masculine [. . .]
De même, bien sûr, dans les différentes religions."

Marina Yaguello

"[. . .] malgré la tentation, je ne raconterai pas les histoires les plus tragiquement tragiques, qui sont celles des personnes qui n'ont jamais eu la chance de transformer leur fatalité en légende."

Hélène Cixous

INTRODUCTION

Through techniques which give "primacy to the thing stated the least over stated things"[1] Duras makes us hear silences and words rearticulated in relationship to them. Decentered, dis-placed, re-placed in other configurations, words themselves resonate differently. Dominique Noguez writes that Duras uses words with "full awareness of their value. [. . .] transfigures them, or, rather, gives them their true timber, their entire plenitude, their glory/halo ['gloire']."[2]

The special aura of Duras' prose has been noticed by numerous critics, but rarely analyzed. Ceremonial in tone, it creates an atmosphere of ritual and legend. In recent decades, women have made conspicuous efforts to articulate our stories, histories and legends. While mediations such as race, class and ethnic origin remain irreducible, the specificities of the feminine condition in all its variations and complexities have prompted the elaboration of gender-specific literary traditions (or at the least gender specific considerations). Defying the "fatality" of oblivion referred to by

177

Cixous in the above epigraph, women are "transforming it into legend," telling tales of silence, and (re)claiming languages.

Transforming the private into the public, when Duras makes fiction from her own life or from other stories, she treats her material in such a way as to ritualize the particular while generalizing it. Duras' texts skip the simply fictional as they skirt the strictly autobiographical, and move directly into the legendary. How Duras makes legends, how she ritualizes, "glorifies" words merits analysis.

NARRATIVE STRUCTURE, THE PERFORMATIVE

Duras' narrative configurations effect a framing conducive to mythologizing. The narrative "ignorance" described in Part I combines with an attitude of reverent fascination for the stories being told. Over and over speakers retell or re-invent multiple reconstructions of inaccessible, absent stories. Repetition, distance, unverifiability characterize the textual matter of legends, while reverence and/or fascination characterize their telling.

In Duras, for whom the binary opposition oral/written has little pertinence, (re)telling is close to (re)writing and to (re)reading. Her narrators are "writers," potential writers, or "reading" speakers. I use the term "reading" in a broad sense, which includes imagining something perhaps unwritten, but which is nevertheless designated as a text (*India Song, Savannah Bay*, etc.). These narrative structures activate in various modalities the etymological meanings of the word "legend": *legere*, in Latin: to gather, select, read.[3]

Webster's Dictionary proceeds with the definition of the word legend: "1. (a) a story coming down from the past; especially one popularly regarded as historical although not verifiable. (b) a body of such stories. (c) a popular myth of recent origin." and: "Popular: of the people, syn.: common."[4] Duras' legends pair the dialectic of the particular and the general with that of the extraordinary and the common. They impart at the same time the uniqueness and the banality for example, of a love affair, which, when it ends, is "what happens every day [and is] at once of no importance and so terrible" (*Savannah Bay*, p. 87). What Duras writes about the Lady in *Le Camion* applies to all her protagonists and stories: "She has that nobility of banality. She is invisible" (Cam, p. 65).

Agents of intertextuality, "ignorance" and "invisibility" also produce communicability. The stories projected and heard often "repeat" themselves by (re)producing love in the fascinated speakers and listeners. "Ignorance," awe and the inherent intertextuality of love deprivatize, transform anecdotes into legends and create a sacralized commonality-communality. Duras identifies this as the *sine que non* of her creative process: "[. . .] each narrative contains what I call its complementarity, that is the openness of the destruction of its singularity. I have a story, I want to destroy it in as much as it is singular. This said, as long as I have not found the complementarity [here of the film script *Véra Baxter*] I won't show it."[5]

Duras frequently establishes the legendary status of her texts through the verbal fiat of performative discourse and/or through "stage directions" specifying the tone and style of narrative delivery. In the introductory remarks to *India Song*, speech-acts prescribe awe to the reader and the internal speakers, both of whom will "rediscover" with "fear" and "emotion" "the story of *India Song*, past, *legendary*, THAT MODEL" (Ind, p. 12). A "stage direction" later announces: "With a culminating softness, the intertwined voices are going to sing the legend of Anne-Marie Stretter. A very slow narrative, a recitative [. . .]" (Ind, p. 40).

Musical metaphors also remove the spoken quotidian into the quasi-sacralized in *Hiroshima mon amour*. After affirming the inadequacy of ordinary speech to render political (or passionate) cataclysms, Duras proclaims about the lovers: "Their first exchange [propos] will therefore be allegorical. *It will be, in sum, operatic [un propos d'opéra]*" (Hir, p. 2). "Stage directions" further assert the solemnity of their dialogue: "A man's voice, flat and calm, recitative [. . .] A woman's voice, very veiled, equally FLAT, a voice of *recitative reading*, without punctuation [. . .]" (Hir, p. 16). One of the readers performs the speech-act in *Le Navire Night*, calling the story "that legend of the only heiress [. . .]" (Nav, p. 45). In *Savannah Bay* "Duras" does it in "stage directions": "Silence. Then Madeleine, relayed by the Young Woman, talks about the legend" (Sav, p. 32) – and, concerning the narrative play the two women engage in : "It is a customary ritual of theirs [. . .]" (Sav, p. 30). In *La Douleur*, the performative becomes an imperative when the author admonishes her readers: "Learn to read: these are sacred texts."[6] *Aurélia*-Paris features a little girl imagining that her mother, murdered by the Nazis, was a legendary "Queen of the Jews" (Aur, p. 185). When we go from the written texts to films and plays actually produced, these "stage directions" and speech-acts are enacted, that-is, the performative is replaced by performance. The reading speakers in *Agatha, Césarée*, the *Aurélia Steiners, Le Camion, Son Nom de Venise dans Calcutta désert, L'Homme atlantique, India Song*, etc, adopt the slow, flat, reverent tones prescribed in the texts. They function like officiants, celebrating the ceremony at hand.

The musicality of Duras' prose, specific features of which I discuss shortly, harks back to ancient oral traditions, both of the transmission of legends, which were often sung, and to the ritual aspects of early theater, Greek or Chirstian. Yet the sacred in Duras is not the divine, God being posited as always already dead. The sacred is human, especially the event of human love, rearticulated in its sublime banality by a woman writer. The absence of God, especially God the Father, informs her work. Its center is the blank space freed by that absence, presented as a space of human creativity, and as an opening for women's creative expression. With this in mind, one can appreciate in the following remarks from *La Vie matérielle* the connections Duras makes between the way her actors read her texts, the style of narrative performance in religious ceremonies, or in Racine's tragedies, or music, and the very recent admission of women playwrights and directors into the sanctified bastions of French theater.

An actor who reads a book aloud, as it would be done with *Les Yeux bleus cheveux noirs*, with nothing else to do [. . .] but maintain immobility, nothing else but carry the text out of the book through voice alone, without gesticulating to foster belief in the drama of the body suffering because of the words said, whereas the entire drama is in the words and the body doesn't move. I know no theatrical speech [parole] equal in power to that of officiants of any kind of mass. Around the pope, one speaks and one sings a strange language, completely pronounced, with no tonic accent, with no accent at all, flat, [. . .]

In recitatives of the Passion [. . .], in certain works by Stravinsky, [. . .] we find these sound fields [champs sonores] created as though each time for the first time, pronounced down to the resonance of the word, the sound it has, never heard in everyday life. [. . .] Bérénice and Titus are soloists [récitants]. The director is Racine, the public is humanity [. . .]

Since 1900 no play by a woman was staged at La Comédie

Française, or at Vilar's TNP [Théâtre National de Paris] or at the Odéon or at Villeurbanne or at the Schaubuhne or Strehler's Picolo Teatro, not one woman author, not one woman director. And then the Barraults began staging Sarraute and me.[7]

GRAMMATICAL MANIPULATION

Duras' manipulation of grammatical elements contributes to the legendary in her style. For instance, the replacement of the expected possessive adjective with a definite article to refer to "the" lover (*L'Amant*), "the" mother (*L'Amant, Un Barrage contre le Pacifique*), "the" mother, "the" son (*Des Journées entières dans les arbres*) constitutes another means of taking the text "outside." Shifting the personal possessive into the general, it makes public property of Duras' private mythology.[8] Regarding *L'Amant*, the author affirms: "I took hold of everything and put it into orbit. That is to say, I put everything about me into external gear, completely avoiding a particular fate for any element, both in the treatment and in the expression of things. [. . .] When I speak of my lover I do not say that I see *his* face again, I say I see *the* face again, and that I remember the name. That takes it outside. To you. I give it to you."[9]

Photographs would have restored the possessive adjective pictorially, because they would have been received as pictures of "her" lover, "her" mother, etc. The definite article has the further effect of imparting uniqueness at the same time it dis-possesses. Although shared with every reader, *the* lover, *the* mother function as models, almost archetypes. Dis-possessed, de-singularized, the definite, becomes definitive yet open to all. Grammatically as well, then, the dialectic between the particular and the general, the banal and the extraordinary, the sacredness of the profane, as it were, comes into play.

Similar results are achieved through alternation between the first person and the third, a distinctive feature of Duras' (primarily) first person narratives. Intensifying the distance between the narrating "I" and the "I" in the story, this creates another dis-possession. The use of "I" and "she" to refer to the same "person" foregrounds the I's internal "otherness," and illustrates grammatically 'Rimbaud's famous "I is an other." It is also absent, something the third person posits automatically. Having undermined the self-possession of identity and autobiography, the female narrating "I"s spin legends

of love and writing.[10] The switch to the third person enables the
speaker to propel the story into the legendary – legends requiring
otherness, distance, absence, i.e. the third person. But the shift
is never stable. Consequently, the continued oscillation between
third person and first maintains the public-private, general-singular
dialectic so peculiar to Duras' sacralization or mythification of the
common.

The treatment of the character of the mother in *L'Amant* combines
this technique with the use of the definite article. "My" mother alternates with "the" mother. This further deconstructs autobiography
by calling attention to the fictional components in writing from
memory. "My" mother is "the" mother "I" remember, forget and
invent. "My" and "the" convey the proximity and distance of a
figure unique in everyone's life and therefore particularly apt for
mythification. Moreover, as I show in Part I, the text makes explicit
the connections between forgetting and fiction. The mother is a
tragic-heroic, passionately painted figure no longer remembered
(Am, p. 38), a "mystery" behind a "closed door" (Am, p. 35) which
fiction opens directly into legend.

ONOMASTICS AND THE LEGENDARY

Lévi-Strauss and Derrida demonstrate the classificatory function
regulating onomastic systems in social organization and the principles of property and propriety underlying the "proper" in proper
names. The relation literature entertains with prevailing onomastic
codes permits play, as Eugène Nicole shows. Therefore, writers have
a margin of freedom to manipulate the three areas in which names
and the vocative operate: identification, predication (meaning), and
revelation of social structures.[11] In a brief paragraph devoted to the
subject, Noguez observes that "the act of naming in Duras [. . .]
is never automatic [ne va jamais de soi]."[12] Effecting distance
through forms of reference which place the person "out of reach,"
and treating the proper name as though it were "taboo," Duras'
onomastic practice "[. . .] takes the named person into the luminous
domain of a sort of lay sacredness, the domain of epic poetry, or of
great human legends."[13]

However, Noguez neglects the other side of the dialectic: the
commonness of the legendary which, paradoxically, seems to
annul the distance created by the sacralization. In Duras, naming

also "destroys the singularity" of her protagonists, framing them so that they become legendary yet at the same time "banal," offered like "the" lover to every reader. Duras' manipulation of appellatives does not simply create taboo, out of reach figures; it renders her characters simultaneously legendary and available in the very laicity of their sacredness. In Duras, not naming as well as naming takes characters "outside," mainly through techniques I call erasure and overuse.

Erasure

Many of Duras' texts contain innominate characters. In addition to its pertinence in the areas of narrative "ignorance" and the rejection of dominant representation, anonymity enhances the legendary. It acts in concert with substitution of the definite article for the possessive adjective, for example in the case of "the" mother in *L'Amant*. The same text refers to "the" lover, not with the form of the title, which appears only once (Am, p. 72) but, most often, with the third person "he," relayed occasionally by the periphrases "the man from Cholen," "the lover from Cholen." Yet beyond its immediate contextual positions, "he" refers each time to the antecedent posed as such in the antonomasia of the title, which "names" this symbol of a woman's desire through its essential quality: loving. In both senses of the term, the title names him definitively yet anonymously, setting up a referent already magnified.

The text situates him geographically, historically, economically, racially and physically, but in the tension between the individual and the general, what identifies him is less these particulars than what he symbolizes, as with legendary figures generally: "He tells me I would remember this afternoon all my life, even when I would have forgotten even *his* face, *his* name. I ask if I would remember the house. [. . .] I say that it is like everywhere. He tells me that's right, yes, like always. [blank space] I still see *the* face, and I remember *the* name" (Am, p. 56 – emphasis added). This passage illustrates the leap from the personal to the general. At the very moment the narrator claims she remembers the lover's name, she erases it by not saying it, and generalizes it through the definite article replacing both the name and the possessive adjective. The description of the house asserts the ordinariness of the extraordinary lovemaking, sacred and common, like everywhere else, for every other passionate couple.

"I still know his name," declares Anna about her eponymous lover in *Le Marin de Gibraltar*, another text whose title is an antonomasia figuring a woman's image of an absolute lover. Onomastic "ignorance" combines with absence, the woman's narrative attitude (she tells the stories about the lover) and her acts, to transform the nameless man into legend. Her search for someone under-identified, absent and perpetually sought, becomes a quest not for a love but for LOVE. "I wanted to live the greatest love on earth," she explains (Mar, p. 160), in conformity with one of Western culture's central myths.

But Anna's love is neither exclusive nor ascetic. A series of temporary substitutes people her quest. The very arbitrariness of the antonomasia naming the nebulous yet absolute figure opens the possibility of this succession. Anna shows the narrator how it was constructed: "He was, [. . .] if you like, a sailor. He was in a small rowboat off Gibraltar when we saw him from the yacht" (Mar, pp. 140–141). The appellative, then, refers to someone probably neither a sailor nor from Gibraltar. ("No one knew where he was from" – Mar, p. 228). The act of telling fictionalizes and expands, transmuting the man into a myth: "[He is] someone one recounts [quelqu'un qu'on raconte] as best one can [. . .] Certain days I wonder if I haven't completely invented him, invented someone based on him" (Mar, p. 167).

Further, slippage between the singular and the plural introduces the particular-general dialectic. *The* sailor becomes sailors: the narrator remarks that he worked for years at a boring job: "not knowing [. . .] that there existed [. . .] women like her who were devoting their lives to looking for sailors from Gibraltar" (Mar, p. 178). Anna herself undergoes onomastic erasure in a synopsis[14] which pluralizes her: "'I had never before met any women of sailors from Gibraltar [femmes de marins de Gibraltar],' I said" (Mar, p. 152). This invites repetition and multiplicity without diminishing the specialness or the specificity either of the legend or of the quest at hand. Moreover, it imparts legendary status to Anna from the narrtor's point of view.

Anna grasps the "meaning" of the past and present love affairs: "since this meeting happened I believe it possible to meet him again, to meet anyone, any time" (Mar, pp. 218). And she does. She meets both him again and "anyone" – the string of substitutes. Yet the uniqueness does not diminish. Private and public interact on the plane of the legendary: "Sometimes I get the impression there are ten stories of the sailor from Gibraltar," complains the narrator to a crew member, who responds: "It's possible, but there is only one sailor from Gibraltar" (Mar, pp. 320–321). Still, like the "original," substitutes need neither be sailors nor come from Gibraltar. The basic requirement is willingness to detach oneself from the bonds of conventional identity before one can join the Siren on the legend making ship. In this respect, the narrator is an excellent "anyone." The subject of the first part of the novel is his repudiation of social identity. Seduced by the Siren's beauty, wealth, and the liberating message of her "song," he leaves a woman he doesn't love, his country and his job at the State Registry, that centralizing French locus of recorded social identity, where he had spent eight years copying *names* from birth and death certificates in the Department of Colonial Affairs. Designated exclusively through the shifters "I" and "you," newly anonymous, he becomes part of the legend extended into the present.

Male anonymity in an exemplary love story told by a named woman coordinates with substitution to foster the legendary in other texts. In *Agatha*, a prototypical love affair's non-occurrence forms the motivating force. The incest taboo having prevented consummation, Agatha replaces her present, unnamed brother, with an innominate, absent lover. The new, enacted love revivifies the impossible legendary one, as Agatha tells her brother: "I knew nothing about loving any more since our separation. (pause). He gives me back to you" (Ag, p. 42).

In *Aurélia*-Vancouver, multiplicity makes legend of an "original" already fictional. Again, the legend's communicability and the play between the particular and the general hinge on the male lover's anonymity. The woman writer-narrator invents an absolute male lover, but as a missing figure. A nameless, imaginary, original father's original absence frees the daughter to imagine her legendary archetype and pluralize an encounter which never occurred . The unique and the many coalesce. Aurélia creates the original from multiple, nameless substitutes: "I assemble them through you and out of their number I make you. You are that which will not take place and which, as such, is experienced. From them all, you emerge always unique, inexhaustible place in the world, unalterable love" (Aur, p. 157).

Multiplicity signifies the free exercise of a woman's imagination and sexuality in the absence of a restrictive paternal function.[15] The nameless father becomes the shifter "you," addressed in the past and the present. The plural dialogues with a new singular, a multiple uniqueness mobile enough to shift to each new lover, so that Aurélia can say: "Today you are a sailor with black hair" (Aur, p. 154). Not unlike Anna in *Le Marin de Gibraltar*, Aurélia produces successive incarnations of lovers who in their anonymity say yes to a woman's desire and self-identification.

Duras assigns anonymity more consistently to male than to female characters, partly to deconstruct the imposition of male names (the patronymic) and male-defined categories on women. Women are already without identity, having been prevented from naming themselves. In their love-legends, her female characters imagine male figures outside the confines of dominant naming.

Several texts feature couples in which both partners are nameless. In *Le Navire night*, *Savannah Bay* and *Hiroshima mon amour* this double onomastic erasure constitutes the focal point of a thematization of identity. Divestment of social identity is posited as the precondition of love and textuality transposed into the legendary. During her visits to Madeleine in *Savannah Bay*, the Young Woman learns how dis-possession converts the tale of passionate love into legend. The unnamed lovers figure love's absolute uniqueness and its generality. Seemingly laying claim to radical belonging, the man "shouts the name of the woman who has definitively become a stranger to anyone other than him" (Sav, p. 51). Yet by leaving both names blank, the speakers de-particularize the couple. It joins the ranks of Duras' prototypes: sacredly common, hypo-identified legendary figures, models which lend themselves to variation in repeatability. In *Savannah Bay*, this is effected on the narrative level. The single, dead couple is resuscitated and pluralized during the ceremonial meetings between Madeleine and the Young Woman, ritual re-presentations of diverse versions of the anonymous, absent, mythical passion.

Banality, passion, substitution revolve around two-tiered ano-nymity in *Hiroshima mon amour*. The French woman never names her "original," German lover, and she and her present, Japanese lover are equally innominate. This permits the two love stories to merge at an intersection with ever-repeatable, ever absolute, legendary love. When the woman recalls Nevers, what she remembers is prototypical: "[she] will remember *Nevers* [. . .], therefore love itself" (Hir, p. 8), which she "recognizes" in the stranger with whom it suddenly reappears.: "I meet you. I remember you. [. . .] Who are you?" (Hir, p. 94). In the fashion of Proust's madeleine, the renewed sensation kindles remembrance, but here the function of memory's narrative is to foster forgetting. When the Japanese man lends his "I" to the "he" of the dead German and the French woman blends both into "you," this facilitates the passage from the past antecedent to the present one. Far from being symptomatic of a loss of subjectivity, this activates a dialectical subjectivity cognizant at once of its own mobility, transience, substitutability and of its supreme individuation in love. "Me, yes. You will have seen me," says the Japanese man (Hir, p. 28 – as does Aurélia Steiner). His listening has the reciprocal effect. The French woman's "Deform me in your image so that no other after you will ever understand the wherefore of so much desire" (Hir, p 94) is the same call for unique specificity as the man's in *Savannah Bay*, articulated within the accepted contradiction of passion's passage and banality. She knows that "like for him [the German], forgetting [. . .] will triumph over you completely [. . .] you will become a song" (Hir, p. 97). Anonymous and banal, love songs celebrate intense particularity with each incantation.

Inherently mobile, these extraordinary, unique passions are, in their anonymity, like *Hiroshima mon amour* "a banal story, a story that happens every day, millions of times" (Hir, p. 3). The French actress's particularity, even her nationality, dissolve symbolically the moment she puts on her Red Cross nurse's costume and becomes "the eternal nurse in an eternal war" (Hir, p. 5). As for the Japanese man, "he is like everyone, like all men, exactly" (Hir, p. 5). However, on the brink of parting, the lovers do name each other: "She: 'Hi-ro-shi-ma.' That is your name.' They look at each other without seeing each other. For always. He: 'That is my name. Yes. [. . .] *Your* name is Nevers. Ne-vers-in France'" (Hir, pp. 102–103). The use of toponyms to "name" nameless lovers is a recurrent trope in Duras. They usually form part of an antonomasia which is also a synopsis: "the man from Cholen" in *L'Amant*, "the policeman from Cahors" in *L'Amante anglaise*, "the sailor from Gibraltar" in the text of that name. In *Aurélia*-Vancouver, an anonymous place serves as onomastic identification for the unnamed, ever re-imaginable lover: "you emerge always unique, inexhaustible place in the world" (Aur, p. 157). As the last example implies, Duras' toponyms do not simply anchor her love stories geographically. Although they do situate the proceedings, often historically as well, like her personal pronouns they also impart the mobile status of shifters. On the one hand, as "Duras" remarks in *Hiroshima mon amour*, "people meet each other everywhere in the world" (Hir, p. 1). On the other, everything is unique in time, place, person. Through "place names, names that aren't names" (Hir, p. 9), Duras removes her protagonists from the subjectivity subject to the dominant social order, which the toponyms re-place with a dynamic subjectivity, participatory of the particular and the general as just described. The patriarchal classificatory onomastic system yields to a more open identification. One is named more accurately by what has marked one most, which can be remembered, forgotten, repeated, an open city evocative of generalizable, mythical absolutes.

At times class more than love replaces names. For example, although *Le Square* hints at potential feeling between the maid and the traveling salesman, its central story is more a tale of class oppression: "*Le Square* – it is the theory of needs."[16] Here anonymity displaces the particular-general dialectic onto a class model, which presents the protagonists as social categories. Hypo-identification signifies not liberation from social identity, but submersion of the personal into socio-economic strata. The "legend" told is one of exploitation and alienation,[17] which pairs with physical deindividuation as well. The characters are nondescript: "Her: A young girl of twenty, about whom nothing attracts attention. [. . .] Him: A man of forty, about whom nothing attracts attention."[18]

L'Homme assis dans le couloir and *La Maladie de la mort* show that in dominant erotic narratives, gender is the determining factor in a namelessness which has disparate effects on the man and the woman. Imposed on the latter, it inflicts reification and repression, as was seen in Chapter 3. These texts illustrate how this conditions standard erotic "legends," and how their "fatality" is fatal to women.

In *Le Vice-consul*, the word "lepers" symbolizes India's hordes, anonymous and undifferentiated in the "legends" of white colonialism. The word connotes exclusion and the decay of discreteness, which the text renders morphologically. The plural "lepers" usually appears in sentences evoking amalgamation into a nameless, numberless mass as perceived by the "on" of white society: "The lepers, one has difficulty distinguishing them from the rest" (V-C, p. 95) and: "the lepers and the dogs, mixed together" (V-C, p. 164). When "leprosy" replaces the expected "lepers," this substitution of the disease for the people conveys their dehumanization: "Dust on leprosy" (V-C, p. 147) and "the heaped up leprosy separates, moves, spreads out" (V-C, p. 166).

Singled out on so many textual levels with relation to this group, the beggar occupies the position of the particular in this particular-general dynamic. But because this particular remains unnamed in her very textual ubiquity, she also "indicates" the general, to the point of symbolizing it. "She" becomes one of a series of referentially equivalent anotonomasias: "the lepers," "leprosy," "the insane," "Calcutta."[19] For example: "Under the street lamp, scratching her bald head, she, Calcutta's skinniness, during this plentiful night, she is seated among the insane" (V-C, p. 149).

Considered separately, the beggar forms another particular general, this one gender-specific. After inventing her personal history, Peter Morgan imagines her meeting thousands of young girls like herself (V-C, p. 14), banished and refused work for becoming pregnant out of wedlock. (People won't hire them for fear they will give birth on their land, creating another mouth to feed – V-C, p. 52.) In a closed society, this type of identity loss leads directly to marginalization, poverty and madness. In addition, then, to symbolizing Calcutta's indigent masses of both genders, the beggar figures the usually unsung legend of a peculiarly female oppression.

Overuse

"She always says the given names: Marcel Proust. Pierre Corneille. Léon Trotsky. Karl Marx . . . An obsession" (*Le Camion*, p. 47). This comment about the lady hitchhiker playfully highlights an important feature of Duras' onomastic practice. Her manipulation of full names nearly always exceeds purposes of identification. Traditional novels usually drop one name in order to impart a sense of familiarity with the character. In Duras, the continual coupling of given name and patronymic – "overuse" – inhibits this by maintaining the form usually reserved for celebrities or people one knows slightly or not at all. Still, because it names characters the reader does get to "know," this procedure produces familiarity within the formal register of the "lay sacred." Its effects often combine the legendary, the social and the symbolic.

In *Dix heures et demie du soir en été*, overuse ritualizes Rodrigo Paestra. Together with the fascinated attitude of Maria, who utters his name more than anyone else, the text's onomastic treatment makes of him, more than a specific individual situated in place and time, "the" perpetrator of "the" crime of passion, unique yet always the same. Within a context of onomastic under-specification (the other protagonists have given names only), the full name over-identifies and de-individualizes, as Maria's question implies: "Who would we save, finally, if we saved Rodrigo Paestra?" (D-H, p. 121). Overuse and underuse produce similar results.This works much the same way in *Moderato Cantabile*. The uniform use of the full name, Anne Desbaresdes, for a protagonist present in every scene, activates a dialectic between proximity and distance. Again, relative over-specification (she alone is designated by a full name) singularizes only to de-singularize on another plane. This prepares the interchangeability between the named protagonist and the anonymous murder victim. The overnamed correlates to the undernamed, becoming one of its possible substitutes in a ceremony which ritually re-enacts the irreducible yet eminently repeatable crime treated by the "narrating" officiants as a legend or sacred rite. All this is also a metaphor for Duras' conception of intertextuality.

The "lay" side of Duras' "sacred" naming has social significations illustrative of ways in which gender functions onomastically in the construction of the legendary. Although "overuse" renders a bored bourgeois housewife's banality extraordinary, it also figures a social trap from which she does not extricate herself. "Anne Desbaresdes" names *the* bourgeois housewife, locked in economic dependency, in roles, ceremonies (the dinner party) and in her husband's patronymic. When Anne Desbaresdes speaks, it is from that social position, and the only fiction she (re)creates is a death ritual. Un-naming herself entails a suicidal identification with an anonymous, murdered woman. The fatality she turns into legend becomes a legend of fatality: she replicates the masochistic, deadening role of the nameless woman in "the" erotic scenario of *L'Homme assis dans couloir*.

Symbolically, Anne Desbaresdes dies twice, in the two, complementary spheres of female social interchangeability: the erotic and the domestic. Before Chauvin "murders" her in the erotic realm, she had already "died" in her role as bourgeois housewife, as had her predecessors in her house. Chauvin remarks; "Many women already lived in that same house, and heard the shrubbery at night, instead of their hearts. [. . .] They all died in their bedroom, behind that hedge [. . .]" (M-C, p. 58). Like the other dead women in *L'Homme assis dans le couloir*, this collectivity inserts historical contextualization and continuity. Leslie Hill's incisive analysis of *Moderato Cantbile* adumbrates a Durassian sense of the apocalypse. He concludes that sexed difference in Duras is an "empty and inhospitable space of division."[20] Trista Selous claims that the text critiques the bourgeois order "in the name of a refusal of ritual or order and a 'return' to a 'natural' world of death and unutterable desire."[21] Yet these readings see advocacy where I see denunciation. Far from glorifying the working-man's "free-flowing sexuality," as Selous maintains,[22] Duras both reverses the classism of that idea (Chauvin "sublimates" into words as much as Anne does), and exposes the male chauvinism in Chauvin's eagerness to "murder" his former boss's coveted possession. Further, exclusive use of the patronymic for him parodies that convention's onomastic connotation of "virility."

Women's fictions in Duras flourish in direct proportion to the extent to which her female characters name or un-name themselves in contexts which free them. In Chapter 2, I discuss how the *Aurélia Steiners* thematize the ways in which a woman's self-naming opens space for the creation of legends of love. In addition to women's creativity, the name Aurélia Steiner signifies Jewishness, which in Duras always evokes the Holocaust (explicitly in these texts), and symbolizes the oppressed ethnic Other, connected in otherness to socially constructed femininity. In the *Aurélia Steiners*, the symbolism and de-singularization produced by overuse contributes to a legend in the making. Loved in her female difference, Aurélia Steiner is also loved in her Jewishness, and both function in the specifically Durassian tension between the particular and the general. Just before making love with the anonymous sailor, the protagonist announces that she is going to give him "a" name, avoiding the possessive adjective "her," as does the "writer," who then informs the reader, "I tell him the name" (Aur, p. 162). This creates enough distance and "ignorance" to disturb traditional identity. Further, writing the name on a piece of paper, which she hands the sailor to read, implicitly places the individual in the fictional or legendary register.

After reading the name, the sailor applies it to the woman before him, whom he thereby discovers: " . . . he comes close to me and looks at me and speaks to me with the name. Carefully, he takes off my dress. [. . .] He begins to discover the body of Aurélia Steiner" (Aur, p. 162). However, this seeming onomastic congruence quickly slips. Repeating the name incessantly as he makes love causes the sailor to "lose the memory of names" (Aur, p. 163). As he continues to pronounce it, he generalizes it to the word "Jew": "He says Juden,

Juden Aurélia, Juden Aurélia Steiner" (Aur, p. 164). The German word links the woman to the past of the Nazi camp where her parents and people died, yet also to a present informed by love. Forged by her, the name affirms a double difference. Onomastic "overuse" thus helps make of Aurélia Steiner a legendary figure singular and plural, unique and banal.

In *Le Ravissement de Lol V. Stein*, the narrator's fascination for the phantasmal legend he is constructing manifests itself in "overuse" whenever Lol's full name appears unexpectedly. After the collapse of her subjectivity at the ball, Lol renamed herself, abbreviating Lola Valérie Stein to Lol V. Stein. The truncated form reflects her truncated existence: "She would pronounce her name angrily: Lol V. Stein – that was how she would designate herself. [. . .] She spoke only to say that it was impossible for her to express how boring it was, and interminable, interminable to be Lol V. Stein" (Rav, pp. 23–24). Marriage notwithstanding, she remains Lol V. Stein, petrified in a temporal immobility further suggested by the patronymic Stein, German for stone. She altered only her first names, which Duras calls "the sole part of [woman's] identity that belongs to her a little, which moreover partakes only of the private sphere."[23] The "legend" of Lol V. Stein is forged by the male narrator. His use of maiden names for Lol and Tatiana encloses them both in the phantasm of "his" book. On the authorial level, the legend told is precisely his silencing of women. In those of Duras' texts which portray the consequences of depriving women of discourse, legend converges with tragedy, the distinguishing feature of which is the fatal effect of closure.

Anne-Marie Stretter is one of these legendary, tragic heroines. In *Le Vice-consul*, a degree of "overuse" of her name, together with other appellative techniques, confers quasi-mythical status. "The Queen of Calcutta" (V-C, p. 202), "the woman of Calcutta" (V-C, p. 93) impart uniqueness whereas "that woman of Calcutta" (V-C, p. 96) conveys banality as well. Her "sacred" role is suggested by allusions to her power to "save" (the "lovers," not herself): "You will be received and saved from crime," the Vice-Consul tells Charles Rossett (V-C, p. 138). She presides over "the Saint-Synod of white Calcutta" (V-C, p. 152). Further, anaphorical overuse magnifies the legend intertextually each time the name recurs in another text.

Finally, those of Duras' female protagonists designated solely by first names fall between "underuse" and "erasure." "Madeleine"

(*Savannah Bay*), "Alissa" (*Détruire, dit-elle*), "Agatha" (*Agatha*), and "Anna" (*Le Marin de Gibraltar*) name women free of the structures connoted by the patronymic. They have access to language, which they use indicatively, acting, living, creating legends not (de)limited by dominant cultural codes.

Although devoid of proper names for the protagonists, *L'Amour* also works like an onomastic hybrid. Because onomastic overuse and other techniques in the preceding texts of the "cycle" (*Le Ravissement de Lol V. Stein* and *Le Vice-consul*) had rendered the characters legendary, the single toponym S. Thala and one or two markers such as "black hair" suffice for the reader to "recognize" Tatiana, Lol, perhaps Jacques Hold and Michael Richardson. "Remembering" unnamed figures in *L'Amour* as hyper-named figures in the other texts, one reconstructs legends, making links Duras does not, despite discrepancies in information, number of characters, etc. This attests to the force of the earlier legends, to the malleability of reader receptivity, and to our tendency towards repetition.[24]

REPETITION AND RITUAL

My discussion of repetition on the narrative level shows that Duras' intertextuality ignores classical tenets of non-contradiction. It functions like the thinking Lévi-Strauss contrasted to rationalism, like "the mythic imagination."[25] Already sacralized in the individual works, characters reappear like mythemes, components which can return in different textual combinations, and which can sustain contradiction and modification. Each recurrence enhances the legendary status of figures "recognizable" despite variation. In Duras, however, no ur-structure regulates transformation. The irreducibility and (per)mutability of her texts are functions of the founding "ignorance" at the heart of her work: the absence of any original underlying her "variants." Derrida critiques the metaphysical postulation subtending the structuralist stance.[26] Duras' "mythic imagination" is closer to his concept of a play of open structures, but with specific social parameters. Starting from the "death of "God – that trick" [ce truc],[27] Duras takes as point of departure the contingent nature of dominant structures – metaphysical, social, psychoanalytic, mythic – especially in relation to women. To be sure, she struggles with their legacy, yet their very arbitrariness implies the possibility of modification. Duras' mythic imagination operates with a view to social change, in part through the production of other narratives.

Noguez notes the paratactic nature of Duras' prose: " [. . .] the Duras sentence is usually rather short [. . .] She does not subordinate. She scarcely coordinates: she juxtaposes. [She is a] writer of parataxis."[28] Duras coordinates parataxis with repetition. Noguez examines the effects of this joint phenomenon in the areas of time, progression and tone. He contends that when Duras' parataxis decomposes an event into its constitutive elements, it "tries" to "restore duration" rather than abbreviate it.[29] As with the repetition of individual words, it dilates reading time, "as though to make it coincide with the supposed duration of what is being described."[30] But this imputes an impulsion towards mimetic realism which, to the contrary, Duras' manipulation of parataxis and repetition contests. Two examples Noguez cites:

> First you see the slight quivering [. . .] and then the eyelids trembling [. . .] and then the mouth opening [. . .] And then you perceive that with your caresses . . . (*La Maladie de la Mort*, p. 39)

> Afterwords, en route towards Calcutta. Calcutta where she will remain. She will remain there, she remains, remains there, in the monsoons. There, in Calcutta, asleep amidst the lepers [la lèpre] under the bushes along the Ganges. (*Le Vice-consul*, p. 60)

The quoted passages do not – could not illustrate coincidence between narrative and diegetic time although they do slow the textual rhythm and confer a special status on what is being evoked, another effect Noguez mentions.

Something else is involved. The scarcity of subordination indeed allows each clause "to form an autonomous sentence, almost a microcosm."[31] Through use of this technique in conjunction with repetition, Duras simultaneously eschews linear causality and linear time. Because of the "autonomy" it creates, parataxis lends itself to a repetition entailing recombination. It frees smaller components for circulation in the permutations of her mythic imagination. Within single passages, elements are rarely repeated verbatim, so that even at this micro level repetition is variation. Not controlled by the determining links of subordination, these smaller sequences can be vehicles of the type of "or else" I described for larger narrative segments. Things could have happened differently, been seen or said differently, and are. In addition to repetition within the initial context, even the smallest components may enter into intra-and intertextual recombination. Variation may consist of morphological, situational, or narrative alteration. My analyses of the reappearance of "rosy reader, rosy" and "profound silence" in *Le Vice-consul* illustrate this on the intratextual level. Sometimes a single sentence enumerates possible permutations, and the "or else" subsumes "repetition": "But you, from where you will be, wherever that is, whether you are connected to the sand, or the wind, or the sea or the wall or the bird or the dog" (Hom, pp. 12–13).

Intertextual examples abound. To cite a few:

"Hiroshima: it's your name" (Hir, p. 102) and "Savannah Bay, that's you" (Sav, p. 7).

"We would have remained at the point we're at now, meeting at the Villa Agatha" (Ag, p. 35) and "We will remain where we are now, then,' said Chauvin" (M-C, p. 113).

"She says she had children, a life, once in an undefined time. [. . .] But she makes mistakes in the number. In the place. The dates" (Cam, p. 57) and a "stage direction" in *Savannah Bay*: "You no longer know who you are, who you have been [. . .] which of your children are alive or dead. Or what the places are, the stages, the capitals [. . .]" (p. 7).

The descriptions of Anne-Marie Stretter in *Le Ravissement de Lol V. Stein, Le Vice-consul* and *India Song* illustrate Duras' parataxis and repetition within individual passages and intertextually. Therefore, I quote them in full.
The male narrator speaks:

She was skinny. She must have always been so. She had clothed that skinniness, Tatiana recalled clearly, with a black dress with a double net sheath, black as well, very low cut. She wanted herself thus formed and clothed, and was so to her desire, irrevocably. The admirable skeleton of her body and face was perceivable. Such as she appeared, such henceforth, would she die, with her desired body. Who was she? They found out later: Anne-Marie Stretter. Was she beautiful? What was her age? What had she experienced, she, that others had never known? By

what mysterious route had she succeeded in [. . .] [*Telle* qu'*elle*
apparaissait, *telle*, desormais, *elle* mourrait, avec son corps désiré.
qui étai*t-elle*? On le sut plus tard: Anne-Marie Stretter. Qu*el*
était son âge? qu'avai*t-elle* connu, *elle*, que les autres avaient
ignoré? Par qu*elle* voie mystérieuse étai*t-elle* parvenue à . . .].
(Rav, pp. 14–15 – emphasis added)

Together with tone, lexical ("irrevocably," "henceforth"), thematic
and other devices (unanswered questions, etc), the repetition of
the words "black," "skinny," "clothed," "such," (telle) and "she"
emphasizes the fascinated focus on a figure who attains legendary
status within this single passage. In French the repetition of "such"
(telle) echoes that of "she" (elle),[32] further intensifying the aura of
awe.
   "Duras" speaks:

She is in black, her dress has a double sheath of black net [. . .]
With the approach of age, a skinniness has come to her which
reveals the fineness, the length of the skeleton. Her eyes are too
light, cut like those of statues, her eyelids have grown thin. (V-C,
p. 92)

Note that the recurring components reappear in different combinations. For example, here the character's slenderness is recent.
Because of the anaphorical charge of the elements repeated from
the former text, the legendary effect can be achieved in a shorter
segment. The same principle underlies playful concision in *India
Song*:

Anne-Marie Stretter will wear a black dress – the one she wore
at the S. Tahla ball – the one described in *Le Ravissement de Lol V.
Stein*. (Ind, "stage direction" p. 57)

In *India Song* as in the other two texts, many other techniques project
the character into the legendary. This and the intertextual factor
permit ever briefer descriptions. Dead or not, older or younger,
recognizable whatever the context, the mytheme Anne-Marie
Stretter enters into multiple textual combinations and functions
in non-linear, mythical time. Thus the continual, varied reappearance of phrases, sentences, paragraphs, whole stories, constitutes a

basic trait of Duras' poetics, affecting everything from the smallest semantic elements to the largest textual units.

Within single texts, devices such as the passive voice and notations of the cessation of action also slow time. In conjunction with parataxis and repetition this creates a ceremonial rhythm and enhances the ritual air: "The Vice-Consul [. . .] reads a letter [. . .] the letter [. . .] has been read. He rereads passages [. . .] it has been read" (V-C, pp. 32–33) – and: "The triangle becomes undone, is reabsorbed. It has just become undone; [. . .] the man must be looking at the woman with closed eyes [. . .] he looks at her [. . .] The woman is looked at."[33]

Noguez interprets these features as a progressive struggle for certainty: "In Duras [. . .] it is as though parataxis were the mark of a slow victory over the uncertain, and repetition a means of gaining assurance little by little."[34] Effecting a "movement towards the concrete"[35], all her stylistic techniques attempt to remedy "not knowing," "silence, a sort of impossibility of saying, a total primordial ignorance that haunts the oeuvre . . . "[36] Her writing is a progressive "conquest over abstraction"[37] which grapples to rid itself of its own "spontaneous," "obstinately abstract" nature.[38] I reiterate my position that Duras' writing does not frame uncertainty as a dilemma. One of the primary purposes of her indicative "discourse of hesitation" is to rearticulate a certain not knowing and not saying into a poetics which acknowledges "ignorance" as a liberating, productive source. Variation and recombination signal the absence of the definitive, not of the concrete. They form the condition of possibility of possibilities. Each group of juxtapositions is definite, yet does not preclude others.

Noguez's metaphor for Duras' repetition is particularly pertinent because it evokes the sea, perhaps the central symbol in and for Duras' writing: "They [the repetitions] move forward, wavelet after wavelet, the second, the third one already there even before the first one has ebbed."[39] This might describe Duras' syntax on every level if interpreted as follows. Wavelets advance juxtaposed (parataxis, metonymy), overlap (paratactic repetition), break and ebb (the sentence, segment, or text ends), and (can) begin again. The image figures positively marked arbitrariness (one wave takes up and follows another), variation (waves don't repeat each other exactly), recombination (each wave or set of waves forms a discrete unit which can enter into other permutations).

Water is, as Gaston Bachelard observed, traditionally symbolized as a female element.[40] Duras states: "The sea is completely written, for me. It is like pages, pages which are full, pages which are empty because they are so full, illegible because they are so written, because they are so full of writing."[41] As a metaphor of textuality, the sea in Duras is informed by an explicitly feminine imagery which figures simultaneously artistic and physical female fecundity and women's sexuality.[42] Endlessly fertile, the sea's full blankness is ever pregnant with multiple possibilities. Waves building to crescendos, non linear, infinitely repeatable and variable, figure women's pleasure. Unrestricted by a fixed origin or linear teleology and therefore unpredictable, this textuality-sexuality also implies a different conception of "feminine caprice" as positively marked variation that is an inherent component in Duras' mythic imagination.

With its non-linear, paratactical permutability, the sea is a preferred metaphor for conveying time. The departure scene in *L'Amant de la Chine du Nord* illustrates this textual-sexual-temporal axis. After a metaphorically sexual description in which the steamer is led through the channel into the feminine element of the sea at the "pure angle of the sea and the river" (p. 217), the young future writer lies on a deck chair looking at the water: "On the planks of the deck, on the sides of the boat, on the sea, with the course of the sun and that of the boat, here is sketched and destroyed with the same slowness an illegible writing [. . .] a fugitive geometry which collapses at the whim of the shadow of the waves of the sea. Only to then, again, tirelessly, again, to exist" (Am-Ch, p. 219). Throughout the oeuvre, phrases such as "today the sea is calm," "this morning the sea is rough," "now the sea is quiet again," "now the sea is blue," "now the sea is sombre," mark time's motion deictically, without limiting it to a single temporal direction. This correlates to the intrasegmental parataxis of the ubiquitous "and then," "and then" and to simple listing, as in, for example: – "Leprosy [la lèpre] moves, mixes, separates" (V-C, p. 114) – or: "They look at each other. Smile at each other. Stop looking at each other" (Nat, p. 42) – or: "She takes him, hugs him, releases him" (Eté, p. 33).

Other media indicate temporal change as non-linear variation in repetition: alterations in weather (rain in *Dix heures et demie du soir en été*, cloud movement[43] in *Le Vice-consul*), walking in multiple directions (*L'Amour*), differences in the "outside turbulence" (*Véra Baxter*), allusions to the lepers, groans, and crepuscular light of Calcutta, (*Le Vice-consul*), the mobility of feminine beauty (it does not follow a straight line from youth to age, but changes according to mood, perspective, etc., which is rendered by sentences such as "now she is beautiful," "now she is ugly") and modifications in the color of female protagonists' eyes. Microcosms of the sea, they mirror its temporality through color change. "There is," for example, "no difference between Aurélia's eyes and the sea, between the breaking through of her glance and the depths of time."[44] Women's eyes go from "light" to "somber" to "transparent," unspecified shades of the sea colors green and blue. (Although male characters may have light eyes, only the women's undergo the modifications expressive of the analogy to the ocean[45].) Duras uses this sort of notation far more abundantly than units of days or years. This predominance of rhythmic variation and repetition over linear chronology corresponds to mythical time.

Duras' handling of verb forms does also. I have shown how, in conjunction with deictics, the present tense situates narration, memory, imagination, desire, legend in the present performative, each narrative creating a different re-presentation of the "myth" at hand. When verbs shift from one tense or mood to another, the first one constitutes a rite of passage into the temporality of the mythic imagination. In *Savannah Bay* and *Le Camion*, we recall, the conditional mood prepares our entry into the "unreal present" of the present tense of play and fiction, in which multiple versions of an originally absent "myth" coexist. In *La Maladie de la mort*, it is a ritual preliminary to the staging and deconstruction of a ritual scenario. In smaller segments as well, the conditional is a prefatory device emphasizing the fictive nature of what follows, on which the ensuing present confers fictional "fact" outside conventional time: – "He would have worn, he is wearing, pants of blue cloth" (H-as, p. 23) – "This bedroom could have been the place where we should have loved each other, it is, therefore, that place, of our love" (Eté, p. 63).

When the future tense has the introductory role, it projects the story into a "possible" equally impossible to locate on a temporal line. The slow, rhythmic repetitions of "you will forget" at the opening of *L'Homme atlantique* evoke the ritual of hypnosis, something the young man seems to require in order to be able to participate in mythic temporality: "You will not look at the camera. [. . .] You will forget. You will forget. [blank space] That it is you, you will forget that. I believe it is possible to do that. You will also forget that the camera is there. But above all you will forget that it is you. – BLANK – " (p. 7).

Noguez reminds us that parataxis belongs to the register of "elevated style," like in the Bible or old French and German epics.[46] In Duras, repetition and parataxis create an "internal rime" akin to that of oral poetry, "nearly sung":[47] "And before anything else, it is perhaps that sublime *aura*, that far away Biblical echo, that tone of incantation or of non profane narrative that one perceives in her juxtapositions and repetitions."[48] If in Péguy, "the certainty of faith"[49] motivates this sort of effect, in Duras "litany" is an effort "against uncertainty"[50] (against lack of faith?). Once more, I draw different conclusions from Noguez' otherwise pertinent stylistic descriptions. Duras' elevated style and ceremonial tone communicate a different message: in the beginning there is no omniscient author of an immutable text. The sacred is not the text. The sacred is textuality, the open source of changeable legends.

MISCELLANEOUS SYNCTACTIC FEATURES

"Je te rencontre
Je me souviens de toi."

Duras

Duras' reversal of antecedents and pronouns effects a repetition which contributes to the ritual qualities of her prose. It is repetition grammatically implied, but of something the reader has not yet encountered. The noun itself then becomes another repetition. Consequently, the reader accepts something similar to the pact presupposed in the hearing or reading of legends: the narrative is received as something being retold and as something extraordinary. Once again, smaller textual segments reinforce what is produced in larger units through narrative framing and "internal" and "external" intertextuality. Switching antecedents and pronouns imparts a sense of the momentous, slows the narrative, and throws into relief what is about to be said, as well as the act of speaking. In the following examples, I have italicised the anticipatory pronoun.

Sometimes certain evenings she [Anne-Marie Stretter] also does *it*, she speaks (V-C, p. 90).

And then he said *it* to her. He had told her that it was like before, that he still loved her [. . .] (Am, p. 142).

He looks at her, suddenly serious and hesitating, then he finally says *it* to her. – Him: 'My family was at Hiroshima' (Hir, p. 29).

She is the one who, suddenly having slowed down, opens the door and says *it*: 'What luck' (D-H, p. 171).

And then she would have succeeded in doing *it*. The strength of the sun is such that in order to endure it she screams (H-as, p. 13).

Non-specific nouns, adverbs, or demonstrative pronouns can have a similar anticipatory function:

When she begins telephoning again, she announces *the news*. She tells him she is getting sicker and sicker (Nav, p. 88).

Never. Never do I separate you from our love (Aur, p. 128).

Sometimes I know *that*: that whenever it is not all things intermingling, going to vanity and to the wind, writing is nothing (Am, p. 15).

Placing "and" in initial sentence positions creates anticipatory repetition with Biblical resonance, especially when coordinated with repeated semantic units and with deictics. The most frequent of the latter is "voici", the French equivalent in Biblical discourse of "lo" (as in "lo! and behold").

And then always, yes, as soon as the night wind [comes], *lo* [voici], it [the sea] begins again, yes, with the coming of night (Eté, p. 91).

And lo [voici]: the sea. Strong. White (Ver, p. 10).

And then you listen to *that* noise which is coming closer, you listen to the sea [The demonstrative adjective functions like the reversed pronouns. "That noise" is "repeated" by the "antecedent," "the sea"] (Mal, p. 41).

And then he does it: he pushes aside the little boys [. . .] *And* then he does it: he takes the little brother by the shoulders (Am-Ch, p. 14).

Within the context of an oeuvre which thematizes discursive practice on every textual level, these syntactic dislocations constitute another means of calling the question of language and of serving up other discursive possibilities. The poetic aspect of these other possibilities connects to the political. Otherwise stated, Duras' poetics is predicated on her critique of the cultural-discursive order.

WORDS, IMAGES AND WORD-IMAGES

"This slowness, this indiscipline of punctuation, it is as though I undressed words one after the other, and discover what is underneath, the isolated word, unrecognizeable, devoid of all relation, of all identity, abandoned."[51] In Duras' highly poetic prose, images are seldom constructed like the dense, lush combinations of lyric poets or the sudden sparks of surrealist juxtapositions. A remarkable simplicity characterizes her language, from sentence structure (parataxis) to vocabulary. After an initial stripping away which detaches the lexical unit from, as Marini says, "the discourse that limits or extinguishes it,"[52] ordinary words become poeticized in renewed networks of signification. Traditional metaphorical substitution is not a major trope in Duras. She tends to compose her images before us, maintaining both components. This has an explanatory role, necessary because she rarely resorts to ready-made cultural metaphors. What results might be called "prepared" metaphors. The preparation itself is usually poetic. In typical Durassian fashion, its presence throws the process into relief. The extraordinary quality imparted through this emphasis, which approaches repetition, places the whole procedure in the realm of the legendary.

Not unrelated to parataxis and metonymy[53] for the larger segments, simple apposition can fulfill this function, as in the description of Betty Fernandez in *L'Amant*: "She is slender, tall, sketched with India ink, an engraving" (p. 83). Without the prefatory poetic image "sketched with India ink," the "engraving" metaphor would make little sense.

In *Le Vice-consul*, the rat metaphor for the pregnant beggar's baby: "Nature, give me a knife to kill this rat," (p. 19) is prepared by several pages describing her acute hunger and consequent sensation of being devoured from the inside. On the page preceding the image, we read: "night and day the child continues to eat her; she listens and hears the incessant nibbling in the stomach whose flesh it is devouring, it has eaten her thighs, arms, cheeks – she searches for them, there are nothing but holes where they used to be in Tonlé Sap

– the roots of her hair, everything, little by little it is taking up the space she used to have, but it has not eaten her hunger" (p. 18). The figurative eating and nibbling anticipate the rat metaphor. Again, images themselves poetic constitute the preparation for the one in question.

A simile prepares the metaphor for the woman's eyes in *Hiroshima mon amour*. "The rivers, too, still flow with impunity. The Loire. Riva's[54] eyes, like the Loire, flow, but *ordered by suffering*, in that disorder. [. . .] Riva is in a corner of the cellar, completely white. There like elsewhere, always. Still with Loire eyes" (pp. 118–120). Appearing pages after the preparation, the anaphorical metaphor "Loire eyes" is explained by the previous juxtaposition of repeated, already poeticized elements.

Previous thematic content prepares many metaphors constructed through agglomeration, or synapses. In *Dix heures et demie du soir en été*, there are two in the passage where Maria watches her husband embrace her friend: "A *Pierre-hand* is all over that *other-woman's-body*. [Une main de Pierre est partout sur ce corps d'autre femme.]" (p. 49 – my emphasis). I add hyphenation to convey the effect created by syntactic irregularity in the French. The construction "corps d'autre femme" becomes a synapsis through the elimination of the article before "autre," and is generalized in its singularity by the demonstrative adjective "ce."

In *L'Amant* the synapsis "the-child-of-the-river-crossing" (Am, p. 113 – hyphenation added) refers to the first encounter with the lover to be. The special status conferred by the form elevates both event and character to a point where metaphor merges with legend. This syntactic treatment "undresses" ordinary words by placing them in unconventional order, so that they "indicate" the extraordinariness of the banal. A synapsis in *L'Homme assis dans le couloir* plays on the polysemy of the French "revenante" (the returning one, or ghost): "He had watched the 'revenante'-from-the-way-of-stones' coming towards him" (H-As, p. 22). The text prepares the meaning "ghost" through allusions to and images of the putting to death of the woman, to which the expression "way of stone" adds Biblical overtones.

Duras' syntactical "undressing" also poeticizes single words. Generally this builds gradually within a text. A word is repeated in numerous contexts and foregrounded through various devices until it acquires exceptional resonance and radiates multiple meanings. Otherwise stated, it becomes what I call a word-image. Denotative, connotative, associative, even etymological significations are activated as well as the material and dynamic imagination described by Bachelard.[55]

In its many morphological variations in *Le Vice-consul*, the word "impossible" is a word-image for the title character. When it first appears (p. 39) it carries no special status. The nature and number of subsequent repetitions, however,[56] render it retrospectively and progressively symbolic. Its opposite, "possible," figures with it in several passages, constituting additional reiteration. In conjunction with this, a pointed lack of explanation progressively complicates the habitually univalent word. Further, some form of emphasis (blanks, suspension points, question marks, explicit metalinguistic references to the word by other characters) nearly always causes the word to stand out. Poetic plurality results, then, from the accumulation of diverse yet interconnected meanings, all of which "indicate" some aspect of the Vice-Consul's unsuitability for life.

He is impossible physically: "How is my face, tell me, Director?' asks the Vice-Consul.' − 'Still impossible'" (V-C, p. 78). Subsequently the text alludes to the disjointed awkwardness of his body, which, like his facial features, does not compose a viable whole. His behavior is impossible in the past (the murders): Anne-Marie Stretter to the Vice-Consul: "I don't know how to say it, . . . in your file there is the word impossible. Is that the word this time? [. . .] Perhaps there is another word?" (V-C, p. 128) and in the present: "'I'm staying,' screams the Vice-Consul. Charles Rossett takes him by the lapels: 'You are, decidedly, impossible.' [. . .] 'Once, keep me with you.' 'That is not possible,' says Peter Morgan" (V-C, pp. 146–147). He is impossible sexually. His inability to love and his virginity suggest the word "impotent" (impuissant), which is etymologically related to the word "impossible." Sexual and emotional non-viability is the central aspect of the Vice-Consul's general existential impotence. Indeed, his very existence is impossible: "'Ah, it's true, it is impossible, completely impossible,' he [Rossett] says, 'to know that he is . . . alive . . . '" (V-C, p. 194).

The word-image "se perdre" symbolizes the legend of loss that is the beggar. She can only resist the temptation to return home if she "gets lost" (se perdre), but she can do that only if the verb acts transitively, with "se" (herself) as direct object. Socially a "femme perdue" (literally a "lost woman", the equivalent to the English "fallen woman"), she finally gets lost (leaves Indochina) after losing her self, her mind to insanity and her body to hunger.

Reticence and ambiguity rather than repetition poeticize the word "ravishing" from the title *Le Ravissement de Lol V. Stein*. The French "ravissement" has meanings of delight, beauty, rapture, theft and violation. The title's syntax prevents determination of whether it implies the active or passive voice, or who the subject is. Who is ravished, by what or whom, and in what sense? The word never occurs in the novel, the narrative structure of which increases the polysemy. Lol is ravished, robbed of her lover and herself (she goes mad), and ravishing: beautiful and a thief (she steals Tatiana's lover). Jacques Hold ravishes Lol doubly: he steals her from her husband and forces himself upon her in the hotel. As narrator, he ravishes her discourse, stealing her story to make it his own. Finally, as narrator and as character Hold becomes a seduced seducer, ravished into phantasm and loss of self.

In Duras' work, the near ubiquity of certain key symbols and the manner in which they are introduced endow the symbols themselves with a sacred quality. The two most significant are the sea and the forest. "Stage directions" in the second edition of *Savannah Bay* specify" "[. . .] a very high door, reminiscent of cathedral portals [. . .] behind this door, there are two immense columns [. . .] behind the columns framed by the doorway, after a nearly black zone of light, there is the sea. It is illuminated by a variable light [. . .] it is framed like the Law".[57] The sea itself is sacred, even divine: "[. . .] at the back of the scenery the door of the sea, a sort of altar opening out on the sea" (pp. 120–121).

In texts not situated near the sea, the author often introduces it metaphorically. Set in an inland Spanish village, *Dix heures et demie du soir en été* opens on a stormy afternoon: "A new phase of the storm is being prepared. That dark blue, *oceanic* mass of the afternoon slowly advances above the city" (p. 14 – emphasis added). As though metonymically elicited, the same paragraph alludes to a woman's changing eye color, that sign of the sea in microcosm: "But now your eyes are blue, says Pierre, this time because of the sky." This sentence, which may represent Maria imagining her husband addressing the woman he desires, introduces the sexual aspect, for, like the sea, women's eye-color is eroticized in Duras. On the same page: "Here is the downpour. The *ocean* is poured onto the city" (emphasis added).

In *Hiroshima mon amour*, a poetically prepared synapsis makes the sea metaphorically present in the inland town of Nevers: "Behind the shutters the [village] square beats like the sea, immense. He

[Riva's father] looked like a shipwreck. [. . .] Alone in my room at midnight. *The sea of the Champs de Mars square* still beats behind my shutters" (p. 114 – emphasis added). The little girl hiding from the Nazis in the countryside "looks [out her window] at the ocean of the forest" in *Aurélia*-Paris (p. 169), and the woman caring for her "bends down and smells the child's hair, nibbling it, she says that in her mouth her hair smells of the sea" (p. 176). With her lover in his room in town, the protagonist in *L'Amant* listens to the street noise: "I caress his body in that noise of the thoroughfare. The sea, the immensity regrouping itself, goes away, returns" (Am, p. 55). These metaphorical waves introduce the repetitive, paratactic rhythms of Durassian desire and "mythic" temporality, as in *L'Homme assis dans le couloir*: "The nakedness of the plain, the direction of the rain should be that of the sea" (p. 22) and: "The sea ought to be flat and warm. [. . .] It is a land that flees before one, ceaselessly seen and seen again, a movement that never stops, that never knows an end" (H-As, pp. 25–26). In *La Maladie de la mort*, the sea figures prominently outside the bedroom. Perhaps in order to stress the association between women and the sea and the man's imperviousness to both, Duras transfers it to the bed on which the woman lies. Another "prepared" metaphor facilitates this: "You [the man] listen to the sound of the sea, which is beginning to rise. That stranger is there in the bed, in her place, in the white puddle of the white sheets" (Mal, p. 30).[58]

Forests in Duras symbolize culture's outside. As such, they are generally received differently by Duras' female and male protagonists, because of the relative cultural positions involved. For Duras, it is axiomatic that the social-symbolic constructs that symbols are, are not experienced in the same way by the constructs that are genders, symbols themselves. Her forests figure "la sauvagerie," that polysemic word so dear to her, evocative at once of wildness, the untamed, the unsociable, savageness and timidity, of whatever is excluded from the social order, taboo. The following remarks offer one of her clearest statements concerning the symbol:

The forest [in *Détruire, dit-elle*] communicates with the grounds [le parc]. The grounds are a foretaste of the forest. The grounds announce its proximity. There are such grounds in *Détruire*. There are some in *India Song*, in *Nathalie Granger*. [. . .] The forest is the forbidden. That is, I do not know exactly what that forest is in *Jaune le soleil*, which I call the forest of nomadism, the forest of the

Jews, I don't know what the link is between that forest and the forest in *Détruire*, which people fear. Which a certain bourgeoisie fears, which men fear, and which they massacre. *We* fit ourselves into it, we weave our way through it, you see. Men go there to hunt, to impose sanctions, to control.[59]

For the dominant groups, the forest is a place of ritual, violent triumph over nature, feared, repressed, "massacred." Because women suffer similar symbolic (and concrete) treatment, they often entertain a different relationship with the forest. Duras' transformation of the his-story of medieval "witches" into a legend of women and language contextualizes the forest symbolism in her fiction. Her version puts it this way: The European crusaders abandoned their wives for the pursuit of murderous glory. In their lord masters' absence, some women revolted against the verbal-sexual silence and solitude to which they were enjoined. They entered forests and talked to plants, animals, trees. Judged sacrilegious, this commerce with the forbidden cost them their lives.[60] "[. . .] all forests in principle date from prehistory."[61] Women exploring, inventing discourse and history outside prescribed limits were burned at the stake in the name of the "sacred" patriarchal stories of the scriptures founding monotheistic Western his-story. Because women are themselves (subject to) taboo, excluded, denied their stories, the forest can figure the site of discursive beginnings of languages of communication rather than conquest.

If the stakes for "witches" were actual death, in Duras they are symbolic death: insanity for isolated women. Sign of the ex-centric outside[62] which is potentially revolutionary, the forest is also the place of madness, where, for example, the exiled beggar's long voyage away from selfhood culminates in depersonalization: "Afterwards, it is the forest, madness in the forest" (V-C, p. 70). Lol V. Stein relives the moment of psychic death prone in the rye field outside the symbolically named Hôtel des Bois (Hotel of the Woods), located at the forest's edge. In *Le Camion*, a mental hospital from which the hitch-hiking lady may have escaped has grounds bordered on one side by a river and on the other by a forest. These two Duras symbols of femininity (there is no sea in the text) frame the insane asylum, a symbol of repression.

Revolt and madness intersect near forests for Claire Lannes (*L'Amante anglaise*) and Alissa (*Détruire, dit-elle*). Relegated by her husband to the "outside" (the grounds of her house), so that her "ravings" won't disturb him, the former's madness is a doomed solitary revolt. (The one man who sympathizes with her lives harmoniously with the forest. But Alfonso is neutralized [feminized?] by foreignness and class, and ultimately exiled himself.). With more effective listeners and lovers, Alissa has better luck, She comes and goes in the forest at will, and speaks a discourse of radical revolution. She is heard by another woman and by sympathetic (Jewish) men, so that the question of her insanity becomes an indictment of the repressive and cooptive powers of the society that limits contestatory "legends" to the "outside" of the sanatorium.

Finally, Duras' use of oxymorons re-"dresses" certain words and concepts, redresses certain connotative wrongs perpetrated by the dominant symbolic system, and creates other symbols and legends. Typically, juxtaposition, repetition and parataxis "prepare," poeticize and intensify the image. In *La Maladie de la mort*, the "strength" in feminine "weakness" so threatening to the man who rejects otherness, is one such deconstructive-reconstructive oxymoron: "You look at that shape [the female body]; at the same time you discover its infernal power, its abominable fragility, its weakness, the invincible strength of its unequalled weakness" (Mal, p. 31). The opening of *Savannah Bay* presents an old woman, one of the most denigrated figures in dominant Western discourse. *Savannah Bay* makes this old, forgetful woman "splendid": "You don't know who you are any longer, who you have been [. . .] You are an actress, the splendor of the age of the world, its fulfillment, the immensity of its last deliverance" (Sav, p. 7).

Conclusion

The "ignorance" generating Marguerite Duras' rearticulation of language does not simply reflect longing for an original lost object. More probably, it reflects the absence of an original, interdicting subject – not a loss, but a potential for liberation from discursive domination and repression. Duras' textual strategies (re)articulate a language "indicative" in several ways. It exposes the unitary language it deconstructs, with its symbolic ordering and mythmaking. It "shows" the silencing of women; it "shows" women's silences in their subversive aspects. And it "points to" one writer's reinscription of these silences in a differently structured discourse, which permits the telling of other stories, transformations into other legends.

Duras' writing traces an historical trajectory in two movements. The first goes from the suppression of women's speech to the inevitable if sometimes unconscious return of this repressed. A passage from *La Pluie d'été* about the foreign woman living in a working class suburb of Paris can read as its metaphor:

> The mother has forgotten the language of her youth. She speaks [French] without an accent, like the populations of Vitry. She makes errors only in the conjugations. What remains to her of her past are irremediable consonances, words she seems to unfold, very soft, sorts of songs which moisten the interior of the voice, so that the words issue from her body sometimes without her being aware of it, as if she were visited by the memory of an abandoned language.[1]

What women have been forced to "abandon" is less an original female language than an original opportunity to speak. The second movement consists in seizing that opportunity. If Marguerite Duras claims so insistently that she writes "as a woman," it is because, women having been silenced *qua* women, when they demand access to language they must do so at first *qua* women, or risk being silenced through discursive assimilation. In the connections Duras' work makes between language and gender and between language and the gendered body, the issue is less one of essentialism by women than of essentialism imposed on women. As Anne-Marie Houdebine writes: "They [those women] who [. . .] speak of their body, claiming it as the site of the beginning of their speech, without forgetting that it is cultural also, spoken, represented, named, already written in a way, [. . .] they have raised the true questions. [. . .] questions of the symbolic, the cultural, the social, of language. Which political party or union has raised them?"[2]

Duras never claims that her speech issues from an unmediated female body. It issues from her struggle against the mediations imposed by dominant language, from her revalorization of negative poles of binary discursive structures and from the rejection of these structures themselves through her reworking of language. Duras proposes and calls for a language which requires different social structures and which would help to effect them. She knows, with Houdebine, that "changing language implies changing history, the socius, mind sets, representations, and ears and words, so that language changes language," that "such transformations are the affair of millions of singularities," and that "it suffices that one voice begin and make itself heard for it to carry others."[3]

Marguerite Duras' is one of those voices. She is one of the "singularities" explicitly thematizing the political dimensions of speech and literature, and transforming language practise. Whether or not one would choose her particular inflection of the signifying instrument, the quality of her work, its popularity among many classes of readers and the continually growing critical attention it is attracting, ensure that Marguerite Duras' voice and the questions she raises do not go unheard.

Notes

Introduction

1. Bakhtin, "Discourse in the Novel," p. 355.
2. *Ibid.*, p. 360.
3. Yaeger, "A Fire in my Head," p. 959.
4. Bakhtin, *op. cit.*, p. 271.
5. *Ibid.*, p. 270.
6. *Ibid.*, p. 263.
7. The term "dialogism" is explained by Bakhtin's translators in the text's glossary: "Dialogism is the characteristic epistemological mode of a world dominated by heterglossia. Everything means, is understood, as a part of a greater whole – there is constant interaction between meanings, all of which have the potential of conditioning others. [. . .] This dialogic imperative, mandated by the pre-existence of the language world relative to any of its current inhabitants, insures that there can be no actual monologue. One may [. . .] be deluded into thinking there is one language, or one may, as grammarians, certain political figures and normative framers of 'literary languages' do, seek in a sophisticated way to achieve a unitary language. In both cases the unitariness is relative to the overpowering force of heteroglossia, and thus dialogism." *Ibid.*, p. 426.
8. *Ibid.*, p. 300.
9. Houdebine, "Les Femmes dans la langue," pp. 11–12. All translations from the French in this book are mine unless otherwise indicated.
10. Beauvoir, *Le Deuxième sexe.*
11. Cixous, "Le Sexe ou la tête," p. 7.
12. Cixous, *La Jeune née*, pp. 115–117.
13. Benjamin, "The Bonds of Love," pp. 46–47.
14. Foucault, *L'Archéologie du savoir*, p. 90.
15. The term is ambiguous because the French "féminin" signifies both "female" and "feminine."
16. Rosalind-Jones, "Writing the Body," p. 374.
17. Moi, *Sexual/Textual Politics*, p. 123.
18. *Ibid.*, p. 126.
19. *Ibid.*, p. 148.
20. Questions Féministes Collective, "Variations on Common Themes," in Marks and Courtivon, p. 226. Among the founding editors were Simone de Beauvoir, Monique Wittig, Christine Delphy, Monique Plaza, and Colette Guillaumin. Within a more Marxist-feminist perspective, they proclaimed women a social class, rather than an essence.
21. *Ibid.*, p. 227. Cf. also Wittig, "The Point of View: Universal or

Particular?" and "One is not Born a Woman." For a clear exposition of the various tendencies in French Feminism, cf. Duchen, *Feminism in France*.
22. Kristeva, "La Femme, ce n'est jamais çà."
23. Kristeva, *La Révolution du langage poétique*.
24. Cf. Rosalind-Jones, "Writing the Body," pp. 363–366.
25. *Ibid.*, p. 363.
26. Cf. for example Moi, *Sexual/Textual Politics*, pp. 167–173.
27. Kristeva, "Un Nouveau type d'intellectuel."
28. De Lauretis "Feminist Studies/Critical Studies," p. 14.
29. *Ibid.*, p. 17.
30. *Ibid.*, pp. 11–12.
31. *Ibid.*, p. 15.
32. Fraser and Nicholson "Social Criticism without Philosophy," in *Feminism/Postmodernism*, p. 25.
33. *Ibid.*, p. 26.
34. Butler, "Gender Trouble," in *Feminism/Postmodernism*, p. 324.
35. *Ibid.*, p. 339.
36. *Ibid.*, p. 338.
37. Huyssens, "Mapping the Postmodern," in *Feminism/Postmodernism*, p. 264.
38. Bordo, "Feminism, Postmodernism, and Gender-Scepticism," in *Feminism/Postmodernism*, p. 151.
39. *Ibid.*, p. 149.
40. *Ibid.*, pp. 146–147.
41. *Ibid.*, p. 155.
42. *Ibid.*, p. 156.
43. Evans, *Masks of Tradition*, p. 8.
44. Duras, "Apostrophes."
45. Duras in *Les Lieux*, p. 102.
46. Unpublished interviews I held with Marguerite Duras, summer 1982.
47. Interviews with me, 1982.
48. See Chapter 4.
49. Duras, "Les Goncourt aimaient *L'Amant*," p. 30.
50. Bakhtin, *op. cit.*, p. 366.
51. Interview, Duras with Husserl-Kapit, *Signs*, p. 426.
52. Marini, "L'Autre corps," p. 27.
53. I retain the French titles of Duras' books, since these are the texts I worked from.

1: "Ignorance" and Textuality

1. Interviews with me, 1982.
2. Duras, in *Marguerite Duras*, p. 81.
3. Duras, *Le Vice-consul*, p. 35. Hereafter referred to as V-C.
4. Genette, *Figures III*, p. 226.

5. Following Elaine Marks' practice in her work on Colette, I put quotation marks around the name "Duras" to distinguish the intratextual "Duras" from the signer. Duras often inscribes a more or less explicitly first person narrating writer in her texts. I read all Duras' onomastically unspecified "writing" narrators as "Duras". When they are male, Duras specifically designates them as such.
6. Kristeva, *Pouvoirs de l'horreur.,*p. 24
7. *Ibid.,* p. 19.
8. *Ibid.,* p. 19.
9. *Ibid.,* p. 17.
10. Marini, *Territoires du féminin,* p. 91.
11. Cf. Chapter 4.
12. Cf. Chapters 3 and 4
13. I discuss the fear of "ignorance" and silence in more detail in Chapter 4.
14. Marini, *op. cit.,* p. 120.
15. Benveniste: "The third person is the form of the verbal (or pronominal) paradigm that does *not* refer to a person because it refers to an object placed outside the allocution. But it only exists and is characterized in opposition to the person, 'I,' of the speaker, who, uttering it, situates it as a non-person" (*Problèmes de linguistique générale,* Vol. 1, p. 265). Buber: "The basic words [. . .] are word pairs. One basic word is the pair I-You. The other basic word is the word pair I-It, but this basic word is not changed when He or She takes the place of It" (*I and Thou,* p. 53).
16. Cf. Part II.
17. Benveniste, *Problèmes de linguistique générale,* Vol. 2, p. 78.
18. ". . . 'nous' is not a quantified or multiplied 'I,' it is an 'I' *dilated* beyond the strict person, which is simultaneously enlarged and given vague contours." Benveniste, *Problèmes de Linguistique générale,* Vol. 1, p. 235.
19. Cf. Chapter 4.
20. When called, one can answer "on vient" for "I'm coming." In the following discussion, I retain the French pronoun due to ambiguities of translation.
21. For example: (1) pp. 99–100, No indication of source of voice: "Tell me about Mme Stretter.' 'Irreprochable and kind [. . .]"; (2) p. 100, Gender specified: "The women,' say the men, 'to see them like in France [. . .]; (3) p. 122, "We" (nous) "We know it, [on le sait bien, nous] she talks about the heat first [..]"; (4) p. 121, General collectivity of white society: "Then all of white India looks at them"; (5) p. 135 Restricted generality: "Some say [. . .]"; (6) p. 139 Generality: " People don't understand"; (7) p. 147 An impersonal singular: "One person muses [. . .]."
22. Cf. Chapter 4.
23. Cf. Chapter 4.
24. Duras, *Moderato Cantabile,* p. 27. Hereafter referred to as M-C.
25. Duras, *Dix Heures et demie du soir en été,* pp. 168–175 (hereafter referred to as D-H).

26. One is reminded of Anne-Marie Stretter's dozing in *Le Vice-consul*. There, however, "Duras" makes all the allusions to her sleeping.
27. For fuller discussion of Lol's phantasm, see Cohen, "Phantasm and Narration."
28. Duras, *Le Ravissement de Lol V. Stein*, p. 137 (hereafter referred to as Rav).
29. Binswanger, "Dream and Existence," p. 243. Cf. also Straus in *Phenomenological Psychology*, p. 116: "the dreamer is alone in his dream world. No one else can enter it, nor can the dreamer leave it."
30. Montrelay, *L'Ombre*, p. 21. She writes on the same page: "The perversion, if there is any, comes from Jacques Hold."
31. Benveniste, *Problèmes*, Vol. 1, p. 244.
32. Straus, *The Primary World of Senses*, p. 391.
33. Pontalis and Laplanche, *Vocabulaire de la psychanalyse*, p. 152.
34. Benveniste, *Problèmes*, Vol. 1, pp. 71–72.
35. Benveniste, *Problèmes*, Vol. 1, p. 72.
36. Cf. discussion Chapter 2.
37. Lol, who "survived" her own existential death at the ball, lives in an existentially posthumous mode. Cf. Cohen, "Phantasm and Narration," pp. 257–259.
38. Benveniste, *Problèmes*, Vol. 2, p. 197.
39. *Ibid.*, p. 200.
40. "He" appears briefly at the opening of the passage (p. 187) and conveys a temporary, and confused division of self into subject and object for the purpose of masturbation. It has little to do with the split under discussion.
41. Cf. Cohen, "Phantasm and Narration."
42. Benveniste, *Problèmes*, Vol. 1, pp. 259–260: "Subjectivity is the capacity to pose oneself as subject [. . .] The one who says 'I' is 'I'."
43. Evans reads this as a rape. Her chapter "Marguerite Duras: The Whore," in *Masks of Tradition*, pp. 123–157, gives an interesting reading of the novel, conducted in terms of vision and anonymity, in relation to which she articulates a concept of Durassian "prostitution" as the radical instability and exchangeability of the subject.
44. Benveniste, *Problèmes*, Vol. 1, p. 228.
45. Evans, *op. cit.*, p. 153.
46. *Ibid.*, pp. 153–154.
47. Evans, introduction *Masks of Tradition*, p. 20.
48. Duras, *L'Amante anglaise*, pp. 191–192 (hereafter refereed to as A-A).
49. For further discussion of the question of Claire's speech cf. Chapter 4.
50. Duras, *Le Marin de Gibraltar*, p. 186 (hereafter referred to as Mar).
51. Duras, *Le Camion*, p. 11 (hereafter referred to as Cam).
52. In the book she can only be "Duras." Because the author plays that role in the film, I dispense with the quotation marks when referring to it.
53. Cf. further discussion in Chapters 2 and 4.

54. Duras, *La Maladie de la mort*, p. 59 (hereafter referred to as Mal).
55. Duras, "Je suis muette devant le théâtre que j'écris," p. 97.
56. Duras, "Entretien avec Marguerite Duras."
57. Duras, *Le Navire Night*, p. 10 (hereafter referred to as Nav).
58. Cf. Chapter 4 for discussion of "indicative language."
59. Cf. Chapter 2.
60. Duras, "Il n'y a rien de plus difficile que de décrire un amour," p. 26.
61. Duras, "Je suis muette devant le théâtre que j'écris," p. 98.
62. Duras, "Il n'y a rien de pus difficile que de décrire un amour," p. 27.

2: Intertextualities

1. Cf. Christian Zimmer: "to build an oeuvre [. . .] ceaselessly annuling the created work by superimposing on it a version that disarticulates its structures [. . .]", in "Dans la nuit de Marguerite Duras," p. 1304. For Sharon Willis, Duras' texts "constitute acts of 'cannibalization,' consuming and re-presenting mutilated fragments of [her] other texts," and "inscribe death itself, the death of the text" – *Marguerite Duras*, p. 164. In "L'écrit,' le jeu de la lecture et la mise en voix," Dominique Fisher proposes a concept of erasure (rature), and the idea of an "original scene" (or scenes) as the principle of Duras' production.
2. Duras, "Sublime, forcément sublime," p. 28.
3. Duras, *India Song*, p. 147 (hereafter referred to as Ind). These statements appear in a "summary" at the end of the text.
4. Duras, *La Femme du Gange*, p. 161 (hereafter referred to as Fem). S. Tahla is spelled S. Thala in *India Song*.
5. In *La Femme du Gange*, Duras uses "outside voices" for the first time to "narrate," in the film and in the text. I focus on *India Song* because it makes richer use of the technique.
6. Bakhtin, *"Discourse in the Novel,"* p. 276.
7. Cf. the interviews with the actors in Bernheim, *Marguerite Duras tourne un film*.
8. Duras, in *Marguerite Duras*, p. 81.
9. The film *India Song* introduces a third variation, with Anne-Marie Stretter participating in the conversation. The film, however, contains only that version, whereas the written text proposes two alternatives. It will be remembered that the film of *Le Camion* projects its possibilities as text not yet filmed.
10. Valéry, "Variété," pp. 467–468. In the pre-realist days of the eighteenth century, writers played on this sort of thing. For example, Diderot included various possibilities of endings in his comic novel *Jacques le fataliste et son maître*. This was largely confined to works of humor, however.
11. For example, *Ind*, p. 13: "At the piano, slowly, a tune named 'India

Song,' [. . .] It is played in its entirety and thus occupies the time –
always long – that the spectator, that the reader needs in order to
leave the common place where he finds himself when the spectacle,
the reading begins."

12.   Duras, "Je suis muette devant le théâtre que j'écris," p. 97.
13.   Duras, *Nathalie Granger*, pp. 23–26 (hereafter referred to as Nat).
14.   Duras, *Agatha*, p. 20 (hereafter referred to as Ag).
15.   Duras, *Hiroshima mon amour*, note to page 107 (hereafter referred to
       as Hir).
16.   The speaking voice thematizes this role in *L'Amant de la Chine du
       Nord*. Presenting the text as a book from which a film might be
       made, she subsumes under the written even "stage directions" such
       as "The camera slowly sweeps over what one just saw" (p. 21) They
       provide indications "in the event of a film" (p. 93) within a text
       identified as a novel (p. 12) Through references to "the first book
       [*L'Amant*]" (p. 13) – and others - with regard to "this book here"
       [pp. 13, 21, etc.), Duras explicitly claims her prerogatives as creator
       of open-ended intertextuality.
17.   For further discussion cf. Part II.
18.   Interviews with me, summer, 1982.
19.   De Man, *Blindness and Insight*, p. 18.
20.   Duras, *Savannah Bay*, p. 31 (hereafter referred to as Sav).
21.   Interviews with me, summer, 1982.
22.   Duras, *Les Yeux verts*, pp. 5–6..
23.   Beaujour, "Autobiographie et autoportrait," p. 453.
24.   For a critique of the Oedipus complex, see Irigaray, *Speculum de
       l'autre femme*, pp. 9–165.
25.   Cf. Bloom, *The Anxiety of Influence*.
26.   Garner, Kahane, and Sprengnether, eds., *The M(o)ther Tongue*, p. 21.
       Their introduction contains a cogent review of these theories.
27.   For American object-theory cf. Chodorow's seminal *The Reproduction
       of Mothering* . Among feminist Lacanians, cf. Mitchell *Psychoanalysis
       and Feminism* and Montrelay, *L'Ombre et le Nom*.
28.   Garner, Kahane, sand Sprengnether, *op. cit.*, p. 21.
29.   Cf. Introduction to this volume.
30.   Cf. *The Private Self*, ed. Shari Benstock; Sidonie Smith, *A Poetics
       of Women's Autobiography*; *Life/Lines*, eds Bella Brodzki and
       Celeste Schenck; *The M(o)ther Tongue*, eds Garner, Kahane,
       Sprengnether; Evans' introduction to *Masks of Tradition*, Leah
       Hewitt, *Autibiobraphical Tightropes*.
31.   Cf.Introduction to this volume.
32.   Cf. Smith, *op. cit.*
33.   Cixous, "Le Sexe ou la tête," p. 14. In this text Cixous opens the
       possibility of such "inscription" to men as well, although her concept
       itself of "femininity" is implicitly essentialist.
34.   Cf. Hewitt, "Rewriting her Story" on positive identifications and
       solidarity between mother and daughter in *L'Amant*.
35.   Bal, Mieke *Narratologie*, p. 72.
36.   On maternal violence cf. Janine Ricouart "La Violence dans la

mère durassienne." For psychoanalytic readings of the question of subjectivity with relation to the mother in Duras cf. Marini, *Territoires du féminin* . See also Willis, *Marguerite Duras*. Willis does not discuss this with respect to the texts where women have access to discourse and articulate different models.

37. Interviews with me, summer 1982.
38. Gallop, *The Daughter's Seduction*, p. xii.
39. But only when treated with distance, non possessively. In *Le Ravissement de Lol V. Stein*, the narrator's attempts to appropriate Lol's memory, from which she can not effect distance, and to displace her as its subject obviates such collaboration.
40. See Irigaray, *Speculum*, on the phallocentric privileging of sight and presence in its relationship to prejudicial definitions of female sexuality, and in connection to this Freud's pejorative historiography of the function of weaving.
41. De Man, *Blindness and Insight*, p. 26.
42. Interviews with me, summer, 1982. Duras' social and aesthetic conception of play accords in this respect with Derrida's critique of Lévi-Strauss: "Play [le jeu] is the disruption of presence [. . .] Now, if Lévi-Strauss, more than another, has shown the play of repetition and the repetition of play, one nevertheless perceives in his work a sort of ethics of presence, of nostalgia for the origin, for archaic, natural innocence, for a purity of presence and self-presence in speech [la parole] [. . .] Turned towards the lost or impossible presence of this absent origin, this structuralist thematic of broken immediacy is, then, the sad, *negative*, nostalgic, guilty, Rousseauist side of thinking on play, of which Nietzschean affirmation, joyous affirmation of the play of the world and the innocence of becoming, affirmation of a world of signs without sin, without truth, without an origin, offered for active interpretation, would be the other side. *This affirmation determines the non-center otherwise than as loss of center* [. . .]" Derrida, *L'Ecriture et la différance*, pp. 426–427.
43. English language grammar books name it the conditional and/or the unreal present.
44. For further discussion of verb tenses cf. Chapter 5.
45. The last two lines are an instance of the women sharing one "I". They both speak the role of the male lover.
46. For further discussion of repetition cf. Chapter 5.
47. In *La Femme du Gange*, the voices of the women "speakers" have the same function as these waves. They "beat the image [on screen or projected in the text], bathe it, wash it" (Fem, p. 82).
48. Duras, *Aurélia Steiner*, p. 135 (hereafter referred to as Aur).
49. Of course, Duras also signs them, but not with a literally counter signature as in those texts in which the intermediary male narrator speaks neither for nor with her. In the film version, Duras' voice speaks Aurélia's lines, with and for her.
50. Following Duras' lead, I use the toponym to distinguish between the three texts. In the Mercure de France edition, the first *Aurélia Steiner* begins on page 117.

51. Duras, *Les Yeux Verts*, p. 76.
52. Cf. Chapter 5 for analysis of Duras' water imagery. Here the bloodied river figures the murder of the Other, whereas the "liquid empty blue" eyes figure the openness of the sea, openness to the other.
53. Cf. Marini, "L'Offrande d'Aurélia Steiner au dormeur millénaire."
54. Yvonne Guers-Villate calls the sea "the analogue of the bedroom mirror, or of the interiority of the woman reflected in it." "Dérive poétique," p. 183.
55. Cf. Chapter 5.
56. Duras, *Les Yeux Verts*, p. 85.
57. *Ibid.*, p. 84.
58. Duras, *L'Eté 80*, p. 63 (hereafter referred to as Eté).
59. Herrmann, *Les Voleuses de langue*, p. 62.
60. *Ibid.*, p. 116.
61. Specialists in cinema studies are more qualified than I to analyze the specifically cinematic qualities in Duras' films. I am far from denying them or Duras' impact on cinema. I make a point Duras herself has made, as will be seen, and especially in connection with verbal language, written textual production, and referential absence expressed in visual terms through words or on screen. See Part II for further discussion.
62. Duras, interview appended to *Le Camion*, p. 86.
63. Duras in *Les Parleuses*, p. 191.
64. Duras, Interview with Blume.
65. Duras, "Entretien avec Marguerite Duras," p. 11.
66. Interview in *Marguerite Duras à Montréal*, p. 18.
67. Duras, quoted by de Gaspéri, "'Le Navire Night' de Marguerite Duras," p. 33.
68. Duras, *L'Homme Atlantique*, p. 17 (hereafter referred to as Hom).
69. Kristeva, *Black Sun*, p. 250. Cf. Chapter 1 in this volume.
70. Duras, in "Veja:" p. 56.
71. Duras, *L'Amant,*, pp. 16–17 (hereafter referred to as Am).
72. Duras, "L'Inconnue de la rue Catinat," p. 52.
73. Duras, *Ibid.*, p. 52.
74. The words "mother" and "brother" each signify "the family," an indissoluble unit for "Duras". The younger brother's death, for example, signals the death of the family as such: "The little brother died in three days, of bronchial pneumonia; the heart could not hold on. That is when I left my mother. [. . .] Everything ended that day. [. . .] She died, for me, of the death of my little brother. So did my older brother" (p. 37). Circulating love includes her mother with her lover and her brothers. She calls the former "my mother, my love" (p. 31), a syntagma resonant with intertextual echoes of Saint-John Perse's "enfance, mon amour." It recurs in *Agatha*, in a passage in which love for the mother joins the passion between brother and sister, as expressed in the polysemic "our love": "He: 'That charming mother, now dead . . . that woman . . . our love.' She: 'Our love . . . our mother'" – p. 65.
75. Duras has equated writing with a certain betrayal. It separates one

from the particular and joins one to the general: "What is writing? What is that parallel road, that fundamental betrayal of everyone and of oneself?" Duras, "Sublime, forcément sublime," p. 29
76. Duras, "L'Inconnue de la rue Catinat," p. 52.
77. Barthes, *La Chambre claire,* p. 120.
78. Duras "L'Inconnue de la rue Catinat," p. 52.
79. *Ibid.,* pp. 52–53.
80. Barthes, *La Chambre Claire,* p. 120.
81. *Ibid.,* p. 134.
82. Barthes, *L'Obvie et l'obtus,* p. 36.
83. *Ibid.,* p. 20.
84. Cf. Chapter 5.
85. Woolf, "Men and Women."
86. Duras "L'Inconnue de la rue Catinat," p. 52.
87. Duras, "Sublime, forcément sublime," p. 29.
88. Duras, *L'Amant de la Chine du Nord,* p. 11 (hereafter referred to as Am-Ch).
89. Cf. note #16.

3: Sleeping Beauties: Discourse, Gender, Genre in the "Erotic" Texts

1. Cf. Anne-Marie Dardigna's seminal, *Les Châteaux d'Eros.* Lucienne Frappier-Mazur notes the "common but fluctuating terminology" and that "eroticism and pornography often blend in the same texts" ("Marginal Canons," p. 113). She adopts the distinction made by Susan Suleiman in "Pornography, Transgression, and the Avant-Garde," according to which pornography aims solely at sexual stimulation, whereas erotic, artistic texts go beyond that limit and are received as "transgressive because they violate both the norms of discourse and of sexual behavior" (Frappier-Mazur, p. 113). The decisive question for me involves the notion of transgression. Within which discursive formations and in which perspective is the concept of transgression elaborated? Against and for what does one transgress? If, as most critics agree, pornography has been written mainly for and by men, in the name of whose sexual freedom does it transgress, and how is sexual freedom defined? Concerning Sade, for example, Dardigna and de Beauvoir (in *Faut-il brûler Sade*) wonder about the revolutionary possibilities of a concept that depends on and actually colludes with that which it transgresses, producing "an eroticism inseparable from our Western Christian values" and class structures, which devalue women and associate us with sinful, abominable nature needing domination ("civilizing") through degradation (Dardigna, *Châteaux,* p. 70). Susan Gubar's "Representing Pornography" reviews the pornography debate within Anglo-American feminism. The issues are, on the one hand, the effects of the production, reproduction and circulation

of images reinforcing dominant sexist ideology, the eroticization of violence done to women, power relations, the representation of sex as violence generally, the correlation between cultural representations and violent acts (Dworkin, Griffin, Barry). On the other hand, there is the view of pornographic art as a valid transgressive use of language which breaks through taboos, conventional consciousness and bourgeois optimism (Sontag, Suleiman), or, for Angela Carter, as something subversive because (in Sade, whose "complicity with the authority he hates" and "ingrained puritanism" she critiques – *The Sadean Woman* pp. 136 and 146) it "diagnoses male political dominance as a symptom of tyrannical relations in an unfree society" (Gubar, p. 727). (Suleiman acknowledges that "there will be no renewal [. . .] as long as every drama, whether textual or sexual, continues to be envisaged [. . .] in terms of a confrontation between an all-powerful father and a traumatized son, a confrontation staged across and over the body of the mother" – "Pornography and the Avant-Garde," p. 132). Gubar asserts the necessity of studying pornography, "for as the most sexually liberating form of art or as the epitome of the sexual oppression reinscribed by art, pornography is crucial for understanding our cultural past" (p. 730). As for the future, presumably our conclusions and analyses will help in the struggle to alter the structures producing works which "represent women as degraded sexual objects" (p. 730).

   In her overview of pornography written by French women, Frappier-Mazur observes that "women's erotica always introduce some love or passion, and grant the female body some integrity" (p. 127), "attach great value to female friendship" (p. 121) and that "women now explore the male/female power relation even when they reproduce it, in ways that either put it in question, or evade the formulaic model, or both" (p. 127). Gubar observes that "the pornographic genre itself frequently produces [. . .] ambiguity through narrative devices meant to frame and justify sexual (and frequently violent) scenes in terms that vary from the scientific and medical to the moral" (p. 730). Frappier-Mazur cites feminist critiques of third person narration in women's erotic fiction (especially Nancy Huston, *Mosaique de la pornographie*), which relate it to "a division of the self through which the writing subject objectifies a portion of herself (ultimately identified with the maternal body) and disowns it . . . " (p. 124). For Frappier-Mazur, the recent use of the first person by women has the effect of presenting the erotic as an integral part of a female *subject*, contextualizing eroticism in social and gender relations in women's everyday life (history), and stressing the cultural component of eroticism (p. 128).

2.   *Marguerite Duras à Montréal*, p. 57. Oddly, Frappier-Mazur elides the speaking narrator-author, stating that *L'Homme assis dans le couloir* and *La Maladie de la mort* are "written in the third person." Although she concedes that the texts "show some awareness of the ambiguous effect of this practice," she maintains that the distinction between character and narrator introduced by first person interventions in

the former text are not "sustained," and that in the latter the use of the second person "tends to reinforce her identification with the female character" ("Marginal Canons," p. 126). She adduces this as evidence of "an inability on the part of the narrator to establish self-boundaries" (p. 126).

3. Marcelle Marini "La Mort d'une érotique," pp. 42–43.
4. Duras, "Je suis muette devant le théâtre que j'écris."
5. Cf. Chapter 4 for her non-verbal strategies.
6. Ducrot, Todorov, *Dictionnaire encyclopédique des sciences du langage*, p. 323.
7. Among the female critics, cf. Marini, "La Mort d'une érotique"; Guers-Villate, "Marguerite Duras' *La Maladie de la mort*, Feminist Indictment or Allegory?"; Makward, "For a Stylistics of Marguerite Duras". Among the male critics, cf. Blanchot, *La Communauté inavouable*, Amigorena "La Dépendance amoureuse" (in his reading, Duras would merely "lend" her voice to the speaking voice [p. 26], which he internalizes and subsequently externalizes).
8. Marcelle Marini, "La Mort d'une érotique," p. 42.
9. Duras, *L'Homme assis dans le couloir*, p. 8 (hereafter referred to as H-as).
10. Littré, *Dictionnaire de la langue française*.
11. *Ibid.*
12. Duras, in *Marguerite Duras à Montréal*, p. 57.
13. *Ibid.*, p. 57.
14. Marini, "La Mort d'une érotique," p. 53.
15. "I see that he is exhausted with love and desire;" and "that love so strong" – H-as, pp. 21, 22.
16. Cf. Guers-Villate, "De l'implicite à l'explicite."
17. Guers-Villate, "De l'implicite à l'explicite;" Lydon, "Translating Duras," pp. 264–265. Lydon suggests that the "voyeuristic structure of the text, the emphasis throughout on seeing and the gaze, could be discussed in relation to the specular grounding of sexuality, of sexual difference in Freud's and Lacan's account . . . " (265)
18. Duras, "Entretien avec Marguerite Duras," p. 11.
19. "Marginal Canons," p. 126. Frappier-Mazur, like Guers-Villate and Lydon, considers that the fellatio episode in *L'Homme assis dans le couloir* presents the woman as a desiring subject. But Frappier-Mazur contends that if the man "is at once the tormenter and the erotic object," this "strengthens the sado-masochistic relation." Yet because she disregards the significance of the speaking first person, she does not distinguish between the position of the female protagonist and that of "Duras," which leads her to conclude that the text does not denounce the woman's alienation (pp. 126–127). Unlike Guers-Villate and Lydon, she sees no undermining of gender roles in the use of the feminine signifier to designate the man's genitals.
20. Selous *The Other Woman*, Kristeva, "The Malady of Grief," Freeman "Epitaphs and Epigraphs."
21. The French is ambiguous: "le songe merveilleux de la mettre à mort de ses propres mains."

22.   Duras, *Outside*, p. 12.
23.   *Le Boa*, p. 112. Cf. Evans and Hewitt on Duras' subsequent re-conceptualization of a certain prostitution as empowerment.
24.   Interviews with me.
25.   Interviews with me.
26.   I translate "le" as him because of the masculine gender of this pronoun, whose antecedent is: "un amant." It remains unclear whether the woman is referring to homosexual partners of the male protagonist, (the reading I consider most probable, in which case the one being killed would occupy the feminine position), whether she is using a "universal" masculine form, or universalizing from a female heterosexual perspective.
27.   Duras, *Outside*, p. 11.
28.   Kristeva, "The Malady of Grief", pp. 221–259.
29.   *Ibid.*, p. 227.
30.   *Ibid.*, p. 225.
31.   *Ibid.*, p. 227
32.   *Ibid.*, p. 222
33.   *Ibid.*, p. 228
34.   *Ibid.*, p. 224.
35.   *Ibid.*, pp. 227.
36.   *Ibid.*, p. 224.
37.   *Ibid*, pp. 258, 259 respectively.
38.   Pierrot, *Marguerite Duras*, p. 302. His meticulous thematic readings are especially insightful for Duras' earlier texts. For him the woman's occasional (desire for) death constitutes punishment for the transgression of incestuous desire for a brother figure, which he considers an originating phantasm motivating most of Duras' work. This autobiographical angle results in slightly reductive readings of the Lol V. Stein cycle (pp. 201–269).
39.   Lydon, "Translating Duras;" Guers-Villate, "De l'implicite à l'explicite."
40.   Willis, *Writing on the Body*, p. 165.
41.   The only female subject of vision Selous acknowledges in Duras is that of the female reader when she reads as the narratee. But because she considers the female characters "always constructed primarily as an object of desire for men," she holds that the woman reader reads as a man, since "the narratee is implicitly constructed in the masculine position." *The Other Woman*, p. 198.
42.   I discuss *Hiroshima, mon amour* and *Le Marin de Gibraltar* more thoroughly in Part II.
43.   Hewitt, "Rewriting her Story." Kristeva writes, concerning *L'Amant*, of "the smooth, sickly pleasure of the prostituted child who gives herself over to the tearful sensuality of a wealthy Chinese grownup" (Malady of Grief, p. 230), whereas the text repeatedly stresses the young girl's agency in desire, indeed the subjectivity of both partners in a sexuality far from "sickly." Again Kristeva misses or dismisses the connection between the girl's discovery of her sexual pleasure, her vocation to write (which prevents melancholia from prevailing)

and the ultimate rewriting of that and familial identities in the text that is *L'Amant*.
44. See also Catharine Stimpson, on lesbian desire and the undermining of feminine passivity, "Marguerite Duras: A W/Ringer's remarks."
45. Cf. *Les Yeux Verts*, pp. 5–6.
46. Interviews with me, 1982.

4: Elements of a Style

1. Noguez, "La Gloire des mots," p. 37.
2. Noguez, *ibid.*
3. Makward, "For a Stylistics of Marguerite Duras," p. 3.
4. Makward, "Structures du silence/du délire: Marguerite Duras/ Hélène Cixous," p. 317.
5. Duras, *Les Parleuses*, p. 109.
6. *Ibid.*, p. 146.
7. *Ibid.*, p. 110.
8. Husserl-Kapit, introduction to interview with Duras, p. 44.
9. Brée, *Littérature française: le vingtième siècle II 1920–1970*, p. 315.
10. Selous, *The Other Woman.*
11. Spender, *Man Made Language*, p. 183.
12. Duras, *Les Parleuses*, p. 175.
13. Duras, *ibid.*, p. 175.
14. Duras, *Les Yeux verts*, p. 87.
15. Duras in *Les Parleuses*, p. 175.
16. Merleau-Ponty, *La Prose du monde*, p. 13: "[. . .] the other, accompanying [my speech] in silence, comes to take it for his own [à son compte] and say it with me, which is understanding" (cf. also Bakhtin, *The Dialogic Imagination*, p. 282: "In the actual life of speech, every concrete act of understanding is active [. . .]").
17. *Ibid.*, pp. 29–30. Merleau-Ponty's conception of listening and silence accords with Duras' texts, except that he does not treat the crucial question of gender.
18. Merleau-Ponty, *Prose*, p. 165.
19. For Duras, receptive seeing is equivalent to listening in the sense of imagining what is being verbally indicated to a listener.
20. Duras in *Les Lieux de Marguerite Duras*, p. 73.
21. The "lovers" can't bear the sight of him for the same reason, for he reflects them as well, which also explains why Richard would "not forgive" Stretter if she saw him. Morgan the "writer" prefers him de-realized, a neutralized object of discourse, like the beggar. He tells the Vice-Consul: "the character [personage] that you are only interests us when you are absent" (V-C, p. 147).
22. Charles Rossett imagines it (V-C, p. 152) and Duras suggests it in the text's final evocation, depicting her in a physical posture of defeat, lying motionless on the path to the beach (V-C, pp. 199–200). Intertextually, this is "confirmed" in *India Song*, which begins years after Anne-Marie Stretter's suicide.

23. Péraldi, "The Passion of Death," p. 21.
24. The text stresses her reading, which associates her with the desexualized "rosy" reader discussed in Chapter 1.
25. Skoller, "Le Vice-consul," p. 161.
26. Cited in Skoller, p. 161.
27. Cf. Chapter 5 for an analysis of her sleeping.
28. Despite his class position of Otherness, the driver in *Le Camion* remains deaf because he has been coopted into the closed discourse of the communist party.
29. de Beauvoir, *Le Deuxième Sexe*.
30. Gilman, *Jewish Self Hatred*.
31. Kabbani, *Europe's Myths of Orient*.
32. Kristeva, "The Malady of Grief," p. 230.
33. One suspects he is far more exotic for a Western reader such as Kristeva than for the young "Duras" growing up in intimate proximity with Asians. Kristeva fails to distinguish between the forbidden familiar Other and the exotic.
34. Kristeva levels a similar accusation regarding the Japanese man in *Hiroshima mon amour*: "He remains if not exotic at least other, from another world, a beyond" (Malady of Grief, p. 232). Yet Duras has the man appear "international" (Hir, p. 137) specifically to avoid "the trap of exoticism and the involuntary racism necessarily inherent in all exoticism." (Hir, p. 136) The text demystifies the concept of exotic otherness subtending artificial demarcations between West and East (Kristeva's "beyond?"), intradiegetically as well. See the female protagonist's stated intention to teach her children "love of other people's countries" (Hir, p. 93) and her denunciation of "inequality posited as a principle by certain peoples against other peoples [. . .] races against other races [. . .] classes against other classes" (Hir, pp. 22–23).
35. I disagree with Willis' otherwise thought provoking reading when she speaks of a "failure to perform or repeat" *(Writing on the Body,* p. 37) and a "failure of mourning" (p. 52).
36. Duras, *Détruire, dit-elle,* p. 101 (hereafter referred to as Det).
37. Marini, *Territoires du féminin,* p. 152.
38. Irigaray, *Speculum,* p. 176.
39. I discuss the episode further on in this chapter.
40. Marini, *Territoires,* p. 53.
41. Merleau-Ponty, *La Prose du Monde,* preface, p. IV.
42. Duras, *Les Parleuses,* p. 15.
43. *Ibid.,* p. 12.
44. I treat this aspect later in this chapter.
45. Duras, *Les Yeux Verts,* p. 49.
46. Irigaray, *Speculum de l'autre femme,* p. 176.
47. Duras , "Les Goncourt aimaient *L'Amant* de Duras," p. 29.
48. Cf. Chapter 2.
49. Selous, *The Other Woman,* p. 130.
50. *Ibid.,* p. 250.
51. *Ibid.,* p. 248.

52. Duras, *Les Lieux*, p. 12.
53. Eco, *A Theory of Semiotics*, pp. 115–116.
54. Duras, *Le Nouvel Observateur*, 14–20 novembre, 1986.
55. Noguez, "La Gloire des mots," p. 32.
56. Kristeva, *The Malady of Grief*," pp. 225–226.
57. *Ibid.*, p. 232.
58. *Ibid.*, p. 235.
59. Cf. note #34.
60. Cf. Chapter 5.
61. Duras in Micciolo, *Moderato Cantabile de Marguerite Duras*, p. 8.
62. Duras, in *Marguerite Duras à Montréal*, p. 18.
63. Duras, *ibid.*, p. 45.
64. Makward, "Structures du silence/du délire," p. 316.
65. Duras, "Le Malheur merveilleux: Pourquoi mes films?" pp. 79–86.
66. Baroncelli, "La Magie de Marguerite Duras." *Le Monde* (February 15, 1977).
67. Cf. Chapter 5, "onomastics."
68. Duras, in *Les Parleuses* , p. 88.
69. Interviews with me, 1982.
70. Gallop, *The Daughter's Seduction*, p. 32.
71. Montaigne, *Essais* , quoted by Erica Stevens in program notes to production of *Suzannah Andler* , summer, 1984, South Street Theater, New York.
72. Note that the narrator, who confirms and aggravates Lol's madness in *Le Ravissement de Lol V. Stein*, is also a doctor (Rav, p. 87).
73. Foucault. *Histoire de la folie*.
74. Duras, *Suzannah Andler*, p. 25 (hereafter referred to as Suz).
75. Cf. Chapter 1.
76. Heidegger, *Essais et conférences*, p. 68.
77. R. Jean quoting Duras in *Le Monde*, March 29, 1974.
78. Noguez, "La Gloire des mots," p. 27.
79. Duras, *Les Parleuses*, p. 117.
80. Cf. Chapter 3.
81. Cf. Chapter 2. In *Hiroshima, mon amour*, in which the female-male looking is reciprocal, the man receives the woman's gaze happily: "Me, yes, me you will have seen" – p. 28.

5: Legends

1. Duras, quoted in Marini, *Territoires du féminin*, p. 50.
2. Noguez, "La Gloire des mots," p. 37.
3. Cf. Chapter 2, for further remarks on the word "legend."
4. *Webster's Seventh New Collegiate Dictionary*, G.&C. Merriam Company, Springfield, Massachusetts, 1961. I use the words legend, myth, ceremony and the sacred more or less interchangeably, for they are close enough to the sense of legend for the purposes of my exposition.

5. Duras, interview "Chroniques de France," cited by Makward in "For a Stylistics of Marguerite Duras," p. 32.
6. Duras, *La Douleur*, p. 134 (hereafter referred to as Dou).
7. Duras, *La Vie Matérielle*, pp. 14–16.
8. In *La Maladie de la mort* and *L'Homme assis dans le couloir*, the substitution of "the" body for "her" body exposes the reification of women into body in masculinist mythmaking concerning women. Cf. Chapter 3.
9. Duras, "Les Goncourt aimaient *L'Amant* de Marguerite Duras," p. 29.
10. Cf. Chapter 1 on the I – He alternation in *Le Ravissement de Lol V. Stein*, which signals a split more than an alternation and is an unhappy loss of self rather than an empowering dis-possession.
11. Cf. discussion in Cohen, "An Onomastic Double Bind," Lévi-Strauss, *La Pensée sauvage*, Derrida, *De la grammatologie*, Nicole, "L'Onomastique littéraire," Perret, "Les Appellatifs."
12. Noguez, "La Gloire des mots," p. 31.
13. *Ibid.*, p. 30.
14. Benveniste proposed the term "synapsie" for this kind of combination. It signifies "joining, connection, collection of joined things." *Problèmes de linguistique générale*, Vol. 2, p. 172.
15. Cf. Chapter 2. Few fathers hold central positions in Duras' texts. The father in *L'Après-midi de Monsieur Andesmas* is only a seeming exception, for his advanced age and open attitude prevent him from exercising the law-giving father function. Much has been made of the fact that Duras had no father. (He died when she was a small child, and her mother did not internalize the paternal function.) Duras' original patronymic, Donnadieu (literally: give to God), is heavy with connotations. Historically, in a gesture of symbolic paternal substitution, it was the name attributed to orphans abandoned on church steps. When Duras rid herself of her father's name, she disencumbered herself of the associative weight carried by the name Donnadieu. The connection between forgetting her - always unnamed – mother and writing about her is made by Duras in *L'Amant*, and discussed in my analyses of that text. One might speculate that Duras' ability to write at all is founded on the absence of the Father function. An exchange in *Les Parleuses* is significant: "Gauthier: 'Can one write if one keeps one's father's name?' Duras: 'That is something that [. . .] never appeared possible for a second. [. . .] I did not have a father [. . .] Well, I had him very little . . . long enough'" – pp. 23–24. If, as has been suggested, the lover in *L'Amant* has a paternal function (he washes the young girl, often referred to as "the child"), it is one without authority. He corresponds to the positive fathers imagined by Aurélia Steiner, who do not dispense law, who listen to the woman/child, look at her without reifying her, and love her in her difference.
16. Duras, *Les Parleuses*, p. 67.
17. The same can be said for the salesman in *Nathalie Granger* and the truck driver in *Le Camion*.

18. Duras, "stage direction" *Le Square,* p. 50.
19. "Calcutta" often symbolically collectivizes the innumerable poor first depersonalized into a toponym, which then undergoes personification: "Again Calcutta cries softly," p. 158; ""again Calcutta grinds in the distance in its sleep," p. 160; "sleeping Calcutta," p. 73.
20. Hill, "Marguerite Duras: Sexual Difference and Tales of the Apocalypse," p. 614.
21. Selous, *The Other Woman,* p. 245
22. *Ibid.,* p. 242.
23. Duras in *Le Nouvel Observateur,* #31, June 20, 1971.
24. For an interesting study of representation and of the "mood" created by Duras' "incantatory prose" in *L'Amour,* cf. Dina Sherzer, "*L'Amour*: Choreography of the Said and the Unsaid."
25. Lévi-Strauss, *La Pensée sauvage.*
26. Derrida, "Structure, signe, jeu," in *L'Ecriture et la différence.*
27. Duras, *L'Amour,* p. 143.
28. Noguez, "La Gloire des mots," pp. 25–26.
29. *Ibid.,* p. 26.
30. *Ibid.,* p. 26.
31. *Ibid.,* p. 26.
32. Verena Conley points out this repetition, and speaks of Stretter's entrance in terms of "sublime grace." "L'affaire Gregory," p. 70.
33. Duras, *L'Amour,* p. 10.
34. Noguez, "La Gloire des mots," p. 29.
35. *Ibid.,* p. 30.
36. *Ibid.,* p. 33.
37. *Ibid.,* p. 30.
38. *Ibid.,* p. 34.
39. *Ibid.,* p. 28.
40. Bachelard, *L'Eau et les rêves.*
41. Duras, in *Les Lieux de Marguerite Duras,* p. 91.
42. Cf. Chapter 2. Duras' male characters almost never immerse themselves in the sea the way the women do. (The man in *Savannah Bay* swims only to pull his young Venus figure out of the water.) In Duras' texts set far from the sea, rivers are usually associated with women (the Mekong in *L'Amant* for example). But river mouths figure the site of sexual difference and ritual joining. (In *Savannah Bay* the man walks along the river path – "masculinity" – and notices the young girl "covered regularly" by the waves on the rock in the sea – "femininity" – the moment he reaches the river mouth, where they enact the rite of love – pp. 43–44). At the confluence of river and sea, different waters-different genders meet and mix, repeatedly.
43. Immobility usually signals blocked time.
44. Duras, *Les Yeux verts,* p. 90.
45. The little boy in *L'Eté 80,* whose eye color moves within the grays of the northern sea, does not constitute an exception. Duras associates children's wildness, openness, "lostness" and capacity for play with women (cf. Chapter 2).
46. Noguez, "La Gloire des mots," p. 27.

47. *Ibid.,* p. 28.
48. *Ibid.,* p. 27.
49. *Ibid.,* p. 28.
50. *Ibid.,* p. 29.
51. Duras, *Les Yeux verts,* p. 49.
52. Marini, "L'Autre corps," p. 5.
53. Cf. Chapter 2 on *L'Amant.*
54. Emmanuelle Riva is the actress who plays the anonymous woman in the film. She is named only in sections appended to the text.
55. Bachelard, *La Psychanalyse du feu.*
56. It recurs eleven times in the text.
57. Duras, *Savannah Bay* nouvelle édition augmentée, p. 93.
58. The woman elicits murderous desires on the part of the man because, metaphorically speaking, he can not see himself in her. Nor can he in the "real" sea, outside. Only a body of still water (in French "dead water" – eau morte) can be a mirror for Narcissus. Alive and mobile, the sea figures a self which refuses to limit herself to reflecting only one set of desires.
59. Duras in *Les Lieux de Marguerite Duras,* pp. 15–16. This passage demonstrates Duras' awareness of the specificity of different oppressions and of their interconnections. One must not fall into readings imputing to Duras universalism regarding women or reductionism regarding men.
60. Duras, in *Les Lieux de Marguerite Duras.*
61. *Ibid.,* p. 27.
62. One thinks of *Outside,* Duras' collection of articles, several of which concern sexual or racial outcasts.

Conclusion

1. Duras, *La Pluie d'été,* p. 27.
2. Houdebine, "Les Femmes dans la langue," p. 15.
3. *Ibid.,* p. 16.

Glossary

antonomasia: substitution of a common noun or name for a proper name

deictic, deixis: words of showing or pointing directly, for ex. "this," "here"

diachronic: concerning phenomena in language as they occur or change over time. cf. synchronic

diegesis: the story considered separately from the act of narration or narrative framing

idiolect: an individual's particular language or speech pattern

paratactic, parataxis: the placing of words, phrases or clauses next to each other without subordinating or coordinating connectives

performative discourse/speech-act: utterance which effects the action it announces, for ex. "I promise"

shifter: expressions such as "I" or "you," whose referent can only be determined with respect to the speakers

synchronic: descriptive of phenomena in language within a certain time period, without regard to historical change. cf. diachronic

Bibliography

Texts by Marguerite Duras

Duras, Marguerite. *Un Barrage contre le pacifique* (Paris: Gallimard, 1950).
——. *Le Marin de Gibraltar* (Paris: Gallimard, 1952).
——. *Des journés entières dans les arbres, suivi de: Le Boa, Madame Dodin, Les Chantiers* (Paris: Gallimard, 1954).
——. *Le Square* (Paris: Gallimard, 1955).
——. *Moderato cantabile* (Paris: Union Générale d'Editions, 1965).
——. *Les Viaducs de la Seine-et-Oise* (Paris: Gallimard, 1959).
——. *Dix Heures et demie du soir en été* (Paris: Gallimard, 1960).
——. *Hiroshima, mon amour* (Paris: Gallimard, 1960).
——. *L'Après-midi de Monsieur Andesmas* (Paris: Gallimard, 1962).
——. *Le Ravissement de Lol V. Stein* (Paris: Gallimard, 1964).
——. *Théâtre I: Les Eaux et forêts, Le Square, La Musica* (Paris: Gallimard, 1965).
——. *Le Vice-consul* (Paris: Gallimard, 1965).
——. *L'Amante anglaise* (Paris: Gallimard, 1967).
——. *L'Amante anglaise, théâtre* (Paris: Cahiers du Théâtre national populaire, 1968).
——. *Théâtre II Suzanna Andler, Des Journés entières dans les arbres, Yes, peut-être, Le Shaga, Un Homme est venu me voir* (Paris: Gallimard, 1968.).
——. *Détruire, dit-elle* (Paris: Editions de Minuit, 1969).
——. *Abahn, Sabana, David* (Paris: Gallimard, 1970).
——. *L'Amour* (Paris: Gallimard, 1971).
——. *India Song* (Paris: Gallimard, 1973).
——. *Nathalie Granger, suivi de La Femme du Gange* (Paris: Gallimard, 1973).
——, and Gauthier, Xavière. *Les Parleuses* (Paris: Minuit, 1974).
——. *Son Nom de Venise dans Calcutta désert*, film (Paris: Distributors Benoît-Jacob, 1976).
——. *Le Camion* (Paris: Minuit, 1977).
——, and Porte, Michèle. *Les Lieux de Marguerite Duras* (Paris: Minuit, 1977).
——. *L'Eden cinéma* (Paris: Mercure de France, 1977).
——. *Le Navire Night, suivi de Césarée, Les Mains négatives, Aurélia Steiner, Aurélia Steiner, Aurélia Steiner* (Paris: Mercure de France, 1979).
——. *Véra Baxter ou les plages de l'Atlantique* (Paris: Albatros, 1980).
——. *L'Homme assis dans le couloir* (Paris: Minuit, 1980).
——. *L'Eté 80* (Paris: Minuit, 1980).
——. *Les Yeux verts* (Paris: Cahiers du cinéma, 1981).
——. *Agatha* (Paris: Minuit, 1981).
——. *Outside* (Paris: Albin Michel, 1981).

———. *L'Homme Atlantique* (Paris: Minuit, 1982).

———. *Savannah Bay* (Paris: Minuit, 1982).

———. *Savannah Bay, deuxième édition augmentée* (Paris: Minuit, 1983).

———. *La Maladie de la mort* (Paris: Minuit, 1982).

———. *L'Amant* (Paris: Minuit, 1984).

———. *La Douleur* (Paris: P.O.L., 1985).

———. *La Musica deuxième* (Paris: Gallimard, 1985).

———. *Les Yeux bleus cheveux noirs* (Paris: Minuit, 1986).

———. *La Vie matérielle* (Paris: P.O.L., 1987).

———. *La Pluie d'été* (Paris: P.O.L., 1990).

———. *L'Amant de la Chine du Nord* (Paris: Gallimard, 1991).

Secondary Sources

Ames, Sanford. "Dead Letters, Impossible Witness," in (ed.) Sanford Ames *Remains to be Seen: Essays on Marguerite Duras* (New York: Peter Lang, 1988) pp. 279–87.

Amorigena, Horacio. "La Dépendance amoureuse," *Les Cahiers du Grif*, (Automne, 1985) 26–29.

Bachelard, Gaston. *La Psychanalyse du feu* (Paris: Gallimard, 1938).

———. *L'Eau et les rêves* (Paris: José Corti, 1942).

Bakhtin, Mikhail. "Discourse in the Novel," in (ed.) Michael Holquist. *The Dialogic Imagination, Four Essays by M. Bakhtin* (Austin: University of Texas Press, 1981) 259–423 translated Caryl Emerson & Michael Holquist.

Bal, Mieke. *Narratologie* (Paris: Klincksieck, 1977).

Barry, Kathleen., "Pornography: The Ideology of Cultural Sadism" in *Female Sexual Slavery* (New York: New York University Press, 1984) 205–53.

Barthes, Roland. *La Chambre claire* (Paris: Gallimard, 1980).

———. *L'Obvie et l'obtus* (Paris: Le Seuil, 1982).

Beaujour, Michel. "Autobiographie et autoportrait." *Poétique* 32 (1977): pp. 442–58.

Benjamin, Jessica. "The Bonds of Love; Rational Violence and Erotic Domination" in (eds), Hester Eisenstein and Alice Jardine, *The Future of Difference* (Boston: G.K. Hall & Company, 1980) pp. 41–71.

Benstock, Shari (ed.) *The Private Self: Theory and Practice of Women's Autobiographical Writings* (Chapel Hill: University of North Carolina Press, 1988).

Benveniste, Emile. *Problèmes de linguistique générale.* 2 vols (Paris: Gallimard, 1966–1974).

Bernheim, Nicole Lise. *Marguerite Duras tourne un film* (Paris: Albatross, 1975).

Binswanger, Ludwig. "Dream and Existence." In Jacob Needleman (ed.), *Being-in-the-World. Selected Papers of Ludwig Binswanger* (New York: Harper & Row, 1968) , pp. 222–49.

Blanchot, Maurice. *La Communauté inavouable* (Paris: Minuit, 1983).

Bloom, Harold. *The Anxiety of Influence* (New York: Oxford University Press, 1973).

Brée, Germaine, ed. *Littérature française. Le XXè siècle II 1920–1970* (Paris: Arthaud, 1978).

Bordo, Susan, "Feminism, Postmodernism, and Gender-Scepticism," in Linda Nicholson (ed.) *Feminism/Postmodernism* (New York: Routledge, 1989) pp. 133–57.

Brodzki, Bella and Schenck, Celeste (eds) *Life/Lines: Theorizing Women's Autobiography* (Ithaca: Cornell University Press, 1988).

Buber, Martin. *I and Thou* (New York: Scribner's Sons, 1970).

Butler, Judith. "Gender Trouble, Feminist Theory, and Psychoanalytic Discourse," in Linda Nicholson (ed.), *Feminism/Postmodernism* (New York: Routledge, 1989) pp. 324–41.

Carter, Angela. *The Sadean Woman* (New York: Harper & Row, 1978).

Chodorow, Nancy. *The Reproduction of Mothering* (Berkeley: University of California Press, 1978).

Cismaru, Alfred. *Marguerite Duras* (New York: Twayne Publishers, Inc., 1971).

Cixous, Hélène. "Le Sexe ou la tête." *Les Cahiers du Grif 13* (October 1976) reprinted as "Castration or Decapitation" in *Signs* vol. 7, no. 1, Autumn, 1981 pp. 41–55 translated Annette Kuhn.

——. "The Laugh of The Medusa." in (eds) Elaine Marks & Isabelle de Courtivon *New French Feminisms* (Amherst: University of Massachusetts Press, 1980) pp. 245–65 translated by Keith Cohen & Paula Cohen.

——. "Sorties," in Cixous and Clément, *La Jeune née* (Paris: Union Générale d'Editions, 1975) pp. 114–246.

Cohen, Susan. "Phantasm and Narration in *The Ravishing of Lol V. Stein*," in (eds) Charney and Reppen, *The Psychoanalytic Study of Literature* (New Jersey: The Analytic Press, 1985) pp. 255–77.

——. "An Onomastic Dougle Bind: Colette's *Gigi* and the Politics of Naming," *PMLA* (October, 1985) 793–809.

Conley, Verena. "L'Affaire Gregopry' and Duras's Textual Feminism." *L'Esprit Créateur* vol. XXX, no. 1 (Spring 1990) 69–75.

Dardigna, Anne-Marie *Les Châteaux d'Eros* (Paris: Maspero, 1980).

De Gaspéri, Anne. "Le Navire night de Marguerite Duras: L'état sauvage du désir," *Quotidien de Paris* (June 27, 1978).

De Beauvoir, Simone. *Le Deuxième Sexe* (Paris: Gallimard, 1949.).

——. *Faut-il brûler Sade?* (Paris: Gallimard, 1955).

De Lauretis, Teresa. "Feminist Studies/Critical Studies: Issues, Terms, and Contexts," in Teresa de Lauretis (ed.), *Feminist Studies Critical Studies* (Bloomington: Indiana University Press, 1986) pp. 1–20.

De Man, Paul. *Blindness and Insight* (New York: Oxford University Press, 1971).

Derrida, Jacques. *L'Ecriture et la différence* (Paris: Le Seuil, 1967).

——. *De la grammatologie* (Paris: Minuit, 1967).

Duchen, Claire. *Feminism in France*. London: Routledge and Kegan, 1986.

Ducrot, Oswald, and Todorov, Tzvetan. *Dictionnaire encyclopédique des sciences du langage* (Paris: Seuil, 1972).

Duras, Marguerite. "Entretien avec Marguerite Duras." *Rouge* (February 11, 1977) 10–12.

——. "Il n'y a rien de plus difficile que de décrire un amour." Interview.*Le Matin* (September 19, 1983) 26–29.

——. Interview. *Le Nouvel observateur* (November 14–20, 1986).

——. "Je suis muette devant le théâtre que j'écris." Interview. *Le Matin* (June 3, 1983) 97–99.

——. "Les Goncourt aimaient *L'Amant* de Duras." *Libération* (November 13, 1984) 29–30.

——. "Le Malheur merveilleux: pourquoi mes films?" *Cahiers du cinéma* (June, 1980) 79–86.

——. "Sublime, forcément sublime." *Libération* (September 4, 1984) 28–33.

——. "Conférence de presse du 8 avril, 1981." in (eds) Suzanne Lamy and André Roy, *Marguerite Duras à Montréal* (Montréal: Editions Spirale, 1981) pp. 15–29.

——, and Blume, Mary. Interview. *The International Herald Tribune* (March 22, 1985).

——, and Husserl-Kapit, Susan. Interview. *Signs* (Winter 1975) 423–34.

——, and Gauthier, Xavière. Interview. In *Marguerite Duras* (Paris: Albatros, 1975) pp. 75–93.

——, and Leite, Paulo. "Veja, excerpts from an interview with MargueriteDuras.". *World Press Review* (September, 1985) 57.

——, and Le Masson, Hervé. "L'Inconnue de la rue Catinat." *Le Nouvel Observateur* (September 28, 1984) 52–54.

——, and Pivot, Bernard, "Apostrophes." French Television Interview (1984).

Dworkin, Andrea. *Pornography: Men Possessing Women* (New York: Putnam's Sons, 1981).

Eco, Umberto. *A Theory of Semiotics* (Bloomington, Indiana: Indiana University Press, 1976).

Evans, Martha Noel. *Masks of Tradition: Women and the Politcs of Writing in Twentieth Century France* (Ithaca: Cornell University Press, 1987).

Fisher, Dominique. "L'Ecrit, le jeu de la lecture et la mise en voix del'écriture dans *La Vie matérielle* et dans *Les Yeux bleus cheveux noirs,*" in *L'Esprit Créateur* vol. XXX, no. 1 (Spring 1990) 76–86.

Foucault, Michel. *L'Archaéologie du savoir* (Paris: Gallimard, 1969).

——. *Histoire de la folie à l'âge classique* (Paris: Gallimare, 1972).

Frappier-Mazur, Lucienne. "Marginal Canons: Rewriting the Erotic." *Yale French Studies* (#75, 1988) 112–129.

Fraser, Nancy and Nicholson, Linda. "Social Criticism without Philosophy: An Encounter between Feminism and Postmodernism," in Linda Nicholson (ed.), *Feminism/Postmodernism* (New York: Routledge, 1989) pp. 19–39.

Freeman, Barbara. "Epitaphs and Epigraphs," in (eds), Adrienne Munich and Susan Squier *Arms and the Woman: War, Gender, and Literary Representation* (Chapel Hill: University of North Carolina Press, 1989), pp. 303–323.

Gallop, Jane. *The Daaughter's Seduction: Feminism and Psychoanalysis.* (Ithaca: Cornell University Press, 1982).

Garner, Shirley, Kahane, Claire, Sprengnether, Madelon (eds) *The (M)other Tongue* (Ithaca: Cornell University Press, 1985).

Genette, Gérard. *Figures III* (Paris: Le Seuil, 1972).

Gilman, Sander. *Jewish Self Hatred* (Baltimore: Johns Hopkins University Press, 1986).

Griffin, Susan. *Pornography and Silence: Culture's Revenge against Nature* (New York: Harper and Row, 1981).

Gubar, Susan. "Representing Pornography: Feminism, Criticism, and Depictions of Female Violation." *Critical Inquiry* (Summer, 1987 vol. 13, no. 5) 712–741.

Guers-Villate, Yvonne. "De l'implicite à l'explicite: de *Moderato Cantabile* à *L'Homme assis dans le couloir*." *The French Review* vol. 58, no. 3 (February, 1985).

——. "Dérive poétique et glissements métaphoriques dans les *Aurélia Steiner* de Duras." in (eds) Danielle Bajomée and Ralph Heyndels, *Ecrire, dit-elle: Imaginaires de Marguerite Duras* (Brussels: Editions de l'Université de Bruxelles, 1985) 179–87.

——. "Marguerite Duras' *La Maladie de la mort:* Feminist Indictment or Allegory?" In (ed.) Sanford Ames, *Remains to be Seen: Essays on Marguerite Duras* (New York: Peter Lang, 1988) pp. 127–37.

Heidegger, Martin. *Essais et conférences* (Paris: Gallimard, 1958).

Herrmann, Claudine. *Les Voleuses de langue* (Paris: Des femmes, 1976).

Hewitt, Leah. "Rewriting Her Story, from Passive to Active: Substitution in Marguerite Duras," in *Autobiographical Tightropes* (Lincoln: University of Nebraska Press, 1990) pp. 93–127.

Hill, Leslie. "Sexual Difference and Tales of the Apocalypse." *Modern Language Review* vol. 84, no. 3 (July, 1989) 601–14.

Houdebine, Anne-Marie. "Les Femmes dans la langue." *Femes et Institutions littéraires. Cahiers de Recherches S.T.D.,* Université deParis (Sept. 13, 1984) 11–19.

Huston, Nancy *Mosaique de la pornographie* (Paris: Denoel, 1982).

Huyssens, Andreas. "Mapping the Postmodern," in Linda Nicholson (ed.), *Feminism/Postmodernism* (New York: Routledge, 1989) pp. 234–64.

Irigaray, Luce. *Speculum de l'autre femme* (Paris: Editions de Minuit, 1974).

——. *Ce Sexe qui n'en est pas un* (Paris: Editions de Minuit, 1977).

Kabbani, Rana. *Europe's Myths of Orient* (Bloomington: Indiana University. Press, 1986).

Kristeva, Julia. "La Femme ce n'est jamais ça," *Tel Quel 59* (Automne, 1974) 12–24.

——. "The Malady of Grief: Duras," in *Black Sun: Depression and Melancholia.* Translated Leon Roudiez (New York: Columbia University Press, 1989) 219–61.

——. *Pouvoirs de l'horreur* (Paris: Le Seuil, 1980).

——. *La Révolution du langage poétique* (Paris: Seuil, 1974).

——. "Un Nouveau type d'intellectuel," *Tel Quel 74* (Hiver, 1977) pp. 3–8.

Laplanche, Jean; and Pontalis, J.-B. *Vocabulaire de la psychanalyse* (Paris: Presses Universitaires de France, 1967).

Lévi-Strauss, Claude. *La Pensée sauvage* (Paris: Plon, 1962).

Lydon, Mary. "Translating Duras: 'The Seated Man in the Passage'," *Contemporary Literature* vol. 24, no. 2 (Summer, 1983) 259–75.

Makward, Christiane. "For a Stylistics of Marguerite Duras," *L'Esprit-*

créateur vol. XXX, no. 1 (Spring 1990) 28–39.

——. "Structures du silence/ du délire: Marguerite Duras/ Hélène Cixous. *Poétique* 35 (September 1978) 314–24.

Marini, Marcelle. "L'Autre corps." in *Ecrire, dit-elle* (eds) Bajomée, Danielle and Heyndels, Ralph (Brussels: Editions Université de Bruxelles, 1985) pp. 21–48.

——. "La Mort d'une érotique." *Les Cahiers Renaud-Barrault* 106 (September, 1983): 37 –57.

——. "L'Offrande d'Aurélia Steiner au dormeur millénaire." *Didascalies* 3 (April, 1982): 38 –49.

——. *Territoires du féminin* (Paris: Editions de Minuit, 1977).

Merleau-Ponty, Maurice. *La Prose du monde* (Paris: Gallimard, 1969).

Micciollo, Henri. *Moderato Cantabile de Marguerite Duras : Lire aujourd'hui* (Paris: Hachette, 1979).

Mitchell, Juliet. *Psychoanalysis and Feminism* (New York: Random House, 1974).

Moi, Toril. *Sexual/Textual Politics* (London: Methuen, 1985).

Montrelay, Michèle. *L'Ombre et le nom* (Paris: Editions de minuit, 1977).

Nicole, Eugène. "L'onomastique littéraire," *Poétique* 54 (1983) 233–53.

Noguez, Dominique. "La Gloire des mots," *L'ARC* 98 (1985) pp. 25–39.

Questions Féministes Collective. "Variations on Common Themes" in (eds) Elaine Marks & Isabelle de Courtivon *New French Feminisms* (Amherst: University of Massachusetts Press, 1980) 225–235, translated Yvonne Rochette-Ozzello.

Péraldi, François. "The Passion of Death. A Free Associative Reading of Freud and Marguerite Duras," in *L'Esprit Créateur* vol. XXX, no. 1 (Spring 1990) 19–27.

Perret, Delphine. "Les appellatifs." *Langages* 17 (1970) 112–18.

Pierrot, Jean. *Marguerite Duras* (Paris: Corti, 1986).

Ricouart, Janine. "La Violence dans la mère durassienne," in (eds) Eunice Myers and Ginette Adamson, *Continental Latin-American and Francophone Women Writers* (New York: University Press of America, 1984) pp. 29–37.

Rosalind-Jones, Ann. "Writing the Body: Toward an Understanding of 'l'Ecriture féminine'," in (ed.) Elaine Showalter, *The New Feminist Criticism* (New York: Pantheon, 1985) pp. 361–79.

Selous, Trista. *The Other Woman: Feminism and Femininity in the Work of Marguerite Duras* (New Haven: Yale University Press, 1988).

Sherzer, Dina. "*L'Amour*: Choreography of the Said and the Unsaid," in *Representation in Contemporary French Fiction* (Lincoln: University of Nebraska Press, 1987) pp. 133–146.

Skoller, Eleanor. "*Le Vice-Consul*: On Leaving Lahore" in (ed.) Sanford Ames, *Remains to be Seen: Essays on Marguerite Duras* (New York: Peter Lang, 1988) pp. 151–169.

Smith, Sidonie. *A Poetics of Women's Autobiography* (Bloomington: Indiana University Press) 1987.

Sontag, Susan. "The Pornographic Imagination." In *Styles of Radical Will.* (New York: Farrar, Straus and Giroux, 1969) 35–73.

Spender, Dale. *Man Made Language* (London: Routledge and Kegan,1980).

Straus, Erwin. *Phenomenological Psychology* (New York: Basic Books, 1966).

——. *The Primary World of Senses* (London: Collier-Macmillan Limited, 1963).

Stimpson, Catharine. "Marguerite Duras: A 'W/Ringer''s Remarks," *L'Esprit Créateur* vol. XXX, no. 1 (Spring 1990) 15–19.

Suleiman, Susan Rubin. "Pornography, Transgression, and the Avant-Garde," in (ed.), Nancy K. Miller, *The Poetics of Gender* (New York: Columbia University Press, 1986) pp. 117–37.

Valéry, Paul. *Variété. Oeuvres Tome 1* (Paris: Gallimard, 1957).

Willis, Sharon. *Marguerite Duras* Writing on the Body (Urbana: University of Chicago Press, 1987).

Wittig, Monique. "The Point of View: Universal or Particular?" *Feminist Issues* vol. 3, no. 2 (Fall 1983) 63–69.

——. "One is Not Born a Woman," *Feminist Issues* vol. 1, no. 2 (Winter 1981) 47–54.

Woolf, Virginia. "Men and Women." In *Books & Portraits* (New York: Harcourt Brace Janovich, 1978) pp. 28–31.

Yaeger, Patricia S. "Because a Fire was in my Head: Eudora Welty and the Dialogic Imagination." *PMLA* vol. 99, no. 5 (October 1984): 955–74.

Zimmer, Christian. "Dans la nuit de Marguerite Duras." *Les Temps Modernes* (February 1970): 1304–14.

Index